D0849727

Global Voices on Biblical Equality

The House of Prisca and Aquila

OUR MISSION AT THE HOUSE OF PRISCA AND AQUILA IS TO PRODUCE QUAL-ITY books that expound accurately the word of God to empower women and men to minister together in a multicultural church. Our writers have a positive view of the Bible as God's revelation that affects both thoughts and words, so it is plenary, historically accurate, and consistent in itself; fully reliable; and authoritative as God's revelation. Because God is true, God's revelation is true, inclusive to men and women and speaking to a multicultural church, wherein all the diversity of the church is represented within the parameters of egalitarianism and inerrancy.

The word of God is what we are expounding, thereby empowering women and men to minister together in all levels of the church and home. The reason we say women and men together is because that is the model of Prisca and Aquila, ministering together to another member of the church—Apollos: "Having heard Apollos, Priscilla and Aquila took him aside and more accurately expounded to him the Way of God" (Acts 18:26). True exposition, like true religion, is by no means boring—it is fascinating. Books that reveal and expound God's true nature "burn within us" as they elucidate the Scripture and apply it to our lives.

This was the experience of the disciples who heard Jesus on the road to Emmaus: "Were not our hearts burning while Jesus was talking to us on the road, while he was opening the scriptures to us?" (Luke 24:32). We are hoping to create the classics of tomorrow: significant and accessible trade and academic books that "burn within us."

Our "house" is like the home to which Prisca and Aquila no doubt brought Apollos as they took him aside. It is like the home in Emmaus where Jesus stopped to break bread and reveal his presence. It is like the house built on the rock of obedience to Jesus (Matt 7:24). Our "house," as a euphemism for our publishing team, is a home where truth is shared and Jesus' Spirit breaks bread with us, nourishing all of us with his bounty of truth.

We are delighted to work together with Wipf and Stock in this series and welcome submissions on a wide variety of topics from an egalitarian inerrantist global perspective. The House of Prisca and Aquila is also a ministry center affiliated with the International Council of Community Churches.

For more information, contact housepriscaaquila@comcast.net.

Global Voices on Biblical Equality

Women and Men Ministering Together in the Church

by

AÍDA BESANÇON SPENCER
WILLIAM DAVID SPENCER
MIMI HADDAD

WIPF & STOCK · Eugene, Oregon

GLOBAL VOICES ON BIBLICAL EQUALITY
Women and Men Ministering Together in the Church

House of Prisca and Aquila Series

www.wipfandstock.com

ISBN 13: 978-1-55635-055-9

Manufactured in the U.S.A.

To Prisca and Aquila

Jewels come in unexpected settings.

Take Corinth in ancient Greece:
more rock than mineral,
rocks piled into rude temples to designer gods,
rocks hewn out with curved grooves where necks were laid so heads
could be severed,
rocks scattered down the Roman highway to bring in refugees from
across the known world.

This pair tumbled in from two other settings:
the soft other-worldly pastel fresco of mystic Judaism
and the bright this-worldly golden brocade of imperial Rome.

The foundation they laid, as they plied their trade together
and with their fellow sojourner Paul,
and risked their necks together to defend him,
and ordered together the doctrine of Apollos more expertly,
and oversaw together the ecclesial settings for other believers in
Ephesus and Rome,
was mineral not rock.

Gemstones of God, buried in stony, multicultural mines.

William David Spencer and Aída Besançon Spencer
May 2008

Contents

Contributors

Ellen Alexander is a homemaker and lecturer in Bangalore, India. After an M.A. in Philosophy (from Hyderabad, India, where she grew up) and a Diploma of Theology from Discipleship Training Centre, Singapore, she spent five years on staff with the Union of Evangelical Students of India (UESI) in Madras and Delhi in the early 1980s. She continues as Chair of the UESI training department and also chairs the board of Interserve India. Ellen is married to Vijay, a banker turned IT consultant, and they have two children. She completed an M.Th. in Pastoral Theology through the University of Wales in 2003. She finds gardening relaxing and enjoyable and hospitality energizes her. Active in her local church, Ellen also teaches philosophy, ethics, and world religions at the Centre for American Education, an undergraduate college in Bangalore.

The **Rev. Dr. Kevin Giles** recently retired from active parish ministry. He has been an Anglican Pastor for thirty-eight years. He has a doctorate in New Testament theology, having studied in Australia (Moore College, Sydney), England (Durham and Cambridge), and Germany (Tübingen). He has written ten books and more than sixty scholarly articles in journals and dictionaries. On the question of women in ministry, he has written *Women and Their Ministry: A Case for Equal Ministries in the Church Today* (Dove Communications), *Created Woman: A Fresh Study of the Biblical Teaching* (Acorn), *Patterns of Ministry Among the First Christians* (Collins-Dove), *The Trinity and Subordinationism: The Doctrine of God and the Contemporary Gender Debate* (InterVarsity), and *Jesus and the Father: Modern Evangelicals Reinvent the Doctrine of the Trinity* (Zondervan). He is married to Lynley, a marriage educator and counselor. The Gileses have four grown children and nine grandchildren. At present, Kevin is assisting in a parish, writing, and lecturing.

The **Rev. Dr. Awilda González-Tejera** was born in Puerto Rico. She received her Doctor of Theology degree from Boston University School of Theology. She received her Master in Christian Education and her

Master of Divinity from Gordon-Conwell Theological Seminary. She is the president, founder, and New Testament professor of the Educational Center for Biblical Studies, Dallas, Texas. Awilda has taught at Gordon-Conwell Theological Seminary, Boston, Massachusetts; Fuller Theological Seminary, Pasadena, California; and The General Theological Seminary, New York City. She has presented at conferences and has preached in North America, the Caribbean, and Central America. Her ministerial experience includes pastoring together with her husband in Iglesia Cristiana Nueva Vida, East Boston, Massachusetts, and Centro Cristiano de Oak Cliff, Dallas, Texas. At present, she is member at large of the Board of Directors of the Asociación para la Educación Teológica Hispana, Austin, Texas, an association that promotes theological education for Latinos/as. The focus of her research has been on Paul's letters and the relation of his writings to social aspects, practices, and understandings of the Greco-Roman world. The title of her dissertation is *Intercession in Paul's Letters in Light of Greco-Roman Practices of Intercession.* She is currently writing the volume *Filipenses, Colosenses, 1 y 2 Tesalonicenses, y Filemón* for the Bible commentary series "Conozca su Biblia" (Augsburg Fortress). Dr. Justo L. González is general editor.

Dr. Mimi Haddad serves as President of Christians for Biblical Equality (CBE, www.cbeinternational.org) and as Adjunct Professor of Church History, North Park Theological Seminary, Chicago, Illinois. A graduate of the University of Colorado, Boulder, Colorado (biology), Mimi completed her Master of Arts in Theological Studies at Gordon-Conwell Theological Seminary (summa cum laude, Phi Alpha Chi member). She was a recipient of the President's scholarship and the Christian Thought graduate award. She holds a Ph.D. in Historical Theology from the University of Durham, England. Her thesis is an assessment of the mystical theology and feminism of Jessie Penn-Lewis, 1861–1927. Ever interested in theology and gender, Mimi is a founding member of the Evangelicals and Gender Study Group and served as co-chair and as a member of the steering committee of the Other Voices in Interpretation study group within the Evangelical Theological Society. Because of her passion for missions and evangelism, Mimi has served on the board of directors of Global Women, a mission organization for women, by women. Mimi convened the 2004 Issue Group 24 of the Lausanne Committee for World Evangelization, Pattaya, Thailand. She has written numerous articles and has contributed to five books. She speaks frequently on issues related to gender and faith for groups and institutions. She lives in the inner city of Minneapolis, where she has been part of an affordable housing initiative that provides accessible housing for low-income and first-time homeowners. Mimi is married to Dale Halladay, whom she describes as "the most wonderful man I have ever known!"

The **Rev. Dr. Roberta Hestenes** is an educator, author, pastor, and speaker. She received her formal education from the University of California in Santa Barbara, the University of Washington, and Fuller Theological Seminary. She served as senior pastor of the two thousand member Solana Beach Presbyterian Church near San Diego, as well as serving other congregations in Washington and Pennsylvania. She taught full-time at Fuller Seminary for twelve years, where she became the first tenured woman faculty member in the Fuller School of Theology and founder of the department of Christian Formation and Discipleship. She served ten years as the first President of Eastern College/University and founder of the Center for Christian Women in Leadership. During her thirty years of association with World Vision, she has served as a Board member, chair of the International Board, and minister at large, preaching and teaching in more than seventy countries of the world. She has received numerous awards, including six honorary doctorates, and in 2008 celebrated forty-nine years of marriage to her husband John. They have three adult children and seven grandchildren.

The **Rev. Dr. Matthew D. Kim** is Senior Pastor of Logos Central Chapel in Denver, Colorado. He earned his B.A. in history from Carleton College, his M.Div. from Gordon-Conwell Theological Seminary, and his M.Th. and Ph.D. in theology and ethics (with a concentration in homiletics) from the University of Edinburgh. He is the author of *Preaching to Second Generation Korean Americans: Towards a Possible Selves Contextual Homiletic* (Peter Lang) and has contributed to various journals and books on Asian American ministry and preaching. He is married to Sarah S. Kim.

The **Rev. Dr. Constantine Matiyenga Murefu** was born in Chivhu, Zimbabwe. He earned a ministerial diploma in 1978 at the then Rhodesian African Bible College (now Living Waters Bible Seminary) in Harare. He went on to earn a teaching certificate with the University of Pretoria in South Africa in 1979 before returning to lecture at his alma mater toward the end of 1979. He graduated from Zion Bible Institute in East Providence, Rhode Island, USA, in 1983, then resumed pastoral ministry within the Apostolic Faith Mission in Zimbabwe and was ordained that same year. Concurrently, he served on the faculty of Living Waters Bible College, lecturing and serving as Dean of Students, Academic Dean, and Vice Principal, respectively. In addition, he is a graduate of International Bible Seminary (USA), Almeida University (USA), and the University of Zimbabwe, and holds several degrees in education, theology, and philosophy, including a Ph.D. Constantine served in the chaplaincy of the University of Zimbabwe from 1985 to 2008. He has pastored and founded several congregations in Harare. He has been the Principal of Living Waters Theological Seminary since 1990, when he became the first indigenous person to head the Institute since its inception in 1974. Concurrently, he is the Senior Pastor of Vessels of Honour Assembly downtown, which he founded in 2007, with ten members then, and now a membership of over one hundred. He is a well-traveled seminary and conference speaker, pulpiteer, marriage officer and counselor, church planter, and teacher. Besides an abundance of seminary lecture notes, he has authored books such as *Biblical Foundation for Believers, Biblical Africa*, and *Azusa to Harare* (Faith Printers).

The **Rev. Darin Vincent Poullard** serves as the Pastor of the Fort Washington Baptist Church in Fort Washington, Maryland, where he has served since October 2002. Pastor Poullard is a graduate of York College, the City University of New York, where he earned a B.S. in Information Systems, and Gordon-Conwell Theological Seminary's Center for Urban Ministerial Education (CUME), where he earned an M.Div. (magna cum laude, Phi Alpha Chi member). He has served as the Family Life Minister at St. John's Baptist Church, Woburn, Massachusetts, and an Athanasian Teaching Scholar at CUME. Since 1990, he has been married to Vicki Delores Poullard. They are parents of two daughters and live in Waldorf, Maryland.

The **Rev. Dr. Eliana Marques Runyon** was born in São Paulo, Brazil. In 1988, at the age of nineteen, she entered into licensed pastoral ministry. Two years after completing a Bachelor Degree in Education, she immigrated to the USA at the age of twenty-three. She earned a Diploma in Practical Theology (Christ for the Nations Institute, Dallas, Texas) and an M.Div. degree (Gordon-Conwell Theological Seminary, Boston Campus, 2004). She has worked in various ministerial roles since her arrival in the United States and later with her parents, Revs. Cairo and Iracy Marques, as a pastoral team within the Brazilian churches they pastored. In 2001,

Eliana was hired as a Technical Assistant at the Consulate General of Brazil in Boston, a role that evolved into an Office Manager function. In 2002, she became a citizen of the United States. That same year, Eliana was ordained with the International Church of the Foursquare Gospel, and in January of 2003 was appointed Superintendent of the Northeast Area of Massachusetts within the New England Portuguese District of the Foursquare Gospel Church. She was released from her role as associate pastor in Malden to plant a new Foursquare church in the city of Lynn. In 2003, John and Eliana were married. In 2004, she was appointed Director and established the Foursquare Theological Institute, a Foursquare Certified Portuguese language institute that trains leaders. In May 2007, Eliana received a D.Min. degree from Gordon-Conwell. As an adjunct professor at Gordon-Conwell's Boston campus, Eliana teaches practical ministry courses in Portuguese. In January 2008, Eliana joined the staff of Massachusetts Institute of Technology as an office manager and continues to serve with her husband John as co-pastor of One Voice Church, a Foursquare multicultural church plant in Lynn, Massachusetts, where they reside with their son, Christopher Joel, born in January of 2006.

The **Rev. John Runyon** grew up as a Missionary Kid in the Dominican Republic. While attending Bethel College, he became involved in the House of Higher Learning, an intentional covenant community committed to addressing racism and cross-cultural issues. After college, he moved to Massachusetts and enrolled in Gordon-Conwell Theological Seminary for his M.Div. (1999) and Th.M. (2001) degrees. While in school, he also served as an assistant pastor in a Brazilian church in Boston. In March 2000, John came on staff at the Center for Urban Ministerial Education, Gordon-Conwell's Boston campus, where he serves as Associate Director for Enrollment Management and also as adjunct professor in the Spanish and Portuguese languages. He currently resides in Lynn, where he and his wife Eliana are Senior Pastors of One Voice Church, a Foursquare multicultural church plant in that city. John served on the Lausanne 2004 Forum Issue Group "Reconciliation as the Mission of God: Faithful Christian Witness in a World of Destructive Conflicts and Divisions," which in 2005 launched a global Reconciliation Network. He recently published an article on that issue, "Reconciliation: Hope for Tortured Histories," *Emmanuel Research Review* 10 (19 July 2005): http://egc.org/research.

The **Rev. Dr. Aída Besançon Spencer** is Professor of New Testament at Gordon-Conwell Theological Seminary, South Hamilton, Massachusetts.

Born and reared in Santo Domingo, Dominican Republic, she earned the Ph.D. in New Testament at Southern Baptist Theological Seminary, Louisville, Kentucky, the Th.M. and M.Div. at Princeton Theological Seminary, Princeton, New Jersey, and her B.A. at Douglass College (Rutgers University). She has authored numerous articles and books including *Beyond the Curse: Women Called to Ministry* (Hendrickson), which was a 1986 *Eternity* Book of the Year; *2 Corinthians* (Hendrickson, Bible Reading Fellowship); and *Paul's Literary Style* (University Press of America). She has coauthored *The Prayer Life of Jesus* (University Press of America) and *Joy through the Night: Biblical Resources on Suffering* (Wipf & Stock), and co-edited *The Global God* (Baker). She has served as a social worker, minister, and educator in a variety of urban settings. An ordained minister of the Presbyterian Church (USA), she is a founding pastor of the Pilgrim Church, Beverly, Massachusetts. She has chaired both the Southeast and Northeast regions of the Evangelical Theological Society and has been a visiting scholar at Harvard Divinity School and El Seminario Evangelico of Puerto Rico. She is married to the Rev. Dr. William David Spencer and has one grown son, Stephen.

The **Rev. Dr. William David Spencer**, who is ordained in the Presbyterian Church (USA), is the author or editor of ten books and more than one hundred articles, reviews, stories, and poems, including *Mysterium and Mystery* (Southern Illinois University Press), *Chanting Down Babylon* (Temple University Press), and *Dread Jesus* (SPCK). Critics have called two of his books the definitive works in their fields, and he has won several awards for writing. Bill is the editor of *Priscilla Papers*, the journal of Christians for Biblical Equality, has taught theology for Gordon-Conwell Theological Seminary since 1983, and is a founding pastor of Pilgrim Church in Beverly, Massachusetts. He previously taught for New York Theological Seminary; the Caribbean Graduate School of Theology in Kingston, Jamaica; and the Louisville, Kentucky Adult Education Program, where he was teaching coordinator in adult literacy for Jefferson County, establishing and supervising eight adult literacy and GED centers. He has also done a variety of other urban ministries, including serving for several years as the Protestant Chaplain of Rider College (now Rider University). He earned his Th.D. from Boston University School of Theology, M.Div. and Th.M. degrees from Princeton Theological Seminary, and B.A. in English Education from Rutgers University. He traces his Lenni Lenape (Delaware) heritage through his father and his Eastern European background through his mother. He is married to the Rev. Dr. Aída Besançon Spencer and is the father of Stephen Spencer, a chef, filmmaker, and musician.

Elke Werner graduated from Duisburg University. By profession a schoolteacher, she is a well-known author and speaker in Germany and Europe. Five books (in German) have been published as of 2008. She also involves herself in mentoring younger women in leadership. Since 2006, Elke is the Lausanne Senior Associate for Women in Evangelism—a ministry that she develops under the name WINGS: Women's International Network in God's Service. She is married to Dr. Roland Werner.

Dr. Roland Werner, having graduated from Marburg University, is a well-known German theologian, linguist (Ph.D. in African languages), church leader, and author. His more than thirty books (all in German) have been translated into other European languages. He coauthored *Day of Devastation-Day of Contentment: The History of the Sudanese Church across 2000 Years* (Paulines). He is also Chairman of "Christival," an evangelical youth congress that brings together thousands of young Christians for training and evangelism. He is married to Elke Werner.

The **Rev. Sandra Gatlin Whitley** is an ordained elder in the African Methodist Episcopal Church. She was appointed in April 2007 to serve as the Pastor of People's AME Church in Chelsea, Massachusetts. Pastor Whitley is a graduate of Alabama State University, in Montgomery, earning a B.S. degree in Business Administration. She served in the United States Air Force for twenty-two dedicated years, earning the rank of Lieutenant Colonel, while also earning an M.A. degree in Management from Webster University. Her military career assignments took her to different parts of the world, including Massachusetts, where she accepted "God's calling." She graduated from Gordon-Conwell Theological Seminary, earning an M.Div. and an M.A. degree in Counseling. She also served as a Byington and an Athanasian Teaching Scholar at GCTS. She is the author of "Security in Christ: Attacked—Fear or Faith?" published in the *Journal for Advent Christian Thought* XXXI: 1 (Spring 2004). She is a preacher, teacher, author, and marriage and family pastoral counselor. Sandra is happily married to her friend and soul mate, Rev. Kenneth Whitley, from Philadelphia, Pennsylvania. He also served in the United States Air Force for twenty-six years. Together, they share the love of travel, photography, people, God's word, and their four nieces, four nephews, and four godchildren. They both now serve together in full-time ministry after having served on the ministerial staffs of the Hanscom Air Force Base Chapel, Bedford, Massachusetts, and the Bethel AME Church, Boston, Massachusetts.

Dr. Beulah Wood, a New Zealander who has worked in India and Nepal for more than twenty years, has authored or co-authored more than thirty books, booklets, and articles published in New Zealand, the United Kingdom, and India, including *Marriage: Patterns of Partnership* (Paternoster), *How Many Chappatis Do You Want?* (SAIACS), *Protect Yourself* (OM), *Writing Is an Art You Can Learn* (Theological Book Trust), and *Turn the Key to Creativity—and Preach More Effectively* (SAIACS), and co-edited or co-authored *Parenting Your Child* (UBSPD), *Pioneering on the Pinda* (ELS), *Building Stronger Families: Sermons that Nurture* (SAIACS), and *Side by Side* (SAIACS). With her B.A. from Auckland University, New Zealand, and B.D. from Melbourne College of Divinity, Australia, she later chose to study the D.Min. in Preaching when in her fifties and graduated from Gordon-Conwell Theological Seminary, Massachusetts (USA), in 2002. Currently lecturing and editing at South Asia Institute of Advanced Christian Studies, Bangalore, India, Beulah has studied and written on gender issues since 1983. She enjoys the hobbies of walking and bird watching. Beulah is the mother of four adult daughters and has been a widow since the age of thirty-seven.

Cecilia Yau was born in China and grew up in Hong Kong. Since 1969, she has been living in the United States and has been serving at the Chinese Christian Mission (CCM) in northern California for more than thirty years. She was the Associate General Secretary in charge of the literature ministry and the personnel department. Currently, she is the Ministry Ambassador of CCM and focuses on writing and preaching. Cecilia has a master's degree in journalism from Wheaton College Graduate School and a Th.M. from Columbia International University. She has written several books, including co-authoring two books on women: *Passion for Fullness* and *Gender Reconciliation*. She also co-authored *Walk in Love, Live in Love, Cults and Extreme Groups, Managing Church Conflicts*. All the above books were written in Chinese. She also edited a book in English, *A Winning Combination: Understanding the Cultural Tensions in Chinese Churches*. She translated *Turning Points* (by Mark A. Noll) and *From Jerusalem to Irian Jaya* (part I) (by Ruth A. Tucker) into Chinese.

Preface

RECENTLY, AN EXPERT IN artificial intelligence made this prediction: "Accepting that huge technological advances will be achieved by around 2050, my thesis is this: Robots will be hugely attractive to humans as companions because of their many talents, senses, and capabilities. They will have the capacity to fall in love with humans and to make themselves romantically attractive and sexually desirable to humans. . . . Humans will fall in love with robots, humans will marry robots, and humans will have sex with robots."[1] The idea of artificially constructing a perfect mate has been in the world since Pygmalion in the ancient Greek legend "saw so much to blame in women that he came at last to abhor the sex," and, instead, "made with wonderful skill a statue of ivory, so beautiful that no living woman came anywhere near it. It was indeed the perfect semblance of a maiden that seemed to be alive," so that "Pygmalion admired his own work, and at last fell in love with the counterfeit creation." We are then told he "caressed it, and gave it presents such as young girls love . . . and called her his wife." Finally, the goddess Venus animated it so that his creation could indeed become his spouse.[2] At the dawn of film, Fritz Lang's groundbreaking 1926 motion picture, *Metropolis*, tells the story of an industrialist who seeks to crush a worker revolt by kidnapping its female Christian leader and substituting a sexbot, that is, just such a robot, designed primarily for sexual purposes, to discredit her and her movement. In many subsequent movies and stories, including such innovative films as *AI*, *Making Mr. Right*, *Bicentennial Man*, and *Cherry 2000*, Pygmalion's struggle to create an artificial human that is perfectly obedient, compliant, and bent entirely to its owner's wishes has been explored.

David Levy, who wrote the book called *Love and Sex with Robots*, with which I opened our preface, is musing on a question raised by Sherry

---

1. David Levy, *Love and Sex with Robots* (New York: HarperCollins, 2007), 21–22.

2. Thomas Bulfinch, *The Age of Fable or Beauties of Mythology* (Philadelphia: David McKay, 1898), 79.

Turkle in her own thoughtful book, *The Second Self,* that we humans should be asking "not what the computer will be like in the future, but instead, what will *we* be like? What kind of people are we becoming?"[3]

That particular question is certainly not limited to our interacting with androids, but is one that humans have been asking since the falling out of Adam and Eve in the garden. What does being woman and man mean in a fallen world? We understand that human relationships were knocked so utterly askew that today we have arrived at the point of considering the rejection of an essential, sentient human life and its replacement by a mechanical doll as one's helpmeet, spouse, and sexual partner. We discover that the church may shortly become the chief voice for preserving the uniqueness of the human being in an increasingly technologically confused society. But have we in the church paused to posit whether the war we have continued to foster between man and woman for gender supremacy has itself been a prelude to this dismal end, which takes us right back to the pagan misanthropy of Pygmalion: to eschew those of the opposite sex and create a being entirely malleable to our own desires? As voices among us continue to clamor that God's intention has always been for one sex to rule the other exclusively, or, in inevitable reaction, that the subsequently oppressed sex seek artificial insemination and construct a life for itself virtually eliminating the need for the other, we need to pause and ask: How can we work with one another to restore the balance first intended for us when God gave us the joint command to steward the earth and its creatures together (see Gen 1:28)? That is the intention of this book: Our goal is to explore around the world the present state of women and men who are together serving Jesus Christ, the great champion and rescuer of fallen humanity by divine and human sacrificial love.

After an introduction by the president of Christians for Biblical Equality, an organization whose primary task is to encourage men and women to work together to bring in God's rule, we begin with representatives from Asia, where Christianity is vibrantly alive and on the move today. Authors from India, China, and Korean America survey the present situation of women and men working on equal footing to serve Christ in their cultures. They explore what positive steps have been made to promote gender cooperation and what stumbling blocks still

---

3. Cited in David Levy, *Love and Sex with Robots,* 21, emphasis original.

stand in the way of full partnerships in ministry. Authors from Africa and African America then investigate the opportunities and challenges facing joint ministry among their constituencies. These are followed by discussions of Native America, Latin America, and Brazilians in the United States. Germany is our representative of Europe, having been the site of the original Reformation. Why is that fitting? This chapter calls for a new reformation—a reforming of the present state of Christianity back to God's original intention at the creation of humanity—that men and women reflect the perfect love within the Triune Godhead, working together in perfect equality and harmony. The book is completed by similar analyses of gender equality in ministry in Australia and the United States. Finally, a conclusion summarizes the main themes and key points that have emerged. I should note this is the first original book to emerge from the ministry of the House of Prisca and Aquila editorial team. Particular gratitude is expressed to Dr. Jewel Hyun, Deborah Beatty Mel, and Rev. John Lathrop. The editors also wish to thank Anastasios Markoulidakis for formatting help and the staffs of the Hamilton-Wenham, Massachusetts, Public Library and the Goddard Library of Gordon-Conwell Theological Seminary for helping obtain resources.

Ultimately, our book is drawing this conclusion: We really do not need to use our technological capability to eliminate the need for each other by substituting artificial facsimiles of the other gender as perfectly controlled and pliable counterparts. That solution to the war between the genders only moves us toward the destination of complete narcissism: the adoration of the self. It takes us totally out of the realm of interacting with someone other. But, such instructive interdependent interaction between two independent others has been God's intention since splitting humanity into two halves at the beginning. The dual nature of humanity, reuniting to become one flesh in marriage and one body in the worshiping church, has been a divine teaching tool to train us to love the other, and thereby learn to love the Wholly Other: God our Creator. God's primal intention was to create us to enter into a love relationship with God, as we learn to love and work with each other, to become more, not less, others-oriented. God has always wanted us to choose to use our capabilities not simply to win our war with each other, but to find a lasting peace as we work together to fulfill at last God's command to steward this wonderful earth in complete cooperation with one another. That kind of cooperation alone will make us the type of people who will be able to bring God's rule back to our world.

We have to confess that we are very enthusiastic about this book. It is the true successor to our previous volume, *The Global God: Multicultural Evangelical Views of God*.[4] In that book, we looked at conceptions of God around the world and discovered that the one true God had a prior claim on all cultures. By assessing the issue of gender equality globally, we are once again examining within the context of all people groupings and nationalities, though space limits us to representative examples. What we have noticed is that prejudice against the other is pervasive. It does not confine itself to a single venue or respect any border. It is all about power and control, not love and self-sacrifice. It isolates individuals rather than promotes community. But God is all about networking multicultural humanity into one great body of Christ. So, in this present volume, we are looking at the state of humanity around the world, exploring how well we are succeeding in fulfilling God's intention for us to work in unity to bring Christ's reign into all our lives together as God has commanded us. It is an energizing and holy search. May it bless you and encourage you too to act for equality in your sphere of influence.

William David Spencer

---

4. Aída Besançon Spencer and William David Spencer, eds., *The Global God: Multicultural Evangelical Views of God* (Grand Rapids: Baker, 1998).

Reform Movements: How They Revive the Church

Mimi Haddad

INTRODUCTION

THROUGHOUT HISTORY, THE CHURCH has altered its perspective on significant theological and social issues. Through scholarly inquiry, debate, and global dialogue, the church has reformed its viewpoint, admitting error in areas such as science, theology, and the impact of ethnicity and gender on church leadership. What have been the more significant areas on which the church has amended its opinion? Consider the following:

Copernicus Reform

Under the Copernicus reform, the church was forced to retract senseless dogma regarding the orbit of the planets, recognizing that the essentials of Christian faith are not compromised by scientific inquiry. Through this challenge, the church was freed to pursue scientific inquiry as God-given and integral to God's purposes for humanity. Scientific discovery not only may advance the wellbeing of human existence, but may also assure us that all truth is God's truth.

Protestant Reform

As a system of indulgences sold by the church overshadowed the doctrine of the atonement, theologians throughout Britain and Europe (especially Martin Luther in Germany) demanded that the church embrace Christ's completed work on Calvary as the only path to salvation and as integral to biblical revelation and Christian faith.

Abolition Reform

The abolitionists considered anew the scriptural challenge to ascriptivism—the notion that one's value and sphere of influence was determined by one's ethnicity or class. Discerning the difference between the moral teachings of the Bible and "Bible culture" (that is, the ancient culture in which God inspired the original authors), the abolitionists advanced a method of biblical interpretation that exposed prejudice, self-interest, and a shallow reading of Scripture that circumvented the biblical ethic to love one's neighbor as oneself.

Gender Reform

Like abolition, the first wave feminists in the late 1800s argued that the whole of Scripture, from Genesis to Revelation, expands rather than limits opportunities for women's service. Christians such as Frances Willard, A. J. Gordon, Fredrick Franson, Katharine Bushnell, Catherine Booth, Sojourner Truth, and others presented a cohesive and comprehensive biblical case that challenged the longstanding view that women are ontologically inferior to men and should therefore submit to male authority in church, home, and society. Like the abolitionists and parallel to them, egalitarians developed methods of interpreting Scripture that freed the church from theological and moral error regarding the treatment of women and the stewardship of their God-given gifts.

Characteristics of Reform Movements

Throughout its earthly pilgrimage, the church continues to undergo renewal and reform. To put it another way, the Holy Spirit "cleans house" in each generation, allowing the church to reflect more perfectly God's holiness and justice in the world. In every age, God corrects error and sin through the work of reformers or prophets who help us to confront our indifference, ignorance, or moral failings as the church.

In assessing reform and renewal movements, it is important to note that its leaders perceive, through a rigorous engagement with Scripture, a truth that has gone unobserved by the church. They articulate the need for biblical reform, and their theological scholarship has sweeping global influence. As God prompts the church to examine the biblical texts anew, the Spirit works within the text, as Gordon Fee points out, leading us, sometimes kicking and screaming, to a better understanding of God's purpose for the church.[1] Thus, throughout church history, Christians continually depend upon their biblical moorings in order to address the challenges of each age.

Thus, a passionate return to Scripture is frequently the first quality noted in reform movements. As reform movements progress, they often move through stages and exhibit similar qualities as they prompt us to perceive and act on truth. Not all reform movements progress in a linear fashion; yet, by outlining qualities shared by reform movements, we hope to develop a framework that assists us in identifying whether a given movement is an authentic reform movement. In general, reform movements often begin with a rigorous intellectual engagement with an issue. Once scholars shape and debate their ideas, artists make academic concepts compelling emotionally, prompting a global discussion. As popular and academic leaders press for reform, the position under critique typically modifies its opinion, often by developing a more moderate perspective. In an authentic reform, the church changes its view both in terms of theology and practice. Let us consider the stages of reform in greater detail.

1. An Intellectual Appeal to Scripture

Reformers see, in profound ways, a deep biblical truth that has not been observed by their peers. As their insights expose error, their scholarship appears initially aberrant to the whole of the church. Eventually, the logic of reformers garners the respect of others, and their work engages and enriches the global church both intellectually and also morally. Ultimately, reform movements call to the church, "Come, let us reason together." A deeper grasp of biblical revelation is often accompanied by another quality of renewal movements—prayer!

2. Prayer

Prayer guides and ignites reform movements. As prayer meets God's reforming work in the church, humans become vibrant vehicles of God's renewing power. Mary Queen of Scots said she "feared the prayers of John Knox more than all the assembled armies of Europe."[2] Prayer fueled the

1. Gordon Fee, *Listening to the Spirit in the Text* (Grand Rapids: Eerdmans, 2000).

2. Mary Queen of Scots, http://www.reformation-scotland.org.uk/articles/lessons -from-john-knox.php (accessed 12 May 2008).

abolitionist movement and the revivals that swept through slave communities as God quickened the oppressed to become leaders of reform. Their prayers and songs of lament and praise awakened reform globally. The arduous work of church reform is accomplished best through the strategic tools of prayer and worship.[3]

3. The Popularization of Theological Ideas

Once the case has been made intellectually for reform, after key visionaries articulate their ideas, God recruits the troubadours—the artists, musicians, activists, and literary geniuses who make intellectual arguments compelling to popular audiences. Artists function as activists by infusing reformist ideas into human hearts, enabling the layperson to perceive the need for reform. While making a reformist case rationally and intellectually is necessary, it is never sufficient. Art enables the human heart first to understand and then to take action. Here are a few examples:

The Protestant reform harnessed the printing press and also music, building consensus among non-intellectuals. A Mighty Fortress is thought to have been a popular German beer-drinking song that reformers shaped into a Protestant hymn. The tune was beloved, though the words were entirely new. The hymn planted Protestant theology into minds and hearts of everyday people. It serves that purpose today.

The abolitionist reform published slave narratives such as the story of Sojourner Truth, African spirituals like Swing Low, and literary works such as Uncle Tom's Cabin to popularize the need for abolition. These songs and literary works enabled non-slaves to feel the injustice of slavery. It was the burden of reformers to expose the moral failings and injustice of slavery, an institution the world had always known and never questioned. Artists taught the world to feel as slaves felt about slavery.

Once the call for reform had been made theologically, spiritually, and emotionally, reformist ideas gained global momentum. A true reform is a global reform.

4. A Global Scope

Reformers find each other across cultural and continental lines. Discussion begins among like-minded individuals who see the same truth, though

---

3. We remember the prayer and worship of Paul and Silas in prison (Acts 16:25), which led many more to faith in Christ.

from within different cultural contexts. What began as a local concern becomes a global conversation. Christians in America join Christians in Europe, who join those in Africa, South America, and Asia. It is the whole body of Christ, praying, writing, thinking, and exploring reformist ideas as the global body of Christ. It is as if reformers wake up the whole church to the need for reform from within their own cultural context.

The engagement of Christians from around the globe inspires a sharpening of reformist ideas and provides clarity, biblical definition, and conviction to the rightness of the reform. The international discussion grows into a global solidarity, and the internal cohesiveness lends a legitimacy and momentum gained through the agreement of the global church. The point is that reformist ideas are impossible to ignore because they are God-given.

5. The Position Under Critique Cedes Ground

As scholars, troubadours, and activists from around the global church offer their support, the position under critique begins to modify its position, slowly admitting error. In the case of abolition, proslavery proponents sought to address the abuses of slavery rather than disassemble the institution. In gender reform, the hierarchical camp confronts the abuses of hierarchy rather than deconstructing patriarchy philosophically.[4] Slave owners are called to be more humane masters in the same way men are urged to remain in all positions of authority, though with compassion. The abuses are confronted rather than the unilateral power base.

6. Reform Brings Change

A God-given reform effects change in both theology and praxis. With some difficulty, the position under critique admits error and yields to the consensus of the global church.

Having assessed the stages or prominent manifestations of reform movements, we will consider key reformers as they manifested these qualities and as they developed theological foundations that inform gender reform.

---

4. For the best example of this, see Steven Tracy, "Headship with a Heart: How Biblical Patriarchy Actually Prevents Abuse," *Christianity Today,* Feb. 2003, n.p. Online: http://www.ctlibrary.com/ct/2003/february/5.50.html (accessed 18 April 2008).

ABOLITION REFORM

William Wilberforce (1759–1833) was perhaps the most prominent abolitionist in Britain. After undergoing a profound religious experience, Wilberforce pursued a rigorous life of spiritual discipline. He discerned that God had called him to a political career. As a member of Parliament, Wilberforce devoted himself to abolition, missions, religious freedom, and social reform. In 1788, Wilberforce spoke for three and a half hours in the House of Commons to advocate for freeing slaves. He said, "Sir, when we think of eternity and the future consequence of all human conduct, what is there in this life that shall make any man contradict the dictates of his conscience, the principles of justice and the law of God!"[5] His motion was unsuccessful, but he advanced abolition for eighteen years until England disassembled their slave trade. Wilberforce propelled the abolition reform on spiritual, intellectual, and popular fronts.

Frederick Douglass (1818–1895) was an American and perhaps the most articulate speaker on behalf of abolitionism. An advisor to President Abraham Lincoln, Douglass is also considered the first great African American public speaker. He insisted that the United States Constitution be amended, giving slaves all the rights of other male American citizens. His capacity as a reformer is most keenly noted in his appeal to intellect, passion, and a consistent Christian witness. Douglass said,

> Indeed, I can see no reason, but the most deceitful one, for calling the religion of this land Christianity. I look upon it as the climax of all misnomers, the boldest of all frauds, and the grossest of all libels. Never was there a clearer case of "stealing the livery of the court of heaven to serve the devil in." I am filled with unutterable loathing when I contemplate the religious pomp and show, together with the horrible inconsistencies, which every where surround me. We have men-stealers for ministers, women-whippers for missionaries, and cradle-plunderers for church members. The man who wields the blood-clotted cowskin during the week fills the pulpit on Sunday, and claims to be a minister of the meek and lowly Jesus. The man who robs me of my earnings at the end of each week meets me as a class-leader on Sunday morning, to show me the way of life, and the path of salvation. He who sells my sister, for purposes of prostitution, stands forth as the pious advocate of purity. He who proclaims it a religious duty to read the Bible

5. William Wilberforce's 1788 House of Commons address. Online at http://satucket .com/lectionary/William_Wilberforce.htm (accessed 1 May 2008).

denies me the right of learning to read the name of the God who made me. He who is the religious advocate of marriage robs whole millions of its sacred influence, and leaves them to the ravages of wholesale pollution. The warm defender of the sacredness of the family relation is the same that scatters whole families,—sundering husbands and wives, parents and children, sisters and brothers,—leaving the hut vacant and the heart desolate. We see the thief preaching against theft, and the adulterer against adultery. We have men sold to build churches, women sold to support the gospel, and babes sold to purchase Bibles for the poor heathen! All for the glory of God and the good of souls.[6]

Sojourner Truth (1797–1887) was an abolitionist, suffragist, preacher, and social reformer who garnered the respect of prominent abolitionists including President Lincoln. Truth had a brilliant theological mind, though she never learned to read or write. A devout Christian, Truth's intimacy with Christ guided her work as an abolitionist and suffragist. During a suffragist meeting in Ohio, Truth argued that to deny women the privilege of voting or preaching because Christ was male was to ignore the fact (posited by Karl Barth years later) that it was Christ's humanity—not his gender—that made him a sacrifice for both men and women. Truth showed that the value, dignity, and service of women is located in their truest identity—as heirs of Christ's sacrifice equally available to men and women. Truth's advocacy of abolition and suffrage had a popular, academic, and spiritual force.[7]

Frances Willard (1839–1898) was one of the most popular women in the United States in her day. When she died, flags were lowered to half-mast in three major cities. Willard served as president of Evanston's Ladies College, which would become Northwestern University, and she was also president of the Woman's Christian Temperance Union, the largest women's organization of its day devoted to evangelism, temperance, suffrage, and abolition.

---

6. Fredrick Douglass, *Narrative of the Life of Frederick Douglass* (1845) n.p., http://gbgm-umc.org/UMW/bible/douglass.stm (accessed 18 April 2008). See also Frederick Douglass, *Life and Times of Frederick Douglass: His Early Life as a Slave, His Escape from Bondage, and His Complete History* (New York: Collier, 1892).

7. Sojourner Truth, "Ain't I a Woman?" speech delivered at the Women's Convention, Akron, Ohio, 1851. Online: http://www.fordham.edu/halsall/mod/sojtruth-woman.html (accessed 12 May 2008).

An activist of the highest order, Willard combated prostitution, exposed the need for laws against rape, fought domestic violence, and called fashion designers to eliminate destructive pencil-thin waistlines. Willard encouraged women's participation in physical fitness (the bloomer's bicycle), and she also lobbied for public drinking fountains to keep men out of saloons.

A reformer with an international view, Willard built a cohesive network of activists in the United States and abroad, who in turn built momentum for evangelism and gender justice in places like India and Britain. Willard's feminism grew out of her commitment to Scripture, evangelism, and social action—loyalties that placed her within the evangelical ethos of her day.[8] D. L. Moody so admired her leadership that he invited her to participate in his Boston campaign where, sadly, her service was limited to the women's meetings. Willard expressed her displeasure in this way:

> All my life I have been devoted to the advancement of women in education, an opportunity I firmly believe God has a work for them to do, as evangelists, as bearers of the Christ's message to the ungospeled, to the prayer meeting, to the church generally and the world at large, such as most people have not dreamed. It is therefore my dearest wish to help break down the barriers of prejudice that keeps them silent. I cannot think that meetings in which "the brethren" only are called upon, are one half as effective as those where all are freely invited, and I can but believe that "Women's Meetings" as such, are a relic of an outworn regime. Never did I hold one of these meetings without a protest in my soul against it. As in the day of Pentecost, so now, let men and women in perfectly impartial fashion participate in all services conducted in His name in whom there is neither bond nor free, male nor female, but all are one.[9]

Abolitionist reformers like Douglass, Truth, Wilberforce, and Willard drove abolition intellectually, spiritually, emotionally, and globally. Abolitionists forever changed the way we interpret Scripture not only

---

8. Mark Noll, *The Rise of Evangelicalism: The Age of Edwards, Whitefield, and the Wesleys* (Downers Grove, Ill.: InterVarsity, 2003), 19. See also David Bebbington, *Evangelicalism in Modern Britain: A History from 1730s to the 1980s* (Grand Rapids: Baker, 1989).

9. Frances Willard, *Glimpses of Fifty Years: The Autobiography of an American Woman* (Chicago: H.J. Smith, 1889), 360.

as it concerns slaves, but also women. Let us now consider the theological work of abolitionists as it illuminates gender reform today.

THEOLOGICAL CONTRIBUTIONS OF ABOLITION TO GENDER REFORM[10]

The interpretive challenges faced by abolition and gender reformists are strikingly similar. Both redress a shallow reading of Scripture. Both insist upon the historical and cultural contexts underlying key biblical passages. Both confront the tendency to confuse the moral teachings of Scripture with Bible culture. Let us consider each in turn.

The Plain Reading of Scripture Challenged

The proslavery camp relied on a plain reading of Scripture as a defense for slavery, insisting that one might read biblical writers such as Paul at face value without considering the historical or cultural background. To do otherwise, they claimed, was to exchange the authority of Scripture for enlightenment ideals. For example, in 1864, John Henry Hopkins said that Scripture's defense of slavery was clear. He wrote:

> The Bible's defense of slavery is very plain. St. Paul was inspired, and knew the will of the Lord Jesus Christ, and was only intent on obeying it. And who are we, that in our modern wisdom presume to set aside the Word of God . . . and invent for ourselves a "higher law" than those holy Scriptures which are given to us as "a light to our feet and a lamp to our paths," in the darkness of a sinful and a polluted world?[11]

In retort, the abolitionists railed at the idea that slavery would seek refuge in Scripture. Theodore Dwight Weld replied to Hopkins, writing:

> Slavery seeks refuge in the Bible only in its last extremity. . . . Goaded to frenzy in its conflicts with conscience and common sense, . . . it courses up and down the Bible, "seeking rest, and finding none." The law of love, glowing on every page, flashes through its anguish and despair.[12]

---

10. Much of what follows can be found in Willard Swartley's excellent book, *Slavery, Sabbath, War, and Women: Case Issues in Biblical Interpretation* (Scottdale, Penn: Herald, 1983).

11. John Henry Hopkins, as quoted by Swartley, *Slavery, Sabbath, War, and Women*, 31.

12. Weld, quoted in Swartley, *Slavery, Sabbath, War, and Women*, 31.

Through a plain reading of Scripture, proponents of slavery confused the attendant features of Scripture (slavery) with its moral precepts. The following is a list of verses, read at face value, to support slavery:[13]

1. Slavery was noted among the Patriarchs (Gen 9:24–27).

2. Abraham owned slaves (Gen 12:5, 16, 14:14, 20:14, 24:35–36, 26:13–14); Joseph bought slaves (Gen 47:15–25).

3. Paul sent Onesimus back to Philemon, since Onesimus was Philemon's property.

4. The angel commanded Hagar to return to Sarah (Gen 16:1–9).

5. Neither Paul nor Jesus opposed slavery.

6. Slavery was part of Israel's constitution.

7. Slave owners were leaders in the early church.

Abolitionists pressed beyond the plain reading of Scripture as an interpretive method, insisting upon an historically researched and biblically cohesive response to those passages which, read at face value, were used to support slavery. Here are a few examples:

It was Noah, not God, who declared the Canaanites slaves, and Noah was drunk (Gen 9:25). Furthermore, Africans are not descendants of Canaanites. If Canaan includes all of Ham's posterity, then "Assyrians, some Persians and all Grecians and Romans should be slaves."[14]

Abolitionists highlighted the daunting differences between American slavery and slavery in ancient Israel. In contrast to the American institution of slavery, slavery in Israel was a method of debt repayment. Slaves in Israel enjoyed all the social and religious benefits of the nation. Israel's slavery in Egypt was viewed as loathsome and her exodus (detailed in the Book of Exodus) is celebrated at Passover every year.[15]

Though neither Jesus nor Paul explicitly opposed slavery, still Christ said that the Son of God came to serve and lay down his life for many. Christ noted that the rulers of the gentiles lord their authority over everyone, but it shall not be so among his followers (Matt 20:25–28). Those

---

13. See Swartley, *Slavery, Sabbath, War, and Women*, 33ff.

14. Swartley, *Slavery, Sabbath, War, and Women*, 39.

15. See Swartley, *Slavery, Sabbath, War, and Women*, 41ff.

who follow Christ must be ready to take up their cross and lay down their lives. Those who want to be great must serve, and those who want to be first must be last. Similarly, though Paul never openly opposed slavery, yet he told slave owners that they are ultimately responsible to God (1 Tim 1:10). Paul instructed Philemon to receive Onesimus as a brother (Phlm 16–17). Paul's words in Galatians 3:28 illustrate the unity and oneness of Christians in Christ.[16]

Confronting the "plain reading of Scripture" as an interpretive method, abolitionists retained the authority of Scripture without embracing the hierarchy of Bible culture. As proponents of slavery relied upon isolated passages, read without consideration of the historical background and without regard to the clear moral and theological teachings of Scripture, abolitionists developed an egalitarian hermeneutic that allowed the spirit of Scripture—the whole teaching of Scripture—to triumph over the letter—isolated texts. Herein slavery met its exegetical doom.

As abolitionists exposed the thin biblical moorings upon which slavery rests, proslavery Christians begin to back-peddle their position by suggesting that it was not slavery that Scripture opposes, but the abuses within slavery: "Let it be said again that support of slavery is not support of all its abuses. . . ."[17] Abolitionists exposed the need for a cohesive hermeneutic that harmonized individual passages not only with the whole of Scripture, but also with the theological and moral teachings of Christian faith. Ultimately, the debate turned to methods of interpretation.

A Question of Hermeneutics

At first, the debate over slavery focused on the meaning of the Hebrew words such as *ebed* ("slave or servant") and *kana* ("to buy") and the Greek word *doulos* ("slave or servant"),[18] just as the gender debate initially centered on the meaning of Bible words such as *ezer* (woman's help likened to the *ezer*-help God gives Israel in Ps 121:1–2), *kephalē* (as "source" rather than "authority" in 1 Cor 11:3), and *authentein* as abusive or domineering authority (in 1 Tim 2:12).

Yet, as abolitionists and egalitarians pressed for an accurate rendering of Bible words, they also demanded a thorough understanding of how

16. See Swartley, *Slavery, Sabbath, War, and Women*, 43ff.

17. Swartley, *Slavery, Sabbath, War, and Women*, 47.

18. Swartley, *Slavery, Sabbath, War, and Women*, 40, 198 &ff.

individual passages fit into a cohesive moral message. For example, why did the apostle Paul direct Philemon to receive Onesimus as a brother in Christ? Why did Paul celebrate rather than condemn the leadership of women as an apostle (like Junia in Rom 16:7), a deacon or pastor (like Phoebe, Rom 16:3), a teacher (such as Priscilla, Acts 18:26), as prophets (noted in Luke 2:36ff; Acts 2:17; 1 Cor 11:3–5, 14:31), as house church leaders (cited in Acts 16:13–15, 40; 1 Cor 1:11, 16:19; Phlm 2; 2 John 1:1), and his coworkers (as those in Phil 4:3)?

Ultimately, abolitionists and egalitarians sought Paul's overarching theological principles as they concerned gender, slavery, and authority in the church. In other words, to what extent do the biblical writers like Paul advance the ontological and functional equality of slaves and women in Christ's New Covenant community? If slaves, like women, are equal recipients of God's gifting and call to service, we should not be surprised to observe an astonishing number of New Testament leaders who were slaves and women,[19] illustrating Paul's theological standards, such as those expressed in Galatians 3:28.

Abolitionists and egalitarians not only sought theological tenets of Scripture, they also assumed the moral teachings of the Bible were part of its theological foundations. For example, patriarchy and slavery are part of Bible culture, yet Scripture does not promote these as moral mandates or as theological absolutes. Abolitionists and egalitarians are accused of ignoring the authority of the Bible,[20] when in fact their focus is on interpretation. How do we read the Bible consistently, theologically, and morally? As part of their search for moral principles in the interpretive process, abolitionists and egalitarians caution against self-interest when reading Scripture.

Ultimately, debate over slavery became a question of hermeneutics. How do we interpret Scripture consistently, theologically, and morally?

19. See Mark Reasoner, "Chapter 16 in Paul's Letter to the Romans: Dispensable Tagalong or Valuable Envelope?" *Priscilla Papers* 20, no. 4 (Autumn 2006):11–17, for examples of Paul's coworkers who were slaves and women.

20. Abolitionists were accused of capitulating to enlightenment ideals; see Swartley, *Slavery, Sabbath, War, and Women*, 199ff. Egalitarians are likewise accused of submitting to a social ethic other than Scripture. See Wayne Grudem, "Should We Move Beyond the New Testament to a Better Ethic? An Analysis of William J. Webb, *Slaves, Women and Homosexuals: Exploring the Hermeneutics of Cultural Analysis*," *JETS* 47, no. 2 (June 2004):299–346. See also *Evangelical Feminism and Biblical Truth: An Analysis of More than One Hundred Disputed Questions* (Sisters, Ore.: Multnomah, 2004).

How do the pieces fit into the whole? How do we interpret Scripture while laying aside self-interest? Were slave owners ready to admit that the ultimate end of slavery was profit and a base love of power rather than the salvation of the slave, as it had been argued? Eventually, the slavery debate gave rise to interpretive methods that include the following:[21]

1. A plain reading of the Bible must include the historical and cultural context.

2. The full testimony of Scripture must be heard. The obscure portions of Scripture must be considered through those passages that are obvious. What is the clear teaching of Scripture? It is love, not bondage.

3. A portion of Scripture should be viewed for its primary emphasis, not for its "attendant features."[22] The history of Sarah and Abraham teaches us that they trusted God's promises, not that they had servants or slaves.

4. Readers should be scrupulous in assessing their own selfish motives when reading the Bible.

Using the interpretive method gained from the abolitionist reform, we can interpret 1 Corinthians 14:34 (a text often assumed to silence or prohibit women's preaching and teaching in the church) and, therefore, texts like it more accurately.

1 Corinthians 14:33b–36: An Interpretive Exercise

(As in all the churches of the saints, women should be silent in the churches. For they are not permitted to speak, but should be subordinate, as the law also says. If there is anything they desire to know, let them ask their husbands at home. For it is shameful for a woman to speak in church. Or did the word of God originate with you? Or are you the only ones it has reached?) (NRSV)

A plain reading of this passage teaches that women may not speak in church and must be subordinate to their husbands. Is this passage

21. See Swartley, *Slavery, Sabbath, War, and Women,* 58 & ff.
22. Swartley, *Slavery, Sabbath, War, and Women,* 60 & ff.

transcultural, applying to all women in all churches? Using the interpretive methods gleaned from abolitionist reform, we turn to the whole of Scripture to discover that women did speak, declare, and prophesy in public.

Anna was a prophet (Luke 2:36ff). Women prophesied at Pentecost (Acts 2:17), and Philip had four prophesying daughters (Acts 21:9). The spiritual gifts (in Romans, Corinthians, and Ephesians) are never limited by gender. Moreover, prophets are named second in the list of those having spiritual gifts (1 Cor 12:28). Paul tells the church in Corinth that all may prophesy, as long as they take turns (1 Cor 14:31). Paul instructs men and women on how to dress when prophesying (1 Cor 11:5).

In considering the cultural background, we discover that Paul's letter to believers in Corinth reveals a troubled and struggling church. Corinth was a rich and decadent city. It was the location of the temple of Aphrodite—a fertility goddess whose temple boasted one thousand prostitutes.

First Corinthians was written about A.D. 55 and concerned a set of difficulties encountered by the church in Corinth. Writing from Ephesus, Paul had been made aware of those specific problems his letter addressed, including the following:

1. Divided loyalties and dissensions (1:10ff, 3:4ff, 6:1–11)

2. Sexual immorality (5:1–11, 6:12–20, 10:7–11)

3. Drunkenness (11:21)

4. Food sacrificed to idols (8:4ff, 10:14ff)

5. Disorder and confusion during teaching and worship (14:23ff)

6. Questions on whether women needed head coverings (11:5–6, 10, 13–15)

7. Questions on whether women should be silent (14:34)

Paul, in dealing with these, initially instructed women to cover their heads, but finally asked them to be silent in the church (1 Cor 14:34). Paul's restriction of women prophets must be viewed in light of his comments three chapters earlier, telling women how to dress when speaking (1 Cor 11:5).

Clearly, Paul's instruction to silence women appears at the end of his exhortation to teach the gospel in an orderly way so others might hear and understand (1 Cor 14:1–36). Paul's primary concern is evangelism. It was probable that married women were crossing into the male section of the synagogue or house church to discuss topics with their husbands,[23] and their chatter was disruptive to the entire church. Thus, the trouble was not *women* speaking, but that their *speaking* was disruptive. Perhaps women in Corinth also spoke with uncovered heads as they did in Corinthian cultic practices. To do so may have proved confusing and also disruptive. This passage works to address a specific problem in Corinth and should not be viewed as universal in application. What is transcultural is Paul's emphasis on preaching the gospel in an orderly way, not restricting the freedom women have to speak in church.

Paul shows a similar concern that the gospel take precedence over speaking in tongues (1 Cor 14:5, 9, 18–19, 32–33). Paul celebrates the gift of tongues, yet when speaking in tongues proves disruptive, like the chatter of women, Paul limits its expression. The highest good is the gospel, which was compromised by the chatter of women and by speaking in tongues. Paul's theological and moral imperative is evangelism—the gospel. While women, wives, and slaves live in a culture that devalues them, in the church they share equally in Christ's New Covenant community where they may use their gifts in mutual service in order to advance the gospel. But, when expressing these gifts brings shame on the gospel, Paul limits their freedom. In many cultures today, women enjoy freedoms inherited from first wave feminists and, thus, limiting women's freedom now brings shame on the gospel. The highest good is the gospel. Therefore, we must confront self-interest and share leadership and authority with women, just as Paul did.

CONCLUSION

The interpretive method garnered from the abolitionist reform has application to the gender debate in the church. This exercise illustrates how helpful, theologically, reform movements are in providing new inroads into Scripture that not only sharpen the church intellectually, but also carry the church to higher moral ground. Reform movements press us to observe not only the words of Scripture, but also how these words were

---

23. Hence, Paul recommends that they ask their husbands at home.

understood at the time Scripture was written and what moral principles they teach us today.

Reform movements also help us to discern not only the meaning of Bible words, but how these words illuminate the overarching moral principles in Scripture. Here we observe the interdependence of biblical and systematic theology. To interpret Scripture accurately, one must not only interpret each passage of Scripture carefully after a thorough understanding of the historical context, but also ascertain the meaning derived from each passage fitting consistently and harmoniously with the rest of the theological doctrines and moral principles of the Bible. For example, our understanding of a particular passage concerning human relationships (or anthropology) must be interpreted consistently alongside our understanding of the Trinity.[24] There is an interdependence and internal consistency among biblical themes. Biblical theology cannot do violence to systematic theology, just as systematic theology must work harmoniously with biblical theology. Scripture must inform Scripture, both biblically and theologically. Reform movements compel us to read Scripture more consistently. The exegetical and interpretive lessons garnered in reform movements assist future generations as they work to read Scripture consistently.

Just as abolitionists learned that, while slavery was embedded in the culture of the Bible, it is in conflict with the moral teachings of Scripture, so too egalitarians discovered that, though patriarchy is part of Bible culture, Scripture never defends patriarchy.[25] Both abolitionists and egalitarians insist that Scripture opposes what philosophers call ascriptivism—the effort to ascribe significance, value, and worth to individuals based on their materiality, gender, ethnicity, or class.

How does our embodiment as men and women, of ethnicities, or of social classes determine our significance and influence in church and in the home? These were the questions that the early egalitarians asked as they noticed the enormous influence that slaves and women had in ad-

---

24. See Kevin Giles, *The Trinity and Subordinationism: The Doctrine of God and the Contemporary Gender Debate* (Downers Grove, Ill.: InterVarsity, 2002) and Kevin Giles, *Jesus and the Father: Modern Evangelicals Reinvent the Doctrine of the Trinity* (Grand Rapids: Zondervan, 2006).

25. For an excellent discussion on this topic, see William J. Webb, *Slaves, Women and Homosexuals: Exploring the Hermeneutics of Cultural Analysis* (Downers Grove, Ill.: InterVarsity, 2001).

vancing the gospel during the Golden Era of Missions, a movement that began in the early 1800s. Women and female slaves outnumbered men two to one on mission fields. Not only did their influence lead to sweeping social reform, but their efforts also shifted the density of Christian faith out of the west into broadly scattered places throughout Africa and Asia.[26] Giving women and slaves greater freedom on mission fields changed the face of missions, which in turn changed the face of the church. The success of slaves and women evangelists and missionaries challenged gender and ethnic prejudices, which led to a vigorous engagement with Scripture and the development of an interpretive method that exposed biblical and theological error as well as self-interest.

Gender reform today—an extension of the first wave feminist reform of the 1800s—has, to one degree or another, embodied the six qualities of reform movements, including as a first priority a rigorous engagement of Scripture. This scholarship is noted in the more than two hundred books and resources published by egalitarians, including the award-winning *Priscilla Papers,* the academic voice of Christians for Biblical Equality (CBE), now in its twenty-first year of circulation, to which more than two hundred institutions around the globe subscribe. Egalitarian scholarship is burgeoning to such an extent that CBE—the largest clearinghouse of egalitarian materials—can carry only representative examples in areas such as biblical and theological studies, church history, marriage and family, ministry, and abuse.[27] In response to the watershed of literature, one critic of egalitarians said that he wonders "if egalitarians hope to triumph in the debate on the role of women by publishing book after book on the subject. Each work propounds a new thesis that explains why the traditional interpretation is flawed. Complementarians could easily give in from sheer exhaustion, thinking that so many books written by such a diversity of authors could scarcely be wrong."[28] Moreover, the dominance

---

26. Dana L. Robert, *American Women in Mission: A Social History of Their Thought and Practice* (Macon, Ga.: Mercer University Press, 2005), ix.

27. In 1989, egalitarian resources fit on approximately two six-foot tables as egalitarians glowed with pride. Today, there are more than two hundred titles, and nearly every week CBE receives notice of a forthcoming title.

28. Thomas R. Schreiner, as quoted by Peter R. Schemm, Jr., "Kevin Giles's *The Trinity and Subordinationism*: A Review Article," *Journal for Biblical Manhood and Womanhood* 7, no. 2 (Fall 2002): 67.

of the internet over local bookstores has rendered egalitarian books not only more accessible, but more affordable as well.

The popularization of egalitarian ideas is keenly noted in the work of CBE founder Dr. Catherine Clark Kroeger and others like her who focus their energy on preventing abuse and violence against women world-wide.[29] Most recently, Christians are exploring the interface of gender and justice, asking how the cultural devaluation of women leads to their abuse globally and how might Christians stand against this theologically and in practice.[30]

As egalitarian scholars continue to expose the exegetical, theological, and moral errors intrinsic to gender hierarchy, as Christians oppose the global abuse that grows out of a philosophical devaluation of women, and as prayer strengthens and guides the work of egalitarians,[31] what was once a local focus has grown into a global movement. Our present book reflects the global gender reform movement that has convened prominent conferences,[32] egalitarian publications in many different languages[33], and a Lausanne issue group commissioned to explore the impact of gender on the Great Commission.[34]

As egalitarians press for reform at academic, popular, and global levels, there has been a modification of the position under critique. A softening of male hierarchy is clearly noted in the article "Headship with a

29. Catherine Clark Kroeger is also founder of the organization PASCH, Peace and Safety in the Christian Home.

30. Organizations such as the Evangelicals for Social Action, the International Justice Mission, InterVarsity Christian Fellowship, PASCH, The Salvation Army, Sojourners, and World Hope International are examples of Christian groups whose egalitarian perspective compels them to oppose the global abuse of women.

31. There is an underground network of prayer partners and praying communities dedicated to advancing biblical truth on gender in denominations, churches, and organizations around the world.

32. CBE has convened or partnered with egalitarians in Australia, Britain, and India to host conferences on biblical equality for women, beginning shortly after incorporating as a nonprofit in 1989.

33. See foreign language listings on EqualityDepot.org, CBE's book service.

34. The 2004 Lausanne Conference for World Evangelization in Thailand assembled thirty-one issue groups to explore the impact of the gospel in the world today. Gender was among these, and members of the Lausanne issue Group 24 published their finding in an Occasional Paper No. 53, entitled *Empowering Women and Men to Use Their Gifts Together in Advancing the Gospel*, edited by Alvera Mickelsen and published by CBE in 2005.

Heart," as the author confronts the abuses of gender hierarchy while also maintaining male authority in the church and the home.[35] Others suggest there is room for a middle position between egalitarians and those who believe Scripture reserves authority for men in the church and home.[36] Whether a middle position is logically tenable or not is a subject of some discussion, but the point is that there is movement away from strident male-only leadership.

Has the church reached the final stage of reform such that churches and denominations are sharing leadership and authority with women? The answer is: almost. Two of the most recent denominations officially to grant women shared leadership alongside men are the Worldwide Church of God, with more than 67,000 members, and the Vineyard Churches, a network of more than six hundred churches. Other organizations like InterVarsity Christian Fellowship give women shared places of leadership with men, both in the ministry and at Urbana conferences. Moreover, at the 2006 Urbana conference, students were encouraged to explore gender policies with exhibitors soliciting their involvement in their ministries, organizations, and institutions.[37]

While the discussion continues in churches and denominations around the world, if the futurists (those who assess the future based on attitudes of the younger generation) are right, egalitarians will be the cultural and theological winners in the gender debate, and those who fail to adopt egalitarian ideals will face some steep losses.[38]

Just as with the abolitionist movement, there is a heavy toll paid by those who ignore God's reforming work in the church. Certainly, the cost will mean a loss in numbers, firstly, because churches, denominations, and institutions have and may continue to split over the issue, and

---

35. See Steven Tracy, "Headship with a Heart."

36. Perhaps the best example of the middle position is put forward by Sarah Sumner in "Forging a Middle Way Between Complementarians and Egalitarians," *Women, Ministry, and the Gospel: Exploring New Paradigms,* ed. Mark Husbands and Timothy Larsen (Downers Grove, Ill.: IVP, 2007), 266–88.

37. See the Urbana 2006 conference program entitled *Global Connexions Guide: The Missions and Schools Represented at Urbana 06,* "Finding the Right Fit" under "Gender" reads, "Does your organization . . . allow women to hold any position in the agency? Have a sexual harassment policy? Have women who serve as members, team leaders, managers, and board members?" (p. 4).

38. See University of Virginia's James D. Hunter's *Evangelicalism: The Coming Generation* (Chicago: University of Chicago Press, 1987).

secondly, because those who embrace biblical equality will show healthy signs of growth, as noted in churches that base ministry on gifts rather than gender. This is particularly the case in places like Africa, China, Asia, and South America.[39] Thirdly, resisting a God-driven reform casts a shadow on the face of God and adds to a cultural disillusionment with the church.[40]

The editors of this book believe that the egalitarian movement is a reform movement given by God to redress a poor reading of Scripture that excludes women from sharing their spiritual gifts in service along-side men. The contributors to this volume represent many ethnicities and cultures whom God has called together as a global egalitarian community to advance the biblical foundations of gift-based rather than gender-based service. We believe that Scripture, rightly interpreted, as guided by the Holy Spirit, teaches the ontological and functional equality of men and women, as taught by Scriptures such as Galatians 3:28. Here we stand; we can do no other.

Our book is dedicated to the founders of Christians of Biblical Equality. First and foremost, we seek to honor Dr. Catherine Clark Kroeger, whom God used and continues to use as a tireless reformer lead-ing and comforting souls around the world to observe biblical truths of equality and gender justice. God called Catherine, and she was faithful to her call. She has greatly furthered the egalitarian reform inherited from the first wave of feminists such as Catherine Booth, Sojourner Truth, Amanda Smith, Katharine Bushnell, and A. J. Gordon. We wish also to honor and thank Gretchen Gaebelein Hull and Alvera Mickelsen for their undaunted tenacity and careful articulation of biblical equality. Their self-less and wise leadership is a legacy to the church. We, the global egali-tarian community, stand on your shoulders, thankful for your sacrifice, wisdom, holiness, and leadership. May you take pride and joy in the work which we dedicate to you, our fearless and beautiful leaders.

---

39. See Loren Cunningham, David Joel Hamilton, and Janice Rogers, *Why Not Women? A Fresh Look at Women in Missions, Ministry and Leadership* (Seattle: YWAM Publishing, 2000).

40. See Catherine Edwards Sanders, *Wicca's Charm* (Colorado Springs: WaterBrook Press, 2005), and Aída Besançon Spencer, Donna F. G. Hailson, Catherine Clark Kroeger, and William David Spencer, *The Goddess Revival* (Grand Rapids: Baker, 1995), which point to the growth of goddess worship and Wicca religion as women and men become disillusioned with sexist practices in the Christian church.

2

Steps Forward on a Journey in India

Ellen Alexander and Beulah Wood

WE LOOK INTO WOMEN'S issues from the angle of worldviews. We respect and eagerly acknowledge the thousands of organizations and people at the grassroots (or is it rice roots?) of work in India who aim to lift the status of women. Our goal, along with some other Christians, is, instead, to step back to examine the umbrella issue of the cultures that control action. The attitudes of millions of Indian women and men are slow to shift, and many of these are, at the back of everything else, religious—Muslim, Hindu, Christian, animist, and others. This is why we have taken a theological and educational approach.

> When mothers can dream of freedom for their daughters—
> freedom to live, to be, and to decide,
> When mothers can dare to see a tomorrow
> without fear in the eyes of their girls,
> When women are empowered and standing shoulder to shoulder,
> side by side with men,
> Then, India's rich culture will truly be rich,
> and this largest democracy
> will be free and empowered indeed.

In a country so vast and diverse, and with a population so large, bringing true freedom seems a mammoth and difficult task, but hope comes from knowing that this is God's kingdom agenda and that even the beginnings of trends can lead to a culture of empowerment, in both society and the church. Helping the church to see the vision that it has lost may call less for resources and more for the commitment of thousands of men and women. In the metaphor of the ambulance at the bottom of the cliff, ambulances are needed, but how much better it is to take away the cliff. This is our goal.

When Jesus told the story of a woman who went to the judge because she was unjustly treated, he praised her persistence and initiative (Luke 18:1–8). In Jesus' view, it was appropriate for her to insist upon her rights. Let this parable summon Christians to come alive to a call to work for rights for women, and for women and men to feel confirmed by Christ in speaking up for a fair deal. This is part of gospel work.

PROFILING INDIAN WOMEN: A PARADOX

The Indian woman through the ages is a paradox. She is worshiped as a *devi* ("goddess") and burnt for dowry. And if being seen at times as a goddess proves no help to women, we point to the extent and variety of a country teeming with inconsistencies. She is the *saas* ("mother-in-law") who holds the keys to her kingdom and the *bahurani* ("daughter-in-law") doomed if she does not produce a male progeny or bring a huge dowry. She may be the prime minister of the world's largest democracy, but she is denied entrance into a temple because she "is a widow." India has produced women like Pandita Ramabai and Indira Gandhi, but also has burnt her widows and buries millions of unborn females before they even take their first breath.

A legacy handed down by the church, along with urbanization and education, is bringing gradual changes. In this chapter we seek to give a picture of India as we see and understand it. So, to set it in a context, we first provide the story of what has been achieved for women. We will then critique the culture today.

WHAT HAS THE GOSPEL DONE
FOR THE WOMEN OF INDIA?

Two hundred years ago, the gospel proved great good news for the women of India. Some of the change is the result of great protagonists for women, such as William Carey and Pandita Ramabai, and much has moved to later Indian organizations.

Health and Safety

William Carey[1] witnessed a *sati* (a newly widowed woman voluntarily burning on her husband's funeral pyre) in 1799 and campaigned against *sati* for thirty years, joined by others like Raja Ram Mohan Roy. When the practice became illegal in 1829, Carey even missed his Sunday preaching to translate the edict into Bengali as fast as possible to save the lives of women. This one legal change has kept thousands of women alive, but we still hear of stray cases in villages. Christian thinking prompted condemnation of infanticide in 1802, saving millions of girls, but female infanticide occurs still today in the Hindi speaking belt and Tamil Nadu. Christians worked against child marriage. Thousands of girls have been saved from voiceless early introduction to childbearing, and, by current law, females may not marry before eighteen years of age, though this too is still frequently breached.

Pandita Ramabai advanced the status of women by both action and modeling. Near Pune in the late nineteenth and early twentieth centuries, she saved thousands of orphans and widows, showing Christians that social action is part of Christian service, and demonstrated that a woman can be a pandit in Sanskrit, Greek, and Hebrew, translate the Bible, and have the business acumen to set up a printing press and train women to print and publish. Amy Carmichael rescued hundreds of boys and girls from the horrors of temple prostitution, yet temple prostitution has not disappeared in the north of Karnataka, where in one ceremony three thousand girls may be dedicated to the goddess Yellamma, becoming prostitutes at age thirteen.

In the hundreds of Protestant clinics and hospitals for women, two pioneers stand out. Edith Brown founded Ludhiana Christian Medical Hospital in Punjab in 1893, and Ida Scudder founded Vellore Christian Medical College and Hospital in Tamil Nadu in 1900. *Zenana*[2] missions and others also served the neglected needs of women and trained nurses, seeking to make nursing an honorable profession due to a Christian worldview.

From 1800 to 2000, the tireless promotion of justice for women encountered the monolithic cultural view that women's purpose is to serve men, as described by Narasimha:

1. William Carey, seen as the founder of modern missions, reached Calcutta in 1793.
2. *Zenanas* were the quarters for women in traditional homes.

Smothered or poisoned at birth, given away in marriage at a tender age, bargained over like some commodity by dowry-hungry in-laws, secluded in the name of chastity and religion, and finally burned for the exaltation of the family's honor, or shunned as an inauspicious widow, the burden of oppression took different stages in a woman's life, from birth to death in a chain of attitudes linked by contempt for the female.[3]

Education

The Christian education of girls and women ranged from teaching in *zenanas* to setting up schools and from kindergarten to college, eventually serving millions. Schools contended with an anti-education ethos that said

- Female education is not approved by our Scriptures.

- Educated girls go astray.

- Educated girls would look down on husbands, parents, and others.

- Educated girls would become widows (and thus cursed).

- Learned girls could not put their minds to domestic work.

- Education interfered with child marriage[4]

Such views notwithstanding, hundreds of women missionaries and then thousands of Indian men and women, trained and employed by Christians, have taught girls in Christian schools and colleges. *The Hindu* newspaper commented about one hundred years ago, "While the educated Indian has not yet got beyond the talking stage in the matter of female instruction, the Christian missionary has honeycombed the country with girls' schools."[5] And in the 1930s, a member of the *Arya Samaj*[6] told

3. Shakuntala Narasimhan, quoted in Ruth Mangalwadi, *William Carey: A Tribute by an Indian Woman* (New Delhi: Nivedit Good Books, 1993), 16.

4. Benoy Bhusan Roy and Pranati Ray, *Zenana Mission: The Role of Christian Missionaries for the Education of Women in 19th Century Bengal* (Delhi: ISPCK, 1998), xx.

5. Helen Barrett Montgomery, *Western Women in Eastern Lands: An Outline of Fifty Years of Women's Work in Foreign Missions* (New York: Macmillan, 1910), 213, quoted in Ruth Tucker & Walter Liefeld, *Daughters of the Church* (Grand Rapids: Zondervan, 1987), 330.

6. Meaning "Noble Society," a Hindu reform movement.

a missionary, "A degenerate Hinduism had enslaved our women. They were condemned to illiteracy, idolatry, superstition, suffering, drudgery and dullness. The lovely things of life were all kept from them. Through Christian Missions the folly and the wrong of this treatment of our women has been convincingly demonstrated."[7]

Social Progress for Women

Dalit[8] women face the triple oppressions of caste, class, and gender. One of the strangest stories came from the far south. Nair women, upper caste, wore a breast cloth, while Nadar women were not permitted to wear anything above their waists. In 1822, when Christian Nadars wore blouses, riots broke out. In a market in 1828, a man stripped a blouse from a woman, causing a further five months of riots. Finally, after further unrest, Nadar women received permission in 1859 to wear blouses—of a different kind than the Nair women.

A Dalit woman, Bama, wrote recently, "Women's labour, sexuality and fertility are controlled . . . and effectively make women believe themselves to be second-class citizens."[9] Sometimes the hardness of their lives comes from their own culture—denial of education, child marriages, forced marriages, and domestic abuse. Sometimes their vicissitudes come from poverty—mud and dust in tiny huts; discriminatory wages; manipulated into paying bribes; lack of toilets; ill health; depending on grazing, gleaning, and gathering; and losing even these with the forces of mechanization and globalization. They can be exploited by politicians, designedly kept down by ultra-Hindu parties, and at times brought by the truckload to vote for a particular politician. Their slum landlords may abuse them economically, or the landlord and any other men around may take advantage of them if there is no male in the hut.

Women Supporting Women

The introduction of a Christian worldview prompted work schemes for women, literacy, legislation, and, later, women's societies such as the

---

7. J. W. Pickett, *Christ's Way to India's Heart* (Lucknow: Lucknow Publishing House, 1938), 69, quoted in Tucker & Liefeld, *Daughters*, 331.

8. Scheduled caste, formerly called outcaste.

9. Nirmala Jeyaraj, ed, *Women and Society* (Madurai: Lady Doak College, 2001), 329.

Young Women's Christian Association, which offered women safe accommodation and a voice. Now there are scores of women's societies working for women—Christian, secular, and those of other religions. They are all needed.

Women at Home

Christian attitudes have considerably improved the treatment of women in the home. A man told a researcher in 1933, "Before these people became Christians they bought and sold wives like we buy and sell buffaloes. Now they choose one woman and remain faithful to her as long as she lives."[10] There is progress, but domestic violence remains an enormous and incalculable problem, even in Christian homes.

PRESENT SIGNS OF HOPE

Independence and Education

Urbanization has overtaken India. Hundreds of women travel city streets on both two- and four-wheelers. Independent and mobile, the number of women in business, banking, and management is increasing, enhancing their economic position and management skills.

The girl child was deprived of education because she was seen solely as the "feeder-breeder" and therefore would not need an education. She could be required to work and at the same time be deprived of food so her brother could go to school or college. But, increasingly, women are educated, and statistics show girls doing much better than boys academically. Notice this recent report:

> Girls have again outscored boys in the SSLC [Secondary School Leaving Certificate] results for 2005, in which 62.46 percent of the total 815,132 students who appeared for the examination have passed. . . . The topper was a girl, and girls outshone boys. 12,034 girls obtained distinction marks as against 8,787 boys.[11]

10. J. W. Pickett, *Christian Mass Movements in India* (New York: Abingdon, 1933), 193, quoted in Tucker & Liefeld, *Daughters*, 332.

11. *Deccan Herald*, April 27, 2005.

Role and Identity

A tiny group of women have moved from the kitchen to the board room, defying the traditional roles. They seek an identity of intrinsic value as against monetary value. For the Christian woman, an identity comes from the recognition that one is created in the image of God and redeemed by his precious Son. Redefining worth and identity in affirmative terms and asking for one's voice to be heard and opinions sought is difficult. Women who assume a level of confidence are branded "aggressive," "feminist," and "unchristian."

Kiran Bedi from another faith is one of our trailblazers. She broke new ground as the first woman to join the elite Indian Police Service in 1972, and is today its most celebrated police officer, awarded several prizes, including the Ramon Magsaysay Prize for drug abuse prevention. Kiran Bedi established two foundations offering education for thousands of poor children; literacy for women; and vocational training and counseling in the slums, rural areas, and inside prisons. The second of four daughters, Kiran Bedi is a tennis champion, holds a law degree, has a doctorate in drug abuse and domestic violence, and revolutionized Delhi's notorious Tihar Jail. She is a role model for many.

Or take Ruth Manorama, a social worker and human rights activist who is deeply involved in issues concerning women from the poorer section of society, from unorganized labor, and from the Dalits. She is known for her immense mobilizing capacity and for the zeal and passion with which she takes up various issues of social justice. Ruth Manorama is currently president of the National Alliance of Women, general secretary of Women's Voice, and the national convener of the National Federation of Dalit Women.[12]

Arts and Film

Media views are gradually changing. A few movies now break with traditional roles for women. One recently had a scene where a woman said, "You are only my husband, not God." (The word for "husband" in Hindi is *Pati-dev*, "husband-god.")

Often, secular women's organizations conduct street plays on issues related to women, and journals carry articles both by men and women that hold women in high esteem.

12. Rithu Memon, ed., *Women Who Dared* (India: National Book Trust, 2002), 215.

WHERE THE GOSPEL NEEDS TO GO

Oppression Remains, Especially in the Home

Changes are evident on the streets and in workplaces, but too little takes place at home and in the church. Some churches work for justice for women, but this is not always characteristic of evangelicals. We wonder if the earlier work by Christians was, in most people's thinking, human rights more than women's rights.

The modern woman is a kind of a schizophrenic. In the workplace, she may have a significant position where she is looked up to and makes strategic decisions. But the moment she steps in the door of her home, she is clothed in the garb of her role as wife, mother, and daughter, with no personal significance and required dutifully to play a role where neither housework nor voluntary work is valued.

The greatest oppressions hide within the four walls of her home where she is often voiceless. *Sati* is extremely rare, but child marriage continues in rural areas, and dowry demands thrive even among educated Christian families.

Renu is a well-educated young woman from a fine Christian family. Her people accepted a proposal for her marriage and the wedding date was fixed and wedding bans published. On the night before the wedding, the groom, a well-educated, believing Christian, demanded that the bride's father assign his property immediately to himself. The groom was taking no risks of the bride's dowry not getting to him. He wanted all his future father-in-law's property immediately. This is far beyond the normal dowry request. The maneuver was planned to take advantage of the bride's father's fear of "losing face," bringing disgrace on himself and his daughter if the wedding were cancelled. Sometimes the bride's family succumbs to the pressure, but in this case neither the bride nor her family yielded. They took the bold step of canceling the wedding. What does society think? Many praised them, but to this day, years later, Renu remains unmarried. In this story, Renu and her family were agreed. Often in families, even if the woman wants to take a stand against dowry, she may not be allowed to do so.

Prema fell in love with a young man from the Christian student group in her city, but her parents did not approve, partly because they did not want it said that their daughter chose her own partner. Prema was packed off to a different town where she was confined within a house while her parents quickly sought another match and married Prema off to this man. Significantly, her brother was able to stand his ground and make his own choice of a wife, but not Prema.

Look at Priya, a beautiful girl trained as a nurse in the top medical college in the country and with a master's degree in psychology. Priya did not have courage to stand up to her Christian father and refuse to marry a man she did not like or want. Neither her mother nor her doctor brother stood with her. From day one, her Christian marriage was a life of oppression. Her husband excluded her from job, friends, finance, her own family, even from going outside the house. She was derided in front of her children. It took her sixteen years to choose to take a requalifying exam to seek a job, and then her husband threatened to deprive her of her home, children, and all official documents. She has courageously told him she will not return without resolving these issues in the presence of a witness. It has taken her this long to accept that her life is intolerable and she must take responsibility to change it. She was able to address this abuse with the support of some of her friends. Now, even her women friends' husbands agree with her decision to assert her rights.

These are just a few stories, and each one of these figures tells a story. The *Deccan Herald* reported[13] that 90 percent of women in Uttar Pradesh State and 80 percent of women in Andhra Pradesh and Madhya Pradesh need permission to go to the market. In Punjab, 70 percent of women need permission to visit friends and relatives. Reporter Khadija Haq says, "The system of Patriarchy is far too strong and so well ingrained in South Asia that it does not allow women's life to change."

Abortion, Another Home-Based Oppression

In India, abortion is seldom about women exercising choice, but instead concerns control by husbands and mothers-in-law who impose the view—often readily accepted by young women—that sons will care for and inherit from their parents while daughters are a liability, and, worse, require a dowry the family cannot afford. This leads to the belief that nobody needs daughters. Abortion in India is almost always female abortion following amniocentesis and ultrasound, and nobody knows its

13. *Deccan Herald*, Feb. 11, 2001.

extent. Perhaps it is two to five million girls a year. Some Christians abort female fetuses, too.

Ruth tells how, feeling uncomfortable since her pastor had taught that wives should obey husbands, she disobeyed her husband's command to get an abortion. A pastor of a large English-speaking church says women come not to ask if abortion is acceptable for a Christian, but to seek help to go through with it in obedience to the husband and/or his mother. Even the *Bangalore Times* of August 2, 2004, reports that there are only 915 women to every 1,000 men in the fast-growing, modern information technology city of Bangalore.

Problems with the Justice System also Affect Women in the Home

A survey[14] showed that, although legislation exists, laws have not been implemented. Women who are raped do not file a case because their families pressure them because they so fear "shame." It was estimated that only 20 percent of rape cases were reported and only five percent of rapes of Dalit women. Of those reported to the police, many were dropped because of political, caste, and class issues or because of religious and gender biases.[15] Besides, the accused often bought off the witnesses. Worse, it takes an average of ten to fifteen years for a case to move from sessions court to Supreme Court. As a result, most crimes against women go unpunished. Families too often feel their only role toward a young woman is to get her married as a virgin. Once married, wives often accept mental torture or criminal behavior, and some commit suicide. There is a significant statistic of suicide by young women in the first six months after marriage. What a tragedy! *The Hindu* newspaper reported on November 30, 2003, that, on average, nineteen women die every day in India in issues related to the husband's family wanting more dowry.

INDIA COMPARED WITH OTHER COUNTRIES

Many of the abuses of women that occur in India are observed in other countries too—rape, domestic violence, unequal pay, and sexual harassment. But India adds oppressions of its own:

14. "Violence Against Women in Uttar Pradesh and Rajasthan," Amnesty International, http://web.amnesty.org/library/Index/ENGASA200292001?open&of=ENG-2S4 (accessed 17 July 2005).

15. At a UNDP training program in 1999, fourteen participants were sent to file complaints. Only two succeeded in filing, and that after waits of six to seven hours.

a. Police condone and even add to the above abuses while holding women in custody.

b. Deep-rooted patriarchy gives rise to female feticide, female abortion, neglect and abuse of baby girls, and deprivation of food and education. While there is celebration and sweetmeats all round at the birth of a boy, for a girl there is gloom.

c. Female dowries, originally to ensure that the woman received her share of property, have turned into a woman's death knell. Growing larger in the last fifty years, dowries now stretch to gold, silver, refrigerators, motorbikes, cars, even apartments. And trailing behind the very word "dowry" are further abuses—devaluing females from the moment they are born (or not born), unequal distribution of parental property, greed, and distorted high valuation of sons. So committed are many to the value of sons and the worthlessness of daughters that elderly people may even reject care offered by their daughter.

d. There is forced prostitution and trafficking of females into prostitution.

e. In poorer homes, girls must work and are given little time for play, sport, or forming their own friends, while boys are encouraged in all these activities. Even in good homes, girls' movement is restricted, and they may be confined to their room if they do not conform.

The sex ratio figures tell of a stark contrast in our country, revealing the prevalence of female abortion and neglect and abuse of females of any age. Where most countries of the world had more females than males, India had 532 million males balanced against 496 million females in the last census.[16] In other words, at least 36 million females are not alive who should be.

But the picture worsens and the disparity increases, again because of son preference and fear of dowry if one raises a daughter. The 2001 census found the discrepancy between males and females had plunged yet further in the zero-to-six-year-old age bracket. Out of 593 districts, most had fewer girls than boys, and 44 had fewer than 850 girls to 1,000 boys. In real figures, that is multiple millions fewer girls than boys. Patiala and

16. Census held 2001.

Fategarh in Punjab had ratios of 764 and 747 girls to 1,000 boys. Salem district in Tamil Nadu had 763 girls. Urban areas can be worse. One Punjab city had 729 girls, and nearby Haryana had the worst of all—678 girls to every 1,000 boys.[17] Significantly, these are among the wealthier states in the country.

The Influence of Religion

Religion plays its part in shaping minds and worldviews. We are all familiar with certain interpretations of the Bible and the writing of certain church fathers which have served women so unjustly in Christianity. To these we add some views from Hinduism.

About 1,500 years before Christ, Manu, regarded as the lawgiver who molded centuries of thinking, said that, no matter what the man is like, he must be worshipped as god. Daughters are raised for someone else and are no advantage to a family. "Her father protects [her] in childhood, her husband protects [her] in youth and her sons protect [her] in old age; a woman is never fit for independence," he said.[18] Giving women no responsibility, he advised men to honor women on holidays and festivals with gifts, ornaments, clothes, and food. This denied women real respect and freedom to choose what kind of people they wished to be.

The sacred Brihadaranyaka Upanishad says, "If she does not grant him his desire, he should beat her with a stick or his hand and overcome her saying with manly power and glory, 'I take away your glory.'"[19] Another sage[20] wrote, "Women can never be their own master. This is the opinion of the Creator himself that a woman never deserves to be independent. There is not a single woman in the three worlds that deserves to be regarded as the master of her own self."

The Islamic invasion of India reinforced such views, as did, probably, some aspects of Christianity later. The teaching in churches and Bible colleges by preachers and lecturers, who said that wives must obey their husbands and find their whole sphere of life within the home, find common ground with the inherent culture of India and fail to regard women with the honor and responsibility granted men. Whole denominations

---

17. Http://www.censusindia.net.results (accessed 27 July 2004).

18. Laws of Manu X 10–3.

19. VI.4.7.

20. Ashtavakra.

still teach that daughters, daughters-in-law, and wives must obey, and that women cannot be leaders. In the disempowered context of Indian women, that can be a recipe for emotional, economic, and physical abuse.

WHERE CHANGE OCCURS

We are saying that change is occurring in India, but there is an interesting question with this: Where is the change? We discover the following places:

In Women, Not Men

Women's self-perception is changing, but the way they are perceived by men changes less often. Often women are seen as roles, things, rather than people who can think. Some urban men have changed enough perhaps to help with chores in the house—as a favor to the woman, not because she is his equal or because it is his responsibility as much as hers. Women carry disproportionate loads of chores and child rearing, thus denying time for personal space or enjoyment.

In Urban, Not Rural, India

Most changes take place in cities with a trickle down to semi-urban India. Rural women still accept the functions of the "ideal Indian woman" along the lines of the Laws of Manu. Perhaps 40 percent of women in urban and 90 percent in rural India are unaware that they are an oppressed class.

In Society, Not the Church

Change has reached the church, but it is often peripheral, cosmetic, and merely tokenism. Real changes of attitude and belief are slow in taking place. Many still believe the Bible requires a treatment of women that confines them to a "feminine" role and regards them as less than first-class members of church or home. In our view, the differences are in fact maintained because of the culture. Since the actions of Christ and the custom of the early church gave equality to women and men, the church should be the trendsetter and pathfinder, but it has lost its impetus. The church does strongly promote education for women and girls, but it also needs to speak out on justice for women.

WHAT CHANGES COULD BRING TRANSFORMATION?

a. Churches and Christian organizations need to be more aware of the issues.

b. Christians need to remember the examples of William Carey and Pandita Ramabai and continue to work against the abortion or infanticide of the youngest females, against child marriage, against child labor, and against forced prostitution, whether it occurs in village or city.

c. Christians must also work for better health, lower maternal mortality, better education for girls, economic justice for women, and equal pay for equal work.

d. All Christians need to come alongside Dalits and work for their full rights and full respect in both church and society.

e. We need new attitudes in both women and men. Women need confidence, independence, and a sense that they are responsible for themselves. Men need to respect women and move aside to make room for them while encouraging other men to change.

f. Marriage needs deeper understanding. Both men and women will benefit if marriage becomes companionship rather than roles restricted to gender, if it welcomes participation for women more than protection, and values fulfillment more than patronage.

g. Christians need a renewed picture of Christ's life on earth so that they see how he empowered and elevated women, moving them toward leadership.

h. In some cases, Christians need to work to reform the justice system, as Mary Roy[21] did to obtain reform of inheritance codes. In many other cases, the legal provisions for better treatment of women are already in place, but not enforced, for the simple reason that police cannot enforce provisions without the agreement and active support of the population.

---

21. Mary Roy worked successfully from Kerala to change the article in Indian Christian family law that required property to go to male heirs.

CAN WE BE A PROPHETIC VOICE?

We evangelicals want to be a prophetic voice to the nations, but we too often choose our battles to suit our inclinations. Christ identified himself with the poor and weak, denounced evils he saw, and confronted those who committed or allowed evil and oppression. Do we believe the gospel can change individual lives? Of course!

Therefore, if we believe this, we should stand against the oppression of women and girls and female fetuses. We know the gospel's goal is to transform unjust structures. That is where a public voice comes in. That is where we need to change the way Christians in India think so that we can influence society around us. Would it not be wonderful if Christians could so put their house in order that they set an outstanding example to the communities around of the equality of all people, male or female? There are indeed Christians working on justice issues. Many more of us need to take up the task.

Let us return to the woman in the Luke 18 parable.[22] She became her own lawyer, even though women were legally powerless. Jesus praised this woman for pressing the unfair judge until he granted her rights. This woman provides us an example in the following ways:

- To be aware that women may be deprived of their rights
- Not to accept the status quo
- To work for justice for women
- That women can protest with their voices and their actions
- That women need to overcome the fear of making a scene, even if a scene is not "ladylike"
- That it is naive to expect immediate results

We may need years of perseverance, but Jesus praised persistence until the goal was achieved. Let us press on together.

---

22. Some thoughts from Mary Aquin O'Neill, *Women, Justice and the Bible,* 2003, http://www.msawomen.org/works/works_lecture_2003_womenjusticebible.htm (accessed June 2004).

3

The Path of Biblical Equality for the Chinese Women

Cecilia Yau

THE PLIGHT OF WOMEN WHEN ROBERT MORRISON CAME TO CHINA

OVER TWO HUNDRED YEARS ago, on September 7, 1807, the first Protestant missionary, Robert Morrison, set his feet on the soil of Canton, China. Canton was the only city open for international trade, and proselytizing activities were forbidden. Morrison had to work as a secretary and translator for the British East India Company in order to take up legal residency in China. In 1809, he married Mary Morton in Macao and later returned to China alone because foreign women were denied entrance to the country.

By the time Morrison came to China, the Qing Dynasty was already in decline. Yet, in its less than three hundred years of reign, the plight of women's lives reached its nadir. It was the accumulating effect of three thousand years of discriminatory customs and traditions.

The following are some of the more distinctive and prevalent traditions toward women at that time.

Polygamy

Although it was clearly forbidden by law for many generations, polygamy had been a common practice during the long history of China. The practice was justified by a patriarchal system intended to perpetuate the patrilineal line and carry on the family name. If a wife could not produce a son, it was only legitimate for the husband to get another wife, or another wife until a male heir was born. Since women were considered part of men's properties, marriage was an exchange of goods. The men who had money and power could get as many wives or "properties" as they wanted.

Three Obediences

The Chinese ideal of womanhood is found in Confucius's ideology. It prescribes that a Chinese woman obey her father before marriage, her husband after marriage, and her eldest son when she is widowed. She is to serve her husband as unto heaven (*tien* or "god"). The spheres of men and women are clearly defined. A woman's place is in the home. She does not need education or talent. In fact, "A woman without talents is considered virtuous."[1] An educated woman was thought to be "licentious."[2]

Double Standards and Extreme Fidelity

In terms of marriage and family, a Chinese husband could divorce his wife for any of seven reasons: sickness, jealousy of her husband's lover, stealing, slander, inadequacy in serving her husband's parents, committing adultery, and inability to bear a son.

A widower was allowed to remarry, but a wife could never divorce her husband nor remarry. In order to show her fidelity to her deceased husband, a "model" widow would self-mutilate by cutting off a part of her body—an ear or a nose. She might also become a vegetarian for life, or she might commit suicide by hanging or drowning herself. Some fathers would go to the extreme to help their daughters to perform such self-destructive "duties" if they were too scared to do so.

Foot Binding

Women were not only properties, but also toys for men. For almost a thousand years, girls of four to five years old, especially those from good and upper-class families, would be forced to have their feet tightly bound so that they could grow no more than three inches. The process was very cruel and painful. Sometimes bones would be crushed and blood would be retained in the cloth for a long time.

1. W.C. Liu, *Women and History* (Hong Kong: Hong Kong Educational Publishing Co., 1993), 89. Liu thinks that the statement first appeared in the Ming Dynasty in *Collection of Wise Thoughts* by Mun Lung Feng, but the thought had been around for a long time.

2. Liu, *Women*, 89. Liu thinks that the statement first appeared in *Guidelines for Womanhood* by Kuen Lui, written in 1927.

The custom caught the fancy of men who enjoyed treating women like playthings. They thought women with bound feet were more sexy when they walked. Others thought this a good way to keep women in the house, as they would be unlikely to walk very far. When men chose their mates, one important criterion was the girl have small bound feet.

Female Infanticide and Girl Slaves

Because of the system of primogeniture, girls were much less valued than boys. In poor families, baby girls were either deserted or drowned. Or, if they were lucky enough to grow up, they might be sold to rich families as maids (*mui tsai* or "slaves").

At the time when missionary Robert Morrison came to China, Chinese women were illiterate, physically weak, and had no financial means nor any future. Of course, there were some women who, for various reasons, could overcome the hurdles and made an impact, but they were as rare as the morning stars. And there were men who could see the injustices done to women and tried to do something about it.[3] But they were far too few.

During the Qing dynasty, voices were targeting the ill treatment of women through novels and articles.[4] The cruelty and barbarianism had reached its limit, and the cries for reform were bursting at the seams of a dynasty that was decaying with political instability and moral corruption.

THE EARLY STAGE OF THE CHURCH'S LIFE AND TWO MAJOR REFORMS

For the first thirty-five years after Morrison's arrival, the work of evangelization progressed very slowly owing to the closed-door policy of China. But after the Sino-British Opium War and the subsequent Treaty of Nanking (1842), the door of China was blasted open by wars and brute force. It brought mixed results. A love/hate relationship began to develop

---

3. Writers wrote prose to attack the patriarchal system. For example, Cham Lee (1527–1602) criticized the practice of extreme fidelity and promoted the cause for widows to have the right to remarry. The Qing ruling nobility had tried to prohibit the custom, but without much success.

4. Writer Yu Chun Lee wrote a famous story, *Chin Hwa Yuen*, in which one hundred talented women were presented and the practice of foot binding was degraded.

between China and the Western countries. Nonetheless, a window was opened, and the Chinese women's fate saw a new light.

At first, as Pui-lan Kwok stated, most female Christians were from the poor and lower classes, as they were marginal members of the society. The rich and upper-class women were forbidden by their families to join a foreign religion, not to mention the physical limitation created by their bound feet.[5]

Since segregation of the sexes was the norm of the day, woman's work had to be conducted by female missionaries who often took up the whole pastoral role, including preaching to the female members of the church. Their ministries became a model for future Chinese Bible women.

Opening of Girls' Schools

A major reform brought by the missionaries was the opening of girls' schools.[5] Missionaries championed female education on the grounds that educated mothers could better develop intelligent children. This had a great appeal for a nation that was frantically attempting to find means to strengthen its human resources. In 1844, the first mission school for girls was established in Ningbo by an English woman, Miss Aldersey of the Society for the Promotion of Female Education in the Far East. Within ten years, eleven such schools were established in the five open ports.[6]

When the Chinese opened their first school for girls in Shanghai in 1897, there were more that three hundred mission schools with more than seven thousand students. A national system of government supported girls' schools was instituted in 1907. In 1908, the number of girls in government-supported schools exceeded that of mission schools.[7]

Banning Foot Binding

Foot binding was another area that missionaries tried to do something about. They taught that women's feet were the creation of a loving God. Distorting them was not only presumptuous, but also bringing unspeakable pain to women for life. In 1874, Rev. John MacGowan of London Mission Society organized "The Natural Feet Society" in Xiamen with

5. Pui-lan Kwok, *Chinese Women and Christianity, 1860–1927* (Atlanta: Scholars Press, 1992), 10–12.

6. Kwok, *Chinese Women and Christianity,* 11.

7. Kwok, *Chinese Women and Christianity,* 17.

other missionaries. Sixty-some career women joined the membership, and the work spread to other cities.

In 1882, Chinese reformer Kang Youwei tried to start a similar society, but it did not materialize until 1894. To the reformers, half of the population being handicapped by foot binding and not being able to contribute to the welfare of the country was deplorable and appalling. The Dowager Cixi in 1902 declared the eradication of such practice. Millions of girls and women were "liberated."[8]

THE FIRST POLITICAL SUPPORT OF GENDER EQUALITY BY THE TAIPING REBELLION

The first Chinese convert to Christianity was a printer called Liang A-fa, whose tract first introduced Hung Hsiu-ch'uan to Christianity in 1836. Hung later started a religious and political movement, the Taiping Rebellion (1850–64), one of the greatest upheavals in modern Chinese history. Hung intended to set up a heavenly kingdom of great peace. He preached a mixture of Christian egalitarianism and traditional Chinese utopian ideas. Initially, the movement won the support of missionaries and other Westerners despite its unorthodox teachings. At its height, the Heavenly Kingdom encompassed much of south and central China and set up its capital at Nanking. Its soldiers numbered between two and three million and posed a great threat to the Dynasty.

The Taiping society was classless. It was declared that men and women were both children of God and should be treated equally. Women were admitted to take examinations for government offices and enlisted for the army. The subject of study for the examinations changed from the Confucian classics to the Bible. Foot binding, prostitution, polygamy including concubinage, and slavery were all banned. Like men, women could own property and had the right to choose their spouses.

However, the policies were short-lived as Hung himself was believed to have eighty-eight concubines, and many of his high-ranking officials also kept concubines. Scholars point out that Taipings did not really grasp the biblical concept of equality. They only wanted to make use of the fe-

---

8. Cecilia Yau, Dora Wang, and Lily Lee, *A Passion for Fullness*, 2nd ed. (Hong Kong: China Graduate School of Theology, May 2004), 263–64.

male resources available at that time to build up their political power base. The kingdom was finally crushed by the Manchu government.[9]

THE BIBLE WOMEN

In the nineteenth century, most female church workers (also called the Bible Women) were minimally educated and generally unskilled. For these women, working in the church could be their first job experience. For destitute widows, it also provided an income for self-support. The early Bible women were recruited from employees of missionary households, preachers' mothers or wives, or other Christian women who had acquired some education. Older or middle-aged women had more opportunities, since it was not appropriate for young women to go out alone. Widows who had no children or other dependents were more desirable because they had more freedom to travel in the villages.[10]

In the church hierarchy, the position of Bible women was much lower than that of ordained pastors or other unordained male evangelists, who could preach from the pulpit and take charge of the church. Many Bible women were employed on a part-time basis. In rural areas, it was more common for them to be volunteers. A survey in 1909 shows that female church coworkers were paid much less—sometimes less than half the salary of the male workers.

Kwok shows that, in 1876, there were a total of ninety Bible women; by 1917, the number had grown to 2,579.[11] The peak came around 1920 when there were 3,304, but, since then, the number has been in decline. By the mid-1930s it was 2,423, and by 1949 it was 2,396.[12] The church lost its female force to secular job markets when women were more educated. Women could get better treatment and had more opportunities to make contributions in the society than in the church.

9. Yau, *Passion*, 263.

10. Kwok, *Chinese Women*, 80.

11. Kwok, *Chinese Women*, 81.

12. Jonathan Chao and Rosanna Chong, *A History of Christianity in Socialist China, 1949– 1997* (Taiwan: CMI Publishing Co., 1997), xxxii.

REVIVALS PRODUCE A CROP OF FINE FEMALE LEADERS

At the turn of the twentieth century, China landed on a very turbulent and chaotic plane. Nationalism was on the rise. China was going through the pain of a new birth. Many intellectuals were swept along by patriotism. They believed that, in order to make China strong, every member of the society had to get ready, including women.

At least thirty periodicals aimed at women were published to promote the "New Woman."[13] The most acclaimed and long-lasting was *The World of Women*, launched in Shanghai in 1904. One of its founding members, Chin Yi, wrote in the first issue, "This is undoubtedly true: to renew China, we have to renew women; to strengthen China, strengthen women first ; to civilize China, civilize women first; to save China, save women first."[14]

Strong winds were also blowing upon Christians and churches. China as a nation was in search of its identity, and the Chinese people were open to new changes. The Chinese church saw great revivals during the first few decades of the new century. A crop of Chinese revivalists and evangelists began to emerge. Among them were some women, namely, Dora Yu and Christiana Tsai.

Dora Yu

Dora Yu was ministering in Korea, but felt the call of God to return to China because she believed that God was going to do mighty things there. When she returned, the prayer movement was spreading like wildfire. She experienced the anointing and filling of the Holy Spirit and became a dynamic preacher at many revival meetings.

In 1920, when Watchman Nee was only seventeen years old, he went to one of Dora Yu's revival meetings and was convicted of his need for God's salvation. He accepted the Lord and immediately felt the call to enter full-time ministry. Years later, God used Nee to launch the "local

13. Hsiao Hung Hsia, *Women of Late Qing and Contemporary China* (Beijing: Beijing University Publishers, 2004), 67.

14. Hsia, *Women*, 77.

assembly" movement,[15] which brought his spiritual visions to every continent of the world.[16]

Christiana Tsai

Christiana Tsai was the daughter of the vice-governor of Jiangsu. Growing up as a devout Buddhist, she vowed she would never "eat" Christianity. But, as was the case with many Chinese girls, education was the stepping-stone toward a newfound faith in Christ. Tsai wanted to learn English and was enrolled in a mission school. Later, she would recall, "God used my love for English to draw me to Himself."[17]

Tsai became an evangelist greatly used by God. In 1918, she and other missionaries organized a gospel team which later came to be known as the Chinese Home Missionary Society. Their initial thrust was to evangelize Yunnan, the second largest province of China at that time, but where very little missionary work was being done.

Yuk Ling Chan

Yuk Ling Chan joined the Chinese Home Missionary Society in 1918 and ended up ministering in Yunnan for twenty-five years. She planted seven churches and was the first Chinese woman to be ordained (in 1938). Chan had a well-rounded ministry that included preaching, teaching (in seminary), writing (commentaries), evangelism, and church planting. She also had the gift of healing.[18]

Wei Chun Chiu

During the 1920s, more female evangelists emerged. Wei Chun Chiu began preaching with great power in Shantung. Within a year, she preached more than three hundred times in many cities to thousands of people.

---

15. Members believe that each locality should have one church, and the name of the place should be the name of the church. The local churches should be self-governing and self-supporting without denominational interference.

16. Silas Wu, *Dora Yu: Harbinger of Christian Church Revival in Twentieth Century China* (Boston: Pishon River Publications, 2000), 193–94.

17. Ruth Tucker, *From Jerusalem to Irian Jaya* (Grand Rapids: Zondervan, 1983), 337.

18. Ka-lun Leung, *Evangelists and Revivalists of Modern China* (Hong Kong: Alliance Bible Seminary, 1999), 144–47.

Later, she taught in coeducational seminaries and started a spiritual center. She was one of the keynote speakers at the Hong Kong citywide revival meetings in 1940.[19]

Bethel Mission

Another mission agency, Bethel Mission, was started by Jennie V. Hughes and Dr. Mary Stone, a Chinese physician-evangelist. The mission was a conglomeration of evangelism, education for girls, nursing education, and biblical training for church leaders.

The fact that Bethel Mission was started by two women has often been eclipsed by its more famous male members, such as John Sung, Andrew Gih, and others. There were many evangelistic teams under Bethel Mission, including teams made up of female evangelists. Ka-lun Leung thinks that Bethel Mission set the pace and model for the revival movement in China.[20] One of its contributions was to raise up female preachers and evangelists.

Leung points out that quite a few other creative ministries were started by women leaders.[21] But, once these ministries became institutionalized with power structures, more male counterparts would join the effort and eventually take over the leadership. Women leaders would be once again marginalized.[22] Leung also compares the female evangelists to their male counterparts. He thinks the former were less ambitious and more likely to be team players. The male evangelists, on the other hand, had more difficulty working with other leaders and would likely split up to start their own work.[23]

Ordination

On the issue of ordination, as mentioned above, Yuk Ling Chan was the first female pastor to be ordained in 1938. However, a few decades later, influenced by the teaching of Watchman Nee, she chose to give it up. She

---

19. Leung, *Evangelists*, 138.

20. Leung, *Evangelists*, 141.

21. Other ministries include China Home Missionary Society and Chung Hwa Women Seminary, etc. They were all started by women.

22. Leung, *Evangelists*, 144.

23. Leung, *Evangelists*, 153.

believed women should be "veiled" and should let brothers take the visible role and the authority of leadership.

Another female minister, Tin Woon Li, was an Anglican pastor. In 1944, China was in the chaos of war. Traveling was difficult. Many Anglican churches lacked ordained priests to perform communion. To solve the problem, Bishop Ronald Hall ordained Tin Woon Li. But, as soon as the war was over, pressure from many Anglican precincts mounted to protest the ordination. The Archbishop of Canterbury from England gave Ronald Hall two options: either he resign as bishop or Li resign as an ordained pastor. Needless to say, Li had to give up her title in 1948.[24]

Causes for the Emergence of These Female Leaders

In light of the low status of Chinese women at that time, the fact that these female revivalists and evangelists were so effective and so widely accepted by people was unprecedented. Leung thinks there are two reasons as to why these women were so successful in ministry.

First, female missionaries set a good example for Chinese women by serving side by side with male missionaries on an equal footing. Many of them were single with college educations and possessed gifts to serve beyond the family circle. Some were as capable as men in their special areas. They more or less modeled the "new woman" image—the independent, self-confident career women—that the Chinese reformers wanted to adopt for Chinese women.[25]

Leung points out that the second reason for the emergence of female evangelists was that female education and theological education both provided space and opportunities for women to develop their gifts.[26] The general education for girls did change their destiny for life. Most Chinese women at that time were illiterate. Education lifted their place in the society and opened up public opportunities for them. Many did come to know Christ while studying under the missionaries. Christiana Tsai was one of those who benefited from it.

Daughters of the Chinese ministers or Bible women often had priority to receive scholarships to study abroad, especially in the United States.

---

24. Leung, *Evangelists*, 155.

25. Leung, *Evangelists*, 95–99.

26. Leung, *Evangelists*, 114–31.

Some of them excelled in their special professions and made an impact through their careers. Mary Stone was one of them.

CONTEMPORARY CHINA AND THE STATUS OF WOMEN

When the Communists took over China in 1949, the party implemented gender equality in its policies. In 1950, a new marriage law gave women equal freedom to choose their mates. It also outlawed prostitution, child marriages, concubinage, and the sale of brides. Literacy programs were launched.

In the 1960s, Chairman Mao coined a famous slogan: "Women hold up half of the sky." Women were encouraged to work and to become officials. In the 1980s and early 1990s, new marriage and employment laws were passed to protect the rights and welfare of women and children. Organizations were established to ensure the implementation process.

In the mid-1990s, 82 percent of working-age women in the cities held jobs; yet, Nicholas Kristof points out a contradicting phenomenon. As women have gained economic independence, many have also become tradable commodities. A huge market emerged in the 1980s in the trafficking of women and children.[27] A government document prepared for the National People's Congress shows that the authorities had investigated 18,692 cases of the sale of women in 1990. The *People's Daily* reported that in a 12-month period between 1989 and 1990, some 10,000 abducted women and children had been rescued by the authorities.[28]

Despite strengthened laws and government efforts to combat human trafficking, it remains pervasive. It has been reported in more than twenty of China's thirty provinces and autonomous regions since the early 1980s. Women and children have been the primary targets of abduction, physical and sexual assault, and sale.[29]

China's one-child policy was launched in 1979 to limit population growth. The most common methods of implementation are abortion and female infanticide. On top of the traditional preference for male offspring, the one-child policy gives couples, particularly those in rural areas, no

27. Nicholas D. Kristof and Sheryl WuDunn, *China Wakes: The Struggle for the Soul of a Rising Power* (New York: Vintage Books, 1995), 214.

28. Kristof and WuDunn, *China Wakes,* 218.

29. Xin Ren, *Violence against Women under China's Economic Modernisation: Resurgence of Women Trafficking in China,* 1. Online: http://www.aic.gov.au/publictions/proceedings/27/ren.pdf (accessed 30 Jan. 2008).

choice but to dispose of a female baby so that they can try again for a boy. According to the Canadian Medical Association, a 1992 survey reported the sex ratio in China had reached 118.5 boys born for every 100 girls, compared to 106 boys to 100 girls in the West.[30] Today, there is a serious shortage of females, and many men cannot find wives to marry. The deficit gives women leverage over men in choosing a life partner. On the flip side, it leads to female trafficking.

Education has always been the pathway for women to elevate to a higher status. In China, the illiteracy rate among women is still very high. It is estimated that women comprise about 70 percent of the illiterate people in China. Among women, 30 percent are illiterate. The majority of the rest have only elementary school education or less.[31]

Women with dual responsibilities of both family and work often have to choose between the two. The divorce rate in urban areas is climbing. Educated women are less tolerant of their husbands. In 1950, women's earnings accounted for 20 percent of family income. Today, it is 40 percent. Girls in China are leading their school classes in grades. In Canton, a recent study shows that 74 percent of divorces were initiated by women with at least one college degree.[32]

Martin Whyte of Harvard observes, "Changes in the Chinese family were imposed quickly and radically. In most societies these changes would take generations. In China they were compressed into a time period of two or three years." A new type of family is emerging where women are more confident and assertive. As Whyte says, "Men in China have trouble marrying up; they usually want to marry down. But the desirable women are moving up."[33]

30. *Infanticide: CNN In-Depth Specials—Visions of China: Social Overview,* n.p. Online: http://www.cnn.com/interactive/specials/9908/China.socialoverview/content/infanticide.html (accessed 30 Jan. 2008).

31. Ning Zhang, "A Conflict of Interests: Current Problems in Educational Reform," *Economic Reform and Social Change in China,* ed. Andrew Watson (London: Routledge, 1992), 155.

32. Robert Marquand, "Women in China Finally Making a Great Leap Forward," *Christian Science Monitor* (17 Dec. 2004): 2.

33. Marquand, "Women in China," 1.

WOMEN AND THE CONTEMPORARY CHINESE CHURCH

The Church in Mainland China

The church in China went through much difficulty and persecution during the first three decades under atheistic communist rule. But when the door of China reopened again in the late 1970s, it was to everybody's surprise that the church was growing so fast. In a decade, the number of Christians jumped from one million before 1949 to at least twenty million. The mushroom effect largely happened in the countryside where house churches were spreading like wildfire.

Ka-lun Leung writes in 1999 that 80 percent of the Chinese Christian population is in the countryside, and most Christians go to house churches where the ratio of male to female is one to five.[34] A logical deduction would be that the majority of Christians in China are women. Many house churches were started and are hosted by women. Some women also lead, teach, and preach. In the underground seminaries, half or more of the students are female. Most house churches are led by laymen or laywomen. Financially, house churches cannot afford a paid pastor. But, more importantly, there are just not enough seminary-trained pastors. Those who are "pastors" often have to work part-time to make ends meet. Those who are gifted in preaching become itinerant preachers, traveling to different cities and villages to help the local churches. Not a few are women.

Wei-Duan Cheng was one of them. A deserted baby by the roadside, she was picked up by a pastor who later died when she was two. Her adopted mother was a Bible woman. She became one herself in her twenties and was an interpreter for Dr. John Sung, an evangelist greatly used by God. She was also an itinerant speaker highly in demand. In 1958, she was arrested in Shanghai. During the next twenty-some years, she suffered imprisonment and torture. The labor camp became her mission field. After she was released, her sickbed became her pulpit, and she was a great inspiration to many who visited her. Another itinerant preacher was Sung Tien Yin, the daughter of John Sung. Xiaomin, still another young woman, has written more than nine hundred gospel songs and touched the lives of many people both inside and outside China.

---

34. Ka-lun Leung, *The Rural Churches of Mainland China since 1978* (Hong Kong: Alliance Bible Seminary, March 1999), 136.

The house churches are in great need of workers and are generally loosely organized. Most do not have a tight authority structure. Perhaps because of this, the leadership of women may not seem an important issue yet. As for the government-controlled TSPM church,[35] women's leadership is not an issue because it corresponds with the government's policy of gender equality.

The Church in the Diaspora

An estimated fifty to sixty million Chinese have spread throughout many countries outside China. As immigrants, many spend their initial years in "Chinatowns." Once they acquire better language skills and accumulate enough money to buy a home, many move out of the "ghetto" and settle down wherever they can make their living. However, most first-generation immigrants still maintain close ties to their mother country or their own people in the same country. A lot of them come to a local Chinese church to associate with other Chinese. Consequently, some of them become Christians.

Regarding the roles of women in these churches, Dr. Hay-chun Maak, the general secretary of the Chinese Coordination Center of World Evangelism from 1996 to 2001, has made the following observations:[36]

In Southeast Asia where gender equality is a far cry, the Chinese churches in general accept women deaconesses, elders, ministers, and ordained pastors, harvesting short-term and long-term spiritual fruitfulness. In Taiwan and Hong Kong where gender equality has made big strides, women's ordination is still uncommon. Nevertheless, the Association of Taiwan Baptist Churches passed a resolution in 1994 to ordain women, and the Association of Hong Kong C&MA Churches did the same in 1999. The Presbyterians and the Methodists have done that a long time ago. Women eldership in these places is widely accepted while installing deaconesses is a common practice. Having women pastors is just a normal part of their church life. In North America, gender equality is a fact of life. Yet the most ridiculous and shameful thing happens within Chinese (evangelical) churches where ordaining a woman pastor

35. The term "TSPM" stands for Three-Self Patriotic Movement, which was created in the 1950s by the government to sanction Protestant churches.

36. Cecilia Yau, Dora Wang, and Lily Lee, *Gender Reconciliation* (California: Fullness in Christ Fellowship, 2004), 62.

is very rare, and most churches do not install woman elders, or deaconesses. Even Bible women are hard to find. Believe it or not, a certain church deacon board discussed for three hours before reaching a consensus to give their full-time female worker the title, "Bible Woman"!

Why is there a gender gap? An obvious reason is the influence of the denominations with which these churches are associated. A majority of the Chinese churches in North America are evangelical, and many belong to the Southern Baptist Convention and Christian & Missionary Alliance—two denominations that do not ordain women. Many of the "independent" churches, which comprise about 40 to 50 percent of all churches have their roots in Watchman Nee's "local assembly," Bible Church, or Plymouth Brethren.

These groups may allow their women missionaries to use their gifts without restraint on the mission fields. But, once they come home, they have to lay aside their leadership gifts and experiences, a double standard that is hard to understand. As the male-leadership-only churches assign women to teach the young and children, do they also feel that people on the mission fields deserve only the "second-best" workers—the women? Such a superiority complex has also polluted the North American Chinese Church.

Dr. Fenggang Yang, a sociology professor at Purdue University, points out another influence: the conservative seminaries where the Chinese pastors have received their training, namely Moody Bible Institute and Dallas Theological Seminary, etc.[37]

In the areas of hermeneutics and theology, in 1994, four seminaries in Hong Kong sponsored a panel to exchange ideas about "Chinese feminist theology." Twenty-three theologians from Taiwan and Hong Kong representing different traditions and denominations gathered to discuss how to resolve the conflicts between biblical authority and church traditions with feminist theology. A general consensus was reached that the aim of feminist theology is not to undermine the authority of the Bible, but to include women's perspectives and experiences in the hermeneutics and the theological process.[38]

37. Fenggang Yang, "Gender and Generation in a Chinese Christian Church," in *Asian American Religions: The Making and Remaking of Borders and Boundaries,* ed. Fenggang Yang and Tony Carnes (New York: New York University Press, 2004), 208.

38. Yau, *Passion,* 230–31.

SUGGESTIONS FOR CHANGE

History has demonstrated that education is the gateway to awareness and change. As more women receive higher education with training in critical thinking, they will be able to make wiser judgments for themselves and for society at large.

Seminary education also provides more opportunities to be involved in church leadership. Those who have struggled to fulfill their calling and develop their gifts in the various fields of leadership will understand more the issues that have been talked about in this chapter and will be able to blaze the trail for women who come after them. Women should grasp every opportunity for further study. They should be diligent in developing their gifts, serving with a humble heart. They should demonstrate to the church that women can be good and effective leaders.

The women leaders who are well accepted by the church should use every opportunity to open the doors for those who are still struggling on the way. Through mentorship, older and more experienced women can help younger women to overcome hurdles and be more confident in answering the call of God.

On a corporate level, Bible study and talks on women's issues should be encouraged in church. Women's studies should be incorporated in seminary curricula. More articles and books on this issue should be written to educate the public. The Chinese church and Christians have yet a long way to go on these fronts. Christians for Biblical Equality (CBE) has set a good example and paved the way for Christians in many countries to follow.

CONCLUSION

Like the women in many ancient cultures, Chinese women had been living under various forms of oppression for thousands of years. Then, missionaries brought the Good News of Jesus Christ, who came to set people free from sins and from oppression. Chinese Protestant history has but two hundred years. Within this short period of time, the destiny of Chinese women has been positively transformed. The same changes might have taken centuries in other cultures. It is hoped that not only the feet, but also the hearts and minds of the Chinese women will never be bound again, and that the freedom in Christ may be a true reality in their lives.

4

Challenging the Patriarchal Ethos:
Gender Equality in the Korean American Church
Matthew D. Kim

D URING THE FOURTH CENTURY, Greek philosophers such as Aristotle
(384–322 b.c.) maintained that "the male is by nature superior, and
the female inferior; and the one rules, and the other is ruled."[1] In fact,
many patriarchal views from the Greco-Roman era have been advocated
and disseminated by leading scholars throughout Christian history.[2]
Although in the West the genesis of patriarchy is often attributed to Greco-
Roman philosophers, notions of patriarchy and the inferiority of women
have been similarly championed in the tenets of East Asian philosophy
which define the socio-cultural-religious pulse of Korean American society.[3] Consequently, a dominant cultural ethos of Americans of Korean
ethnic descent is one of universal male headship and leadership to the exclusion of females' exercising their abilities and gifts within domestic and
ecclesial contexts. In essence, Korean American Christians' cultural and
theological presuppositions with respect to gender equality are shaped
by dual patriarchal systems deriving from past Confucian philosophy as
well as more recently adopted Greco-Roman conservative evangelical
patriarchy.

---

1. Aristotle, *The Works of Aristotle-Politics* 1.5.B4v (Oxford: Clarendon, 1921), 1253.

2. Mimi Haddad, "Egalitarian Pioneers: Betty Friedan or Catherine Booth?" *Priscilla Papers* 20, no. 4 (Autumn 2006): 53.

3. This chapter concentrates solely on biblical equality among those of Korean ethnic descent living in the United States and not native Koreans in North or South Korea.

This chapter will explore current perspectives on gender equality among first generation Korean immigrants[4] and second generation Korean Americans[5] in the United States. Although biblical equality is becoming a flourishing movement spanning the globe, these harmonious patriarchal systems have stymied its reform in the Korean American context. For this reason, a more biblical model of gender equality will be suggested that advocates unanimity and egalitarianism within a socio-cultural-religious system that often impedes gender equality from occurring in Korean American congregations.

THE FIRST GENERATION AND CONFUCIAN PATRIARCHY

For the most part, Koreans have arrived later in United States immigration history than their East Asian neighbors from China and Japan. Whereas the first group of Chinese immigrants arrived in San Francisco prior to the "fabled Gold Rush of 1849," the first large wave of Japanese migrants came to Hawaii initially in 1885 as indentured laborers, but later established a Japanese American community on the West Coast by the late 1880s.[6] The first cluster of Korean immigrants to America, however, appeared between 1903 and 1905, replacing these Japanese workers in the Hawaiian sugar fields.[7] During this span of two years, 7,226 Korean workers immigrated to these islands.[8]

However, the twenty-first century witnessed the greatest numbers of Korean immigrants who made their way across the Pacific as beneficiaries

4. First generation Korean immigrants are foreign-born Koreans who immigrated to the United States after the age of eighteen. The first generation prefers to speak in the Korean language and tends to retain Korean culture rather than embrace American culture.

5. Americans of Korean ethnic descent either born in the United States or who emigrated from Korea before the age of five whose primary cultural affinity is American and whose primary spoken language is English.

6. Harry H. L. Kitano and Roger Daniels, *Asian Americans: Emerging Minorities* (Upper Saddle River, N.J.: Prentice Hall, 1988), 21, 57; In-Jin Yoon, *On My Own: Korean Businesses and Race Relations in America* (Chicago: University of Chicago Press, 1997), 51; and Stephen S. Kim, "Seeking Home in North America: Colonialism in Asia; Confrontation in North America," *People on the Way: Asian North Americans Discovering Christ, Culture, and Community*, ed. David Ng (Valley Forge, Pa.: Judson, 1996), 18.

7. Wayne Patterson, *The Korean Frontier in America: Immigration to Hawaii, 1896–1910* (Honolulu: University of Hawaii Press, 1988), 114.

8. Illsoo Kim, *New Urban Immigrants: The Korean Community in New York* (Princeton, N.J.: Princeton University Press, 1981), 20.

of the United States Immigration Act of 1965.[9] This act permitted a larger immigration quota to those of Asian descent, especially to those who sought reunification with their families.[10] William Gudykunst reports the exponential growth of the Korean community in America in this way: "In 1970, there were 69,155 Koreans in the United States. The corresponding numbers for 1980 and 1990 are 354,974 and 798,849."[11] More recently, the United States Census for 2000 indicates that there are now 10,242,998 Asian Americans in the United States, comprising 3.6 percent of the total American population. Within the Asian subcategory, 1,072,682 represent those of purely Korean ethnic descent, or 10.5 percent of the total Asian American population.[12] Those reporting mixed heritage with Korean and one or more other ethnicity/race constitute a slightly higher figure of 1,226,825.[13]

While the vast majority of present-day Korean immigrants have lived on American soil for over a quarter of a century, they have often been hesitant to embrace wholly American cultural values. Rather, the ideological values of Confucianism, originally established in Korea during the Yi Dynasty (A.D. 1392–1909), have been upheld.[14] In East Asian countries like Korea, "Confucianism is not so much a religion as it is a philosophy of life and an ethical and moral system."[15] The teachings of Confucius, or Kong Fuzi (551–479 B.C.),[16] created a class system through

9. Pyong Gap Min and Jung Ha Kim, eds., *Religions in Asian America: Building Faith Communities* (Walnut Creek, Calif.: Altamira, 2002), 2.

10. Sucheng Chan, *Asian Americans: An Interpretive History* (New York: Twayne, 1991), 145; and Kitano and Daniels, *Asian Americans: Emerging Minorities,* 17.

11. William B. Gudykunst, *Asian American Ethnicity and Communication* (London: Sage, 2001), 77.

12. U.S. Census, http://www.census.gov/prod/cen2000/doc/sf4.pdf (accessed 30 April 2008).

13. U.S. Census, http://www.census.gov/prod/cen2000/doc/sf4.pdf (accessed 30 April 2008).

14. Xinzhong Yao, *An Introduction to Confucianism* (Cambridge: Cambridge University Press, 2000), 117.

15. In-Gyeong Kim Lundell, *Bridging the Gaps: Contextualization among Korean Nazarene Churches in America* (New York: Peter Lang, 1995), 57.

16. Confucianism is attributed to Confucius of China "who explored deeply and elaborated extensively on the basic principles of what was to become Confucianism, and it was Confucius and his disciples who succeeded in transmitting and transforming their ancient culture." Confucianism is called "*ru jia, ru jiao, ru xue* or simply as *ru* in China and other East Asian countries" representing "the doctrine, or tradition, of scholars." See

social hierarchy.[17] Thus, Confucianism was founded primarily on moral virtues and hierarchical relationships. There are five central virtues that Confucius held in high esteem: benevolent love or humanness (*ren*), righteousness (*yi*), proper conduct (*li*), wisdom (*zhi*), and faithfulness (*xin*).[18] It was believed that these virtues would maintain harmony and social order in society if preserved by members of the five basic relationships: king and subject, father and son, husband and wife, elder and younger, and friend and friend.[19]

Reflected in these human relationships are Confucian notions of collectivity that prioritize hierarchical relations. In general, the Korean immigrant culture endorses Confucian hierarchy where seniority is paramount.[20] This principle has unavoidably penetrated first generation Korean ethnic church walls.[21] First generation Korean pastor Jason Kim explains, "For male members in Korean churches, there are four hierarchical levels. The first level is the layman level, second is the appointed deacon level, third is the elected deacon, and the last and highest level is the eldership."[22] Since many Korean immigrant men cope with marginalization and downward mobility in American society, the Korean ethnic church has become the primary site to meet their needs for higher social status through holding ecclesial positions.[23] Sociologists Eui Hang Shin

---

Yao, *Introduction to Confucianism*, 17, 22.

17. Chan, *Asian Americans: An Interpretive History*, 66.

18. Yao, *Introduction to Confucianism*, 34.

19. Lundell, *Bridging the Gaps*, 57.

20. Nak-In Kim, "A Model Ministry to Transitional and Second Generation Korean-Americans" (D.Min. diss., School of Theology at Claremont, 1991), 50–51.

21. According to Pyong Gap Min, "Korean Christian immigrants participate in a Korean congregation very frequently; about 80 percent go to a Korean church once or twice a week. Korean Christian immigrants preserve ethnicity mainly by practicing Korean culture (not necessarily Christian rituals) and increasing their co-ethnic fellowship through their active participation in a Korean congregation." See Pyong Gap Min, "A Literature Review with a Focus on Major Themes," *Religions in Asian America: Building Faith Communities*, eds. Pyong Gap Min and Jung Ha Kim (Walnut Creek, Calif.: Altamira, 2002), 18.

22. Jason Hyungkyun Kim, "The Effects of Assimilation within the Korean Immigrant Church: Intergenerational Conflicts between the First and Second Generation Korean Christians in Two Chicago Suburban Churches" (Ph.D. diss., Trinity International University, 1999), 140.

23. Pyong Gap Min, "The Structure and Social Functions of Korean Immigrant Churches in the United States," *International Migration Review* 26 (1992): 1389.

and Hyung Park relate that "Korean immigrants strive seriously to acquire such lay leadership positions and the struggle for status building in
the church turns into a fierce competition among candidates."[24]

Not only are Korean ethnic churches hierarchical, but they also sanction Confucian patriarchal tendencies that downplay the role of women.
This does not come as a complete surprise, as the deprecation of women
is highly consistent with Confucian doctrine.[25] In fact, Korean females in
the church have often been precluded from participating fully in the work
of God's kingdom. A number of recent sociologists have attempted to understand the basis for the lack of gender equality in Korean immigrant
churches. For example, Kwang Chung Kim et al. recount:

> Many [Korean] churches have no women elders, and when women
> do have the formal status of elder, they are often only symbolic fig-
> ures without real authority. Church women are expected to serve
> in such areas as the Sunday school, the choir, and the kitchen. . . .
> The [Korean] immigrant church seems designed to serve the needs
> of men.[26]

Similarly, Inn Sook Lee writes, "The older [Korean] men who largely
control church and community organizations are naturally reluctant to
relinquish their superior status and influence. So, [Korean] women usually must content themselves with supporting roles and rarely become
officers or board members."[27] On a denominational level, Jung Ha Kim
reports that only 8 percent of Korean American church elders in the
Presbyterian Church (U.S.A.) are women, and that the vast majority of

24. Eui Hang Shin and Hyung Park, "An Analysis of Causes of Schisms in Ethnic
Churches: The Case of Korean-American Churches," *Sociological Analysis* 49 (1988):
242.

25. Chenyang Li has edited a helpful volume which places Confucianism in dialogue
with feminism. Throughout this work, scholars emphasize the patriarchal tendencies of
Confucian thought which convey a "degrading and repressive attitude toward women
and [is known] for its history of women-oppressive practice." See Chenyang Li, ed., *The
Sage and the Second Sex: Confucianism, Ethics, and Gender* (Chicago: Carus, 2000), 1.

26. Kwang Chung Kim, R. Stephen Warner, and Ho-Youn Kwon, "Korean American
Religion in International Perspective," *Korean Americans and Their Religions: Pilgrims
and Missionaries from a Different Shore*, eds. Ho-Youn Kwon, Kwang Chung Kim, and R.
Stephen Warner (University Park: Pennsylvania State University Press, 2001), 14.

27. Inn Sook Lee, "Korean American Women and Ethnic Identity," *Korean American
Ministry*, eds. Sang Hyun Lee and John V. Moore (Louisville, Ky.: General Assembly
Council PCUSA, 1987), 200.

ordained United Methodist female Korean American clergy are not presented with the opportunity to serve as senior pastors. Rather, they often
hold clergy positions as assistant/associate pastors or youth/educational
ministers who are under the strict management of male senior ministers.[28]
Lastly, Korean females entering parish ministry also find themselves hit-
ting an imaginary "glass ceiling" where many encounter structural frus-
trations as well as economic impediments. For instance, Timothy Tseng
and his colleagues report how one first-generation Korean clergywoman
discussed her disappointment with receiving a lower salary at a congregation that, for her, crossed racial and cultural lines. She responds, "I don't
know what is an acceptable package of equitable salary any more [*sic*].
. . . I don't know whether it's due to my gender or ethnicity or the [cur-
rent] appointment that is the core reason for my under-pay."[29] At present,
this second-class treatment of Korean females occurs regularly not only
in the Korean immigrant community, but also as Korean women coexist
with members of the dominant American culture.[30] A clear portrayal of
sustained Confucian patriarchy in Korean immigrant churches can be
found in *More than Serving Tea: Asian American Women on Expectations,
Relationships, Leadership, and Faith*, where Christie Heller de Leon
writes,

> There are times too, though, when our struggle to be respected
> is in situations with Asian men. Jessica, a campus minister in
> Georgia, talks about an encounter with a pastor in her city: "There
> have been times where I feel like I have no voice. I met with a
> pastor who was new to my area. He was coming to start a church
> and wanted to meet up to 'partner together.' When we met, he
> was very nice, but at the same time I felt belittled. I was a woman,
> a Taiwanese American woman, and he was a Korean pastor. He
> shared his vision, and I shared my thoughts and asked follow-up
> questions. In the end, he was going to do what he was going to do.
> Later I asked my Korean male supervisor to meet with the pastor,

28. Jung Ha Kim, "Cartography of Korean American Protestant Faith Communities
in the United States," *Religions in Asian America: Building Faith Communities*, eds. Pyong
Gap Min and Jung Ha Kim (Walnut Creek, Calif.: Altamira, 2002), 199.

29. Timothy Tseng et al., "Asian American Religious Leadership Today: A Preliminary
Inquiry," *Pulpit and Pew: Research on Pastoral Leadership* (Durham, N.C.: Duke Divinity
School, 2005), 32.

30. Jung Ha Kim, "The Labor of Compassion: Voices of Churched Korean American
Women," *New Spiritual Homes: Religion and Asian Americans*, ed. David K. Yoo
(Honolulu: University of Hawaii Press, 1999), 206.

to speak on my behalf, because I honestly wasn't sure if the pastor respected me, my work or my thoughts."[31]

Thus, the damaging effects of Confucian patriarchy are both prolific and deep-rooted in the Korean immigrant church context. Many first generation Korean females harbor acrimonious feelings toward the Korean culture and church in general and toward chauvinistic Korean males in particular. As Rose Kim relates, "Some of my earliest memories are of suffering the degradation of being female, and for a long time I could not help but associate Korean culture with the oppression of women."[32] Similarly, in my research in the Korean American ecclesial context, I have found that female degradation has led, as one female respondent remarked, to "a lot of low self-esteem among the women."[33]

Interestingly, one reaction to this oppression in Korean culture has been to seek marriage partners outside of the Korean ethnicity. For instance, Ruth Chung states, "As I observed the inequality between men and women in Korean culture, I was determined not to perpetuate the pattern. . . . Needless to say, my father was quite displeased when I asked for permission to marry a non-Korean."[34] However, eliminating innate Korean cultural values like Confucian patriarchy is not always as straightforward as marrying a person outside of one's ethnic group. Akin to members of other Asian cultures, Koreans are by nature a dyadic people group who place enormous demands on their members to conform to tradition.[35] In addition, as we shall observe later in our discussion of second generation Korean Americans, it is often the case that females have accepted their "lower" status in the Korean American church and have not been willing to challenge the status quo.

31. Christie Heller de Leon, "Sticks, Stones, and Stereotypes," *More than Serving Tea: Asian American Women on Expectations, Relationships, Leadership and Faith*, eds. Nikki A. Toyama and Tracy Gee (Downers Grove, Ill.: InterVarsity, 2006), 27.

32. Rose Kim, "My Trek," *Struggle for Ethnic Identity: Narratives by Asian American Professionals*, eds. Pyong Gap Min and Rose Kim (Walnut Creek, Calif.: Altamira, 1999), 50.

33. Matthew D. Kim, "From Corporate Silence to Real Talk: A New Contextual Homiletic for Second Generation Korean Americans" (M.Th. diss., University of Edinburgh , Ann Arbor: UMI, 2004), 85.

34. Ruth Chung, "Reflections on a Korean American Journey," *Struggle for Ethnic Identity*, 63.

35. Nikki A. Toyama, "Perfectionist Tendencies," *More than Serving Tea*, 57.

As we have observed to this point, the first generation Korean immigrant church has been largely persuaded by Confucian patriarchal tenets where it is culturally accepted that males hold leadership positions in the church often, to the exclusion of female participation. In many Korean immigrant congregations, gender inequality has become the norm rather than the exception. Unfortunately, the legacy left by first generation Korean immigrants to their children has also been one mired in the patriarchal ethos. This patriarchal ideology is not solely attributable to Confucianism, but also to Greco-Roman ideas advanced in conservative evangelical theology on gender.

THE SECOND GENERATION AND GRECO-ROMAN PATRIARCHY

While second generation Korean Americans presume an American cultural affinity and primarily speak English as their dominant language of choice, their bicultural tendencies have generated a "complex interplay of two sociocultural systems, the Korean ethnic heritage and the American way of life."[36] This dichotomy in cultures ironically produces both conflict and synergy for second generation Korean Americans. It generates conflict in that members often have difficulty choosing which cultural tradition to embrace and practice. At the same time, however, when it comes to gender roles in the home and in the church, second generation Korean Americans can easily synthesize the tenets of both Confucian and Greco-Roman philosophies to solidify their arguments for male supremacy and gender role distinctions. The adherence to patriarchal values among second generation Korean Americans can be witnessed daily within their homes and within their churches on Sunday morning.

First of all, in a domestic capacity, many second generation Korean Americans subscribe to a more complementarian, rather than egalitarian, approach to gender roles. That is, as Kevin Giles explains, "This new theology subordinating women to men in the church and the home has had a tremendous impact on evangelicals. It sounded acceptable to modern ears: 'Men and women are equal, they simply have been given different roles: they complement each other.'"[37] In other words, rather than see-

36. Kwang Chung Kim, et al., "Korean American Religion in International Perspective," *Korean Americans and Their Religions*, 13.

37. Kevin Giles, "Post-1970s Evangelical Responses to the Emancipation of Women,"

ing marriage as a way of reinforcing "mutual submission," as I believe Paul advises in Ephesians 5:21–22, second generation Korean Americans normally take Paul's instruction for wives to submit to their husbands literally and without questioning, which then permits "husbands [to] make critical and final decisions and [to have] wives willingly submit to the husband's authority over them."[38] The assumption is that husbands have a God-given privilege and right to make all family decisions irrespective of their wives' beliefs and opinions. Put simply, Korean American husbands often have the final and only word. In addition, in various homes, first generation Korean mothers teach their second generation sons early on not to wash the dishes or to assist with any other household chores, because these are the duties of daughters and their wife to be.[39] Obviously, these pejorative perspectives on female gender roles are at variance with today's Korean American women who are socially trained to be "assertive, independent, and competent," rather than simply to accept roles as only mother, caretaker, and domestic servant.[40] It is no surprise, then, to observe how comparable attitudes toward women spread into the second generation Korean American church context.

Within a conservatively minded church milieu, the difficulty of advancing biblical equality in second generation Korean American churches is again the staunch commitment to a traditional understanding of texts from Paul, most notably 1 Corinthians 11 and 1 Timothy 2. Influenced heavily by traditionalist pastor-scholars like John Piper and Timothy Keller, many second generation Korean Americans uphold the ecclesial positions of pastor, elder, and teacher as reserved strictly for men, as Paul's chapter on worship in 1 Timothy 2 is often interpreted. In fact, during my search for a full-time pastoral position, I encountered one Asian American congregation where the sole elder of the church, who was a second generation Chinese American male, questioned my view on the

---

Priscilla Papers 20, no. 4 (Autumn 2006): 47.

38. Judith K. Balswick and Jack O. Balswick, "Marriage as a Partnership of Equals," *Discovering Biblical Equality: Complementarity without Hierarchy*, eds. Ronald W. Pierce and Rebecca Merrill Groothuis (Downers Grove, Ill.: InterVarsity, 2005), 449.

39. Peter Cha and Grace May, "Gender Relations in Healthy Households," *Growing Healthy Asian American Churches*, eds. Peter Cha, S. Steve Kang, and Helen Lee (Downers Grove, Ill.: InterVarsity, 2006), 166.

40. Ken Uyeda Fong, *Pursuing the Pearl: A Comprehensive Resource for Multi-Asian Ministry* (Valley Forge, Pa.: Judson, 1999), 181.

authority of Scripture because I held to an egalitarian position on women in ministry. He went as far to say that, if I believed that Paul's argument in 1 Timothy 2 was indeed context-specific to the situation in the Ephesian church, then my theology would also be susceptible to homosexuality as being a culturally condemnable practice only in the particular context of the ancient world.

Likewise, during my doctoral research, one second generation male pastor defended his position of women's subordination and prohibition to serve as pastors and elders in this way:

> [In] 1 Timothy 2, Paul says that he doesn't permit women to teach or exercise authority over men. The pattern that's given there is even from creation when God created Adam first and Eve fell first . . . and so there is a timeless principle involved. Even in the image of Christ and the church, just as Christ is the head of the church, the husband is the head of the wife and you see that in the church.[41]

As a result of this gender discrimination, many second generation Korean American females feel that Korean American preachers cater to men and usually fail to address the needs of women parishioners. Employing sociological terms, Alice Mathews introduces one category of gender identification as *type-A error* or *alpha-bias*. Korean American preachers known for alpha-bias would tend to "exaggerate the differences between men and women."[42] For example, one research respondent explained how his pastor "talks a lot about biblical standards [in marriage] . . . when male-female are as one the man is to take over as . . . the main role leader and that women are supposed to submit."[43] The reality is that Korean American pastors often communicate one-sided arguments toward which congregants are expected not to challenge their pastors' teachings. In fact, Korean churches have a penchant for pastoral clout where "the spiritual authority of pastors is seldom questioned."[44] This ab-

41. Matthew D. Kim, "Preaching to Second Generation Korean Americans: Towards a Possible Selves Contextual Homiletic" (Ph.D. diss., University of Edinburgh, 2006), 171–72.

42. Alice P. Mathews, "Preaching to the Whole Church," *Preaching to a Shifting Culture: 12 Perspectives on Communicating that Connects*, ed. Scott M. Gibson (Grand Rapids: Baker, 2004), 159. See also Alice P. Mathews, *Preaching that Speaks to Women* (Grand Rapids: Baker, 2003), 23–24.

43. Matthew Kim, "Preaching to Second Generation Korean Americans," 171.

44. Myungseon Oh, "Study on Appropriate Leadership Pattern for the Korean Church

sence of cognitive reasoning is clearly indicative of what Mark Noll has poignantly termed "the scandal of the evangelical mind."[45]

Moreover, in Kelly Chong's study of two second generation Korean American congregations in Chicago, she found that, for her second generation participants, their Christian and Korean identities are not estranged or treated hierarchically, but instead are fused.[46] Therefore, since both Christian and Korean values hold to conservative ethics, second generation members feel that their Koreanness becomes validated or reinforced through conservative, evangelical Protestantism.[47] As Chong states, "The religious dimensions of Christianity interact with Korean culture to provide legitimation for Korean culture and values, thereby supporting a sense of Korean ethnic identity and group consciousness."[48] Again, this dual patriarchal understanding rears its ugly head and complicates matters for gender relations to make headway in many second generation Korean American churches. As demonstrated, second generation Korean American females have been commonly barred from leadership capacities due to Confucian and patriarchal Christian ideologies. Consequently, Korean American females have been forced to "bury their gifts and even deny a part of God's call in their lives because they believe a stereotype of what they ought to be."[49] How then can we properly challenge the Korean American community to embrace a more balanced and inclusive attitude toward gender within our homes and churches?

A BIBLICAL UNDERSTANDING OF GENDER EQUALITY

A helpful starting place to confront gender inequality is to refocus Korean American Christians on the word of God. For Korean Americans, both first and second generations alike, the word of God still holds authority in their lives and represents a salient framework for their earthly sojourn. The problem, thus far, has been that, in terms of biblical hermeneutics,

---

in Post-modern Era," *Journal of Asian Mission* 5, no. 1 (2003): 132.

45. Mark A. Noll, *The Scandal of the Evangelical Mind* (Grand Rapids: Eerdmans, 1994), 3.

46. Kelly H. Chong, "What It Means to Be Christian: The Role of Religion in the Construction of Ethnic Identity and Boundary among Second-generation Korean Americans," *Sociology of Religion* 59 (1998): 271, 278.

47. Chong, "What It Means to Be Christian," 261.

48. Chong, "What It Means to Be Christian," 275.

49. Mathews, *Preaching that Speaks to Women*, 61.

many Korean American pastors and lay persons are blinded by their predisposition to patriarchy and female subordination, as we have observed above. Accordingly, they simply take Paul's instructions literally without considering his teachings on gender equality in light of the biblical canon in its entirety, and also without taking into account their cultural context.

In *Women Leaders and the Church*, Linda Belleville asks, "What if any positions of authority can women hold in the church?"[50] In this study, Belleville concludes that "(1) God gifts and calls women and men equally, [and that] (2) God intends the male-female relationship to be mutual."[51] In what remains, we will explore some scriptural passages that support Belleville's conclusions for women's inclusion and participation in senior ecclesial leadership with the objective of enlightening the Korean American Christian culture on this relevant topic.[52]

God Gifts and Calls Women and Men Equally

As Rebecca Merrill Groothuis suggests, I would argue that first and second generation Korean Americans commonly espouse the perspective that "men and women are 'equal in being' but 'different' (that is, unequal) in 'function' or 'role.'"[53] With this traditional understanding, Korean Americans in the church often set apart men's roles from women's functions in church life. Pragmatically, as discussed, this means that men universally hold positions of leadership (including teaching, preaching, and senior pastor roles), whereas females are relegated to women's ministry, children's ministry, or catering responsibilities. However, for those who hold to the perspective of equal gifting and calling, there is much freedom for women to become servant-leaders in their respective congregations.

---

50. Linda L. Belleville, *Women Leaders and the Church: Three Crucial Questions* (Grand Rapids: Baker, 2000), 181.

51. Ronald W. Pierce, "Contemporary Evangelicals for Gender Equality," *Discovering Biblical Equality*, 69. For the sake of space, we will not explore Linda Belleville's third conclusion that "in the church 'there is not . . . male and female.'" See Belleville, *Women Leaders and the Church*, 181.

52. I borrow insights from N. T. Wright's article "The Biblical Basis for Women's Service in the Church," *Priscilla Papers* 20, no. 4 (Autumn 2006): 5–10.

53. Rebecca Merrill Groothuis, "'Equal in Being, Unequal in Role,'" *Discovering Biblical Equality*, 302.

Scholars note how many women in Scripture have been affirmed in positions of leadership. For example, like others, Linda Belleville cites Miriam in Numbers 12:15 as a leader whose "congregation of Israel viewed her role as essential to its mission, refusing to move ahead on one occasion until she was restored to leadership after her criticism of Moses."[54] She also mentions Deborah, the judge, and Huldah, the prophet, who led Israel in the context of prominent male leaders like Moses, Barak, Josiah, Jeremiah, etc.[55] The prophet Joel's testimony that both males and females would prophesy in chapter 2 is not something to take casually, especially in light of the entire biblical witness. For, in the New Testament, Belleville makes special reference to female leaders like Junia in the church of Rome, who was noted by Paul as "outstanding among the apostles" and who was "in Christ before [he] was." In addition, Paul names noteworthy women leaders in the church of Philippi, such as Euodia and Syntyche, who shared in Paul's ministry by preaching the gospel and leading the congregation.[56] We also receive word in Romans 16 and 2 Timothy 4 of female leadership in the persons of Phoebe and Priscilla who ministered with Paul as coworkers in Christ.[57] And Luke the physician affirms equal gifting and calling when he discusses the roles of Philip's four daughters as prophets in the church of Caesarea in Acts 21:9, among others.[58] With such biblical support, it is difficult to proceed blindly with the argument that women were not gifted and called by God to serve in leadership capacities. The setback in Korean American culture has been that the "stories of women are through the lens of patriarchal attitudes, contributing to the tendency to view female characters negatively."[59] Yet, it is clear that, in certain Asian American ministries, some are beginning to challenge the status quo with respect to views on equal gifting and calling. For example, Duke University's *Pulpit and Pew* study on Asian American women in

54. Linda L. Belleville, "Women Leaders in the Bible," *Discovering Biblical Equality*, 111.

55. Belleville, "Women Leaders in the Bible," 113.

56. Belleville, "Women Leaders in the Bible," 120.

57. Belleville, "Women Leaders in the Bible," 121.

58. Belleville, "Women Leaders in the Bible," 123. Belleville also refers to "[a] woman named Ammia in the Philadelphian church" who "is also said to have prophesied during New Testament times" and Nympha who "had legal responsibility for and hence authority over the church that met in her house (Col 4:15)." See "Women Leaders in the Bible," 123–24.

59. Lisa Wilson Davison, *Preaching the Women of the Bible* (St. Louis: Chalice, 2006), 9.

ministry found that one Japanese American professional brought about significant cultural change

> when she was invited to the church's leadership council meeting. [She] initially understood her role was to serve the men snacks. But when the council chairman told her she was to make decisions and not serve, she realized her internalized patriarchal image of leadership. As a professional woman, it did not take her long to shift gears. She invited more women to the group and gradually brought about significant cultural change. It took nudging by two male leaders for her to see herself as a decision maker in her church.[60]

Therefore, Tseng and his colleagues conclude, "Rather than blaming women in the church for their lack of support of female leaders, proactive male elders are needed to break through the internalized sexism that families and churches have inculcated."[61]

God Intends the Male-Female Relationship to Be Mutual

From 1 Timothy 2:11–15, Korean American pastors have commonly taken the position that the creation order precludes women from having authority over men, particularly in the forms of teaching or preaching in mixed-gender congregations. However, as Kevin Giles aptly explains, "The word rendered 'authority' by most modern translations is the Greek word *authentein*, found only this once in the whole Bible. In the first century it was a very harsh word implying domination or usurping authority. This exceptional word clearly indicates an exceptional situation."[62] Further clarifying this position, N. T. Wright observes:

> The key to understanding the present passage, then, is to recognize that it is commanding that women, too, should be allowed to study and learn, and should not be restrained from doing so (v. 11). They are to be "in full submission"; this is often taken to mean "to the men" or "to their husbands," but it is equally likely that it refers to their attitude, as learners, of submission to God or to the gospel—which of course would be the same attitude required of male learners.[63]

60. Tseng et al., "Asian American Religious Leadership Today," 34.

61. Tseng et al., "Asian American Religious Leadership Today," 34.

62. Giles, "Post-1970s Evangelical Responses," 51.

63. Wright, "The Biblical Basis for Women's Service in the Church," 9.

Later, Wright continues that verse 12, which has spawned much controversy, should not be read as "I do not allow a woman to teach or hold authority over a man," but rather "I don't mean to imply that I'm now setting up women as the new authority over men in the same way that previously men held authority over women."[64] As we know, the Apostle Paul in this letter to Timothy sought to correct any false teachings and distorted doctrines prevalent in the church of Ephesus.[65] Thus, arguing from the stance of cultural sensitivity, Wright suggests that Paul was most likely challenging the primary pagan religion in Ephesus, based on the Temple of Artemis, where women held positions of authority as priests who "ruled the show and kept the men in their place."[66] To make himself perfectly clear, Wright argues that Paul was not promoting a skewed philosophy, where "Christianity would gradually become a cult like that of Artemis, where women did the leading and kept the men in line."[67] On the contrary, Wright construes that "Paul is saying, like Jesus in Luke 10, that women must have the space and leisure to study and learn in their own way, not in order that they may muscle in and take over the leadership as in the Artemis cult, but rather so that men and women alike can develop whatever gifts of learning, teaching, and leadership God is giving them."[68] Through this more evenhanded point of view, Wright justly maintains that Paul's text, which has been so often employed to abuse and oppress women, is truly intended to build up God's people, God's church, women and men mutually.

CONCLUSION

Culturally ingrained philosophies, such as Confucian or Greco-Roman patriarchy, cannot be easily detached from one's socio-cultural-religious consciousness. Rather, as Kathy Khang asserts, it is generally easier in the Korean American context to conform to "the expectations of the world around me and identify so closely with my failures to meet those

---

64. Wright, "The Biblical Basis for Women's Service in the Church," 9.

65. James Choung, "Can Women Teach?: An Exegesis of 1 Timothy 2:11–15 and 1 Corinthians 14:33–40" (unpublished paper, La Jolla, Calif., 2006), 2.

66. Wright, "Biblical Basis for Women's Service," 9.

67. Wright, "Biblical Basis for Women's Service," 9.

68. Wright, "Biblical Basis for Women's Service," 9.

expectations that I forget who God created me to be."[69] Prior to attending Gordon-Conwell Theological Seminary for the Master of Divinity degree, I was educated similarly during my formative years in a conservative Korean American church that women should never teach, preach, or be ordained as ministers of the gospel. To believe otherwise would lead to an arduous and isolated road. Consequently, I naturally conformed to this more convenient mode of thinking. Fortunately, a host of seminary professors properly instructed their students to commit themselves to the word of God and to investigate thoroughly the text in its historical, literary, and grammatical context.[70] While the vast majority of first and second generation Korean Americans in the United States still preserves notions of female subordination and male supremacy in the home and in the church, I testify to the possibility that biblical equality is still achievable in Korean American society, albeit in time. In examining the Scriptures holistically, one cannot deny God's mutual equipping and calling of women and men to serve the entire body of Christ. When Korean American churches wholly understand and embrace this constructive biblical perspective, there is no telling what God will accomplish through an assembly of united and obedient servant-leaders within our respective faith communities—irrespective of gender.

In conclusion, then, how can we achieve this objective of making gender equality a more significant priority in Korean American churches? Stated differently, what practical steps are necessary to facilitate biblical equality in our specific ethnic and cultural context? Admittedly, while the task before us is rather voluminous, it begins at the grassroots level as one congregation launches reforms that will optimistically influence its neighboring churches. Allow me to share how we, at Logos Central Chapel, have sought to advance gender equality and later bring our discussion to a close with final initiatives to mobilize second generation Korean American pastors in promoting biblical equality.

---

69. Kathy Khang, "Pulled by Expectations," *More than Serving Tea*, 41.

70. See Douglas Stuart, *Old Testament Exegesis: A Handbook for Students and Pastors*, 3rd ed. (Louisville, Ky.: Westminster/John Knox, 2001), 1; and Haddon W. Robinson, *Biblical Preaching*, 2nd ed. (Grand Rapids: Baker, 2001), 21. In particular, I thank Dr. Aída Besançon Spencer, Professor of New Testament, and Dr. Scott M. Gibson, Haddon W. Robinson Professor of Preaching, at Gordon-Conwell Theological Seminary, for helping me to receive this important insight.

At Logos Central Chapel, we have pushed the envelope in regard to how second generation Korean Americans perceive the role of women in ministry. Coming from patriarchal and traditionalist Korean Presbyterian roots, many of our parishioners felt strongly that women should not hold positions of leadership, especially as pastors or elders. However, over the past year, through the mediums of preaching and teaching, I have taught my congregants scripturally how God has equipped men and women equally to share in parish ministry and leadership.[71] Specifically, I conducted a six-week sermon series on "Women in the Old Testament," exploring biblical characters like Deborah, Jael, Huldah, Rahab, Ruth, and Hannah, with the aim of revealing God's heart for and commitment to female ministerial leadership. In addition, as part of our adult Sunday school classes, we have engaged in discussions on topics like biblical leadership through the narratives of male and female leaders from the book of Judges. Through the faithful proclamation and corporate study of the word, we have witnessed several scales that have fallen from the eyes of both male and female congregants with respect to gender equality. Thus, it is imperative that the first step in advancing biblical equality is conscientious and cogent instruction from God's word. We must properly inform our church members vis-à-vis God's intention for mutual partnership and shared leadership among men and women in the church.

Secondly, we must be intentional in appointing females to lead in substantial ecclesial positions. For example, in previous years, women have not served as moderators for our Sunday worship service. This year, however, through our collective encouragement, two females have stepped forward to preside over our worship gathering. Moreover, in our church's brief nine-year history, the governing structure has taken the form of a steering council where six leaders oversee different ministry committees, which include administration, discipleship, education, ministry, outreach, and worship. Prior to my arrival, these leadership positions were reserved strictly for men. Yet, in the years to come, we will open these steering council roles to both genders. Accordingly, in these purposeful ways, Logos Central Chapel, a predominantly second generation Korean

---

71. Logos Central Chapel is an independent second generation Korean American congregation in Denver, Colorado, that branched out from a first generation Korean immigrant church in the fall of 1999. To put things into perspective, I became the senior pastor of Logos Central Chapel in September 2006.

American church, is breaking away from its traditional, patriarchal heritage to one that fully welcomes and practices gender equality.

And, finally, how we can mobilize second generation Korean American pastors toward biblical equality?[72] On a local level, an initial suggestion would be to rally the lead pastors of second generation Korean and Asian American congregations in one's city or state who uphold an egalitarian ministry philosophy to participate in roundtable discussions and forums with the objective of praying together and sharing both successful and fruitless methods for gender equality implementation in their respective local church contexts. Further down the road, as these egalitarian pastors build relationships and solidify their beliefs, regional or national conferences may be held where experts on gender equality inform non-egalitarian senior pastors via teaching a hermeneutical perspective of biblical equality as well as developing corporately practical strategies across select egalitarian Korean and Asian American congregations. Although egalitarians will undoubtedly face myriad forms of resistance from clergy and laity alike, we must press forward and challenge the patriarchal ethos in Korean American churches with God's help and for God's glory.

72. In this final paragraph, I have included insights from Dr. Jewel Hyun, who provided valuable feedback on this chapter.

5

Biblical Equality in Zimbabwe, Africa

Constantine M. Murefu

GENESIS 1:27 STATES THAT God created man "male and female," and Genesis 2:18b also states that God made man "a helper comparable to him." These statements alone should be correctly viewed as the foundation of biblical equality. They describe the way in which God intends women and men to relate to each other and thus provide a blueprint with which each culture should build its own paradigm for gender relationships. The present chapter attempts to pursue the general African views embraced by the Shona people in Zimbabwe with regard to the role of men and women, including the three types of African families; societal changes that caused the church to review its position; successful attempts made toward the ordination of women within the Apostolic Faith Mission (AFM) in Zimbabwe, the oldest and certainly one of the largest Pentecostal denominations in the country; and the way forward if we are going to make this equality a workable truth.

GENERAL AFRICAN VIEW OF THE ROLES OF MEN AND WOMEN AMONG THE SHONA PEOPLE IN ZIMBABWE

Gender equality appears to be an elusive issue to many fraternities or sororities (communities of men and women) at home and abroad. Assessment is further complicated by the lack of consensus on the subject definition. The following questions need to be considered and satisfactorily answered by society: What is equality? Who defines it? Whose equality is it? What is the basis of equality? These questions should not be approached simply with relativism or mere cultural anthropology, which may simply report patriarchal traditions and thereby limit thinking. Let me try instead to define equality focusing on the general understanding in Zimbabwe, particularly among the Shona ethnic group. (Shona is an indigenous language spoken by more than 70 percent of the black population in Zimbabwe. The author happens to be of Shona origin.) Among the Shona people, men are viewed in elevation over women.[1] Manhood is associated with strength, boldness, courage, decisiveness, and tenacity. On the other hand, womanhood is associated with childbearing, dependency upon men, need for protection, and homemaking;[2] hence, we see that such "equality" is ethnically based and defined, but it lacks a biblical foundation and is not universal to all people.

This traditional approach may have been relevant during yesteryear when there were no career women. However, with technological development and the dawn of modern time, some things had to change. Women began to venture into areas that were previously regarded as the preserve of men. Professions like engineering, construction work, running a business, and university professorship had been dominated by men, but within the past three decades we have seen women also entering such occupations. Church leadership, also dominated by men, became the last area to awaken to this reality. The dynamics of change started in the secular world and penetrated into the church, while the church was not quite ready for it. It is a bit embarrassing to note that the church did not respond rapidly, probably because the men had viewed the change wrought by salvation and sanctification as only affecting the heart and not gender roles. Something had to change.

The general African traditional culture views a woman as belonging to her husband while a girl belongs to her father, but a widow is in limbo.[3] Widows are deprived of a husband, breadwinner, and social status. They are often haunted by the accusation that they killed their husbands.[4] Turning to this African paradigm for reference would make gender equality a regional issue founded on cultural anthropological relativism; hence, the subject becomes elusive to universal definitions.

1. Brendah Siamanzime, "The Reporter," Zambian National Broadcasting Television Channel, 9 a.m., 11 Feb. 2007.

2. Agnes Murefu (author's eighty-one-year-old mother), interview, 998 Chitunya Road, Chitungwiza, Zimbabwe, 17 June 2007.

3. Siamanzime, "The Reporter," 11 Feb. 2007.

4. Siamanzime, "The Reporter," 11 Feb. 2007.

Gender equality could be defined as competence in playing the assigned gender roles accepted by the community. I am not necessarily referring to equal pay for equal qualifications as espoused by the feminist movements today, since this conclusion is fairly indisputably acceptable in Zimbabwe. The main focus of this treatise is more related to personhood. Since God created for man a helper comparable to him, the Bible means someone of equal, comparable, complementary competence. God did not create an inferior dependent.

Although the Zimbabwean African culture has traditionally and historically accepted a certain equality based on roles played, or expected to be played, within the family, it must be understood that terms such as *brother, sister, mother,* and *father* have a different meaning within the Zimbabwean Shona culture in particular. Within such confines, I have as many mothers as my mother has sisters. I have as many fathers as my father has brothers, giving me many brothers and sisters in these families. Every one of my father's brothers is also my father; every one of my mother's sisters is also my mother. Their children are my brothers and sisters as well.

Hence, the term *orphan* had no real place or value until the dynamics of change caught up with us. The mother is associated with love, care, and nurturing, while the father is associated with breadwinning. It was from such a conceptual framework that the roles were derived. A married woman belongs to the family into which she marries. She has a corporate identity, and her life, property, and identity are seen as belonging to it.

The payment of the dowry or the bridal price meant that her parents have replaced her with material wealth given by the son-in-law. This was meant to prove to the father-in-law that the young man could take care of the woman he marries while he and his wife find solace in the bridal price.[5] This practice was not originally commercialized as has often become the tendency nowadays. In its original state, it compares with Isaac sending some jewelry and other ornaments for Rebecca (Gen 24). The woman's major role was to raise children for her husband, cook for him, and take care of him at all costs while he supplied all the family economic needs. Such needs included fending for the family, purchasing enough land for growing food crops, buying animals for draught power and for meat, and providing for clothing and education for the family. Apparently, the boys

5. Interview with Agnes Murefu.

were encouraged to go on for further education, but not the girls. Girls prepared for marriage while boys got more education in order to fend for their future families.

These roles were played well since the people lived together in family and tribal communities. However, industrialization, urbanization, and other related technological developments began to take their toll on such communal living. Women and men began to flock to urban centers in search of a healthier economic living arrangement. They would become employed and send money home for the care of parents and family members who remained behind. Money became the medium of business transactions as opposed to the previous years when cows, goats, silver, gold, and movable property were the business transaction media. There were no longer fixed marriages when parents befriended each other, resulting in the planned marriages between their sons and daughters.

Up until the influx of Western culture and the exodus of Zimbabwean Shona people into the diaspora, gender roles remained undisputed. The entrance of Christianity in Zimbabwe did not quite address these issues; it seemed to concentrate on salvation through Jesus' efficacious death, oftentimes ignoring the fiber of deep cultural values that shaped the African views. To a large extent, the African views are not documented, but are passed on effectively orally from generation to generation. The missionaries did a phenomenal job in getting the African saved, but then failed to cross the cultural bridge, oftentimes presenting the gospel in a Western cultural casing. The African at times became more Western than Christian.

Three Types of African Families

The current situation in most of Africa, as I observe it, is that we now have at least three main distinctive African family models in Zimbabwe, and, possibly, in the rest of the African world. The first is the traditional family, which is quite conservative as it regards itself as the custodian of culture. Such a family would have basically two homes: one in the urban center and another one in the rural roots of communal family living. It oftentimes practiced ancestral worship and animism. The second type is the transitional family, which adopts a composite of both African and Western evils and positive values. Children from such families often regarded themselves as the elite of society. They often dressed better, had a better education, and had a profession. Each culture has its own evils and positive values; there are both good and bad aspects of it. Family choices often helped to preserve family integrity, but they deprived people of their individuality and independent choices. Every decision is crosschecked with the senior family members, grand parents, and elders. The third type is the westernized family. (Very few African families are in this category; one will find that out among those who purport to be so.) They emphasize elements of the African traditional practices at one time or the other. These are featured mainly at family functions like funerals and marriages and result in a cultural dualism of Western and African practices. Each culture is then preferred above the other when it is both convenient and suitable.

On the religious front, the African religions acknowledge God as Creator, but fail to know him as the Father of our Lord Jesus Christ, through whom we are saved.[6] They regard all Africans as believers who derive their cultural values and interpretations from their religious paradigm. Any diversion or change is deemed to be offending the ancestral spirit world. The church accepted these structures as they are, literally interpreting such Bible texts as 1 Corinthians 14:34 to mean that women must keep silent in the church and that they are to be submissive; however, the advent of female missionaries from the West began to effect certain changes. The African women began to ask questions as to whether there were concrete differences between the Westerner and the African.

Societal Changes Affect Women's Roles in the Church

The church was forced to review its position. Various dynamics began to change age-old presuppositions on women's role in society and in church. The 1996 Revised Edition of the Maintenance Act of Zimbabwe[7] established that any man fathering a child out of wedlock is bound by statutory laws financially to support and maintain that child until adulthood. The same applies when a marriage breaks up and the minors are staying with the mother. It made men more careful and responsible. Such acts have had a tendency to emancipate women from the retrogressive cultural

6. Constantine M. Murefu, *Biblical Foundation for Believers* (Harare: Faith Printers Foundation, 2001), 9.

7. Revised Edition Maintenance Act, Chap. 5:09 (Harare, Zimbabwe: Printflow Printers, 1996), 258–59.

practices which oftentimes silenced them. Often, women had been looked upon as existing for men's pleasure. Of particular significance, then, is the Domestic Violence Act of 2006. It interprets domestic violence, among many other considerations, as abuse derived from cultural or customary rites or practices that discriminate against women or degrade them.[8] Anything that would cause emotional, psychological, or mental pain is considered an offense.[9] While men have cried foul, the women have heartily welcomed such a bill. Ropafadzo Mapimhidze (former assistant editor of *The Herald*, a Zimbabwean newspaper) lobbied for the banning of the word *prostitute* being applied to women alone, since it takes two to tangle. This practice reflected how society frowned on women's immorality while condoning similar behavior from their male counterparts. Her point was well articulated. Feminist movements around the world have had a dynamic impact on African gender equality and have even helped some churches change their views on ordination of women into pastoral positions.

SUCCESSFUL ATTEMPTS TOWARD THE ORDINATION OF WOMEN IN THE AFM

The Apostolic Faith Mission (AFM) in Zimbabwe, the oldest and arguably one of the largest Pentecostal denominations in the nation, had struggled with the issue of non-recognition of women as full-time ordained pastors. For many years, it had recognized women only as deaconesses[10] and full-time "lady workers," even though women had the capacity for higher ecclesiastical posts. Most likely, the term *lady worker* was coined to accommodate female missionary preachers from the Western countries who came to minister in Zimbabwe. Other than this reason, I do not see any logic in it. The pendulum began to swing in the other direction when women started enrolling for pastoral training at Living Waters Bible College in Harare. Living Waters Bible College operates under the auspices of the AFM in Zimbabwe as a theological seminary. More and more women were graduated by the seminary. Some became pastors' wives; others felt a stronger call to ordination as ministers of the gos-

8. Domestic Violence Act, Chap. 5:16, 213–14.

9. Domestic Violence Act, Chap. 5:16, 214.

10. Apostolic Faith Mission in Zimbabwe, Constitution and Regulations (Harare, Zimbabwe: Marden Printers, 2003).

pel. Comparison was drawn from other Pentecostal denominations like Zimbabwe Assemblies of God Forward in Faith, wherein a number of women became pastors and began excelling. Non-Pentecostal churches like the Anglicans and other evangelicals did not seem to have a problem in ordaining women into pastoral ministry.[11] The problem within the AFM was mainly historical interpretations of the role of women in an African society. The elderly people in particular felt it to be an anathema to ordain women pastors while the younger ones felt that the dynamics of change were irresistible. Then, in the mid-'nineties, the first group of AFM women was taken on probation as pastors. This was after I, in my position as principal of Living Waters Bible College, had presented a solid position paper on non-gender-based ordination to the Apostolic Council. The Apostolic Council is the supreme governing authority of the Apostolic Faith Mission in Zimbabwe, of which I am an ex officio member by virtue of being the Bible college principal.[12] Since women were already accepted elsewhere in pastoral roles often played by men, the Apostolic Faith Mission in Zimbabwe found itself with no choice but to break away from the status quo.

The paper I presented centered on the call of God upon an individual, irrespective of gender. The purpose was to accept women into ministry on an equal basis with men. The women who were taken on proved their mettle through the anointing of the Holy Spirit, showing that God can use any vessel regardless of gender, color, or creed. Some of the first female pastors to be ordained by the Apostolic Faith Mission in Zimbabwe were Sifelipilo Dube, Auxillia Ngoreta, and Scholastic Kwaramba, with many more thereafter. The first ordination of these women pastors was in 1996 during a general conference at Rufaro Mission, an AFM conference center in Chatsworth, about 270 kilometers south of the capital city, Harare. The majority of these female pastors have gone beyond what most male pastors have achieved. This ruffled a few feathers among their male counterparts as they were pragmatically proven wrong.

It is the nature of most people to resist any form of change. It disturbs the status quo and their comfort zones. Part of ministry is to comfort the afflicted and to afflict the comfortable. Be it known that God and the Holy Spirit are neither male nor female, neither Jew nor Gentile, and certainly

11. My personal observations.

12. Reference is made to the minutes of the Apostolic Council sitting, February to March 1994.

not African, European, or Asian. There is a dynamic cultural transformation in Zimbabwe as we see God working through his vessels of honor. In the secular world, we are also seeing women venture into previously male-dominated professions such as engineering, automobile mechanics, agricultural extension work, and many more.[13] The challenge now is to redefine equality in the face of these dynamics of change.

In Acts 10:34–35, the Apostle Peter perceived that "In truth . . . God shows no partiality" (NKJV) and is no "respecter of persons" (KJV). "But in every nation whoever fears God and works righteousness is accepted by God" (v. 35). This text is in reference to Peter preaching to the gentile house of Cornelius when the Holy Spirit descended on them without the laying of the prejudiced Apostle Peter's hands. The parallel truth that God shows no partiality means that God wants truth and righteousness channeled through and into any person created in God's own image—which refers to all of us, regardless of nationality, gender, ethnic group, or any such barrier. Galatians 3:26–29 states, "For you are all sons of God through faith in Christ Jesus. For as many of you as were baptized into Christ have put on Christ. There is neither Jew nor Greek, there is neither slave nor free, there is neither *male* nor *female*; for you are all one in Christ Jesus. And if you are Christ's, then you are Abraham's seed and heirs according to the promise" (NKJV, emphasis added). In Christ, distinctions of race, rank, and gender neither hinder fellowship nor grant special privileges. This is our rightful heritage in Christ. Faith in Christ has made us full-grown heirs with the rights of heritage. The law kept us in bondage and in immaturity while grace delivered us into heirship and freedom.

Even the earthly ministry of Jesus Christ went against culturally accepted exploitive practices and rituals. Jesus' ministry to several culturally undeserving women throughout the gospels presents to us a paradigm shift. Such cases as the cleansing of the leper (Matt 8:2–3), healing of Peter's mother-in-law (Matt 8:14–15), a girl restored to life and a woman healed (Matt 8:18–26), the dialogue with the unchaste Samaritan woman (John 4:1–37), the forgiving of the woman caught in the very act of adultery (John 8:1–11), and many more gospel accounts tell of Jesus' way of dealing with society against popular opinions and practices.

Of particular interest in the case of the woman caught in adultery in John 8 is the fact that the society appeared to care less about the equally

13. My personal observations.

immoral contribution of the male culprit. The woman, but not the man, is brought before Jesus. When Jesus freed the woman, it was now the man who was actually bound, since the man never experienced the freedom of the forgiveness of sin as the woman did. Indeed, society is bound in its bias.

The Zimbabwean situation has presented us with a new era of re-defining and transforming our mentality. Landmarks that brought about this transformation include the various acts of parliament toward social and gender balance, the feminist movements, research on violence against women and children by the World Health Organization,[14] World Council of Churches Africa Desk, and United Nations–funded programs and seminars. In 2004, Zimbabwe elected its first woman vice president, Joyce Mujuru, into the presidium. There are now several key government posts occupied by women. The church has also awoken to such realities and has begun ordaining women without gender preference or prejudice. More and more people are becoming enlightened on the issue. Of particular en-couragement is the way in which women in Zimbabwe have taken up the novel challenge of rising up and being seen and heard. Of course, there are always a few fanatics who end up in reverse discrimination against men as well. A few men have suffered as casualties and a few marriages have also broken up because of the intensity and misunderstanding of the changes; however, good, steady progress has mainly been realized.

THE WAY FORWARD

We have noted significant progressive changes on gender equality within the Zimbabwean secular and sacred communities. More and more women are finding themselves playing roles that were traditionally the preserve of men. There are some men who are even jobless while their wives become the breadwinners. To some extent, some men even deliberately neglect work, though job opportunities are wide open to them, so that they take advantage of the new openness of society to women's employment.

The church has begun addressing such realities and is recognizing its responsibility to nurture the process and preach the gospel of equal-ity in righteousness and in truth. To do so, the church needs to conduct seminars and workshops to address these relevant issues. The church also

14. Mary Ellsberg and Lori Heise, *Researching Violence against Women*, World Health Organization (Geneva, Switzerland: PATH, 2005).

needs to compare notes about what is happening with other churches across the globe in order to assess where it should make necessary adjustments. It must start with the bishops, reverends, and pastors. The church is the salt of the earth and the light of the world (Matt 5:13–14); therefore, it must be on the forefront of events. Since we have heard so many voices on the subject, the church cannot afford to sit on the fence anymore. It is a bit embarrassing that, for the greater part, the church has only reacted or responded to voices of change. The church needs to be proactive. It must make its voice loud and clear. Gender equality is ethical, biblical, and progressive. How long shall the church drag behind positive societal change? If the church does not take such responsibilities seriously, it may deflect the nation into a post-Christian era, making itself irrelevant.

Women also need to be encouraged not to look down on themselves and on each other. This propensity of women to look down on fellow women who take up challenges by venturing into previously male-dominated arenas has often become debilitating. It is better to fail in a cause that eventually will succeed than to succeed in a cause that eventually will fail.

Men must not feel threatened by progress-minded women. They should encourage them, applaud, and accept them as equal partners in societal governance. We are all made in the *imago Dei*, the image of God. Therefore, that image in us, not our gender, must give impetus to progress. We have been created in royalty as rulers and priests. I hope to get a few amens on this.

I believe that women have always had a better view of life because they carry life in their wombs for nine months and then give birth to life. All this is done with much pain, patience, joy, and endurance. After all, almost all of us have been taught our elementary foundational life lessons by our mothers. It is about time that we love, respect, and give a chance to these "mothers" to take us further in every aspect of life. We have nothing to lose and everything to gain. Theological seminaries and institutions must also not lag behind change. They must be on the forefront in research, practice, and curricula.

Biblical texts like 1 Corinthians 14:34 ("Let your women keep silent in the churches, for they are not permitted to speak: but they are to be submissive as the law says," NKJV) must be understood within their traditional historical and cultural contexts. We should note that such a text was written to correct an imbalance whereby priestesses of goddess

Diana or Artemis were involved and leading in sexual orgies as part of worship to such a goddess. She was believed to be a goddess of fertility, life, and vegetation. Sexual intimacy with these priestesses was believed to be an act of worship that would increase the fertility of the land in an agro-industrial economy.[15]

Ephesians 5:22 ("Wives submit to your own husbands as to the Lord," NKJV) should also be understood to mean that husbands ought to demonstrate a Christlike character that will make it easier for the wife to submit. The text states "as unto the Lord," not as unto the devil. A husband cannot demonstrate a satanic character and expect his wife to submit to it; that is not the biblical injunction. Submission is a mutually responsive act. Christ sacrificially loved the church, and, therefore, it becomes easier for the church to respond in submission. Husbands also need sacrificially to love and respect their wives for them to respond in loving complementary submission.

However, such a domestic setting is not retrogressive at all. It is rather a benchmark on how harmony needs to be engendered. There is something that each one of us is talented to do. Let us give way to those who can do other things better than we can, regardless of gender. Such an attitude will create a better world for all of us Africans, Europeans, Americans, Japanese, Chinese, and the rest of the globe. The extent, respect, and promotion to which we accept women can determine our degree of achievement, progress, and advancement. To God be the glory! Amen!

15. Constantine M. Murefu, lecture notes on 1 and 2 Corinthians, Living Waters Bible College, Harere, Zimbabwe, April 1995.

6

Gifted for Leadership: Gender Equality from an African American Perspective

Darin Vincent Poullard and Sandra Gatlin Whitley

INTRODUCTION

GENDER AND BIBLICAL EQUALITY in the African American culture has had its metamorphosis in seven mainline black church denominations.[1] Without a doubt, it has been "not without a struggle," as the first African American female bishop, the Right Reverend Vashti McKenzie, attests. Bishop McKenzie coined the phrase "the stained glass ceiling has been broken" following her election as the first female African Methodist Episcopal Church (AMEC) bishop in 2000.[2] Gender and leadership struggles in the African American church have been largely due to the political and economic climate since slavery in America. As early as the 1700s, the black church served two purposes for its people: a place where individual souls communed intimately with God and a place where the people freely discussed, debated, and devised an agenda for their common good.[3] The black church was a source of comfort, nurture, and care for an

---

1. The seven mainline black church denominations are three Baptists (Progressive National Baptist Convention [PNBC]; National Baptist Convention [NBC] USA, Incorporated; and the National Baptist Convention of America [Unincorporated]), three Methodists (African Methodist Episcopal Zion Church [AMEZC]; African Methodist Episcopal Church [AMEC]; Colored Methodist Episcopal Church, renamed in 1956 the Christian Episcopal Methodist Church [CMEC]); and one Pentecostal (Church of God in Christ, or COGIC).

2. Marvin A. McMickle, *An Encyclopedia of African American Christian Heritage* (Valley Forge, Pa.: Judson, 2002), 35.

3. Evelyn Brooks Higginbotham, *Righteous Discontent: The Women's Movement in the Black Baptist Church, 1880–1920* (Cambridge, Mass.: Harvard University Press, 1993),

outcast people. The black church became "a refuge in a hostile world," where the people would sing, shout, laugh, and cry among those who understood and shared their pain.[4] Even in its earliest beginnings, the black church was typically comprised of a predominately female membership and a largely male leadership.[5] The foci of this chapter will be the reasons African American women have been denied access to positions of leadership. We will examine the evolution of the black church in regard to women in leadership in order to observe contemporary perceptions on gender equality within that community, to ascertain whether the present views on gender equality are consistent with the Scriptures, and to present practical benefits to the African American community when there is a biblical framework for understanding gender equality.

WHAT OTHERS HAVE WRITTEN

As Evelyn Higginbotham points out in her book *Righteous Discontent,* "the black church is presented not as the exclusive product of a male ministry, but as a product and process of male and female interaction."[6] Therefore, the black church milieu is used to present the historical, contemporary, and biblical evolution of gender equality from the African American perspective in the American society. One key factor is that the black church scarcely could have survived without the active support of black women.[7] African American women were not received as equals in areas of leadership or power, and some may surmise that it was due to the political and economic unrest experienced by the black community as early as the 1700s. Evelyn Higginbotham points out that the strides black women made in their fight for women's rights in the church and in our American society were largely due to the most respected source within their community: the Bible.[8] Based on historical reflections, the black church spurred African American women unawares by "stirring up their gifts" and thus encouraging them to become leaders in their own right

---

16–17.

4. C. Eric Lincoln and Lawrence H. Mamiya, *The Black Church in the African American Experience* (Durham, N.C.: Duke University Press, 1990), 272.

5. Lincoln and Mamiya, *The Black Church,* 275.

6. Higginbotham, *Righteous Discontent,* 2.

7. Lincoln and Mamiya, *The Black Church,* 275.

8. Higginbotham, *Righteous Discontent,* 2.

(2 Tim 1:6). The women's giftedness and ingenuity contributed to their venturing and pioneering in areas of leadership, not carved out for them by males, but by the Lord God within and outside the church.[9] Despite the many attempts to mute female voices and to accentuate their subordinate status vis-à-vis males, the women still persevered in steadfast faith.[10] In the larger society, black men faced similar challenges in losing their rights due to the process of "disenfranchisement" in, for example, the Mississippi south—through literacy tests, poll taxes, other state election laws, and social and psychological sanctions.[11] In addition to losing many rights that the constitution and federal civil rights laws protected, such as sitting on juries, holding public office, and receiving adequate tax dollars for schools and other social services, they had to protect their families and themselves from insult and victimization and struggle for their fair share in other basic human and citizenship rights.[12] While black men faced these challenges, women experienced additional gender struggles in church denominations, whether black or white. As the church's survival was largely due to the active support of women, the values, the symbols, and the experience of church work and its struggles contributed to the women congregants gaining wider recognition. Outside of the church, they became social activists, resulting in the establishment of the largest number of woman-led voluntary associations in the black community because the black church and their Christian beliefs were the central values of their lives.[13] Women also resorted to other means within the church until their voices were heard and denominational missionary societies were established, such as the AMEC Missionary Department in 1844 and, later, the Women's Home and Foreign Missionary Society in 1896; the AME Zion Ladies Home and Foreign Missionary Society in 1880; the Christian Methodist Episcopal Church (CMEC) General Women's Missionary Society in 1886 and Women's Connection Missionary Council in 1918; the Baptist Women's Missionary League in 1900; and others.[14] Without fail, as male leadership became aware of the giftedness

---

9. Clarence Taylor, *The Black Churches of Brooklyn* (New York: Columbia University Press, 1994), 172.

10. Higginbotham, *Righteous Discontent*, 3.

11. Higginbotham, *Righteous Discontent*, 4.

12. Higginbotham, *Righteous Discontent*, 4.

13. Lincoln and Mamiya, *The Black Church*, 284–85.

14. Lincoln and Mamiya, *The Black Church*, 286. Also Henry H. Mitchell, *Black*

of women congregants, women were given roles and titles in ministry, such as exhorters, teachers, missionaries, evangelists, and religious writers. However, the leadership roles of pastor or preacher still remained off limits and a privilege for men only.

It was a former slave from Maryland, referred to as Elizabeth, who persevered, but "not without a struggle." She developed the black church's oral tradition and its highest art form by preaching publicly. Virginia government officials did not succeed in their efforts to mute this preaching woman's voice until 1796. The officials threatened to arrest Elizabeth. When she was asked if she was ordained, her response was, "not by the commission of men's hands; if the Lord has ordained me, I need nothing better." They let her go.[15]

Another black woman's example is that of Jarena Lee attempting to answer her call to preach and respect the church's hierarchal tradition of male leadership. But it was clearly "not without a struggle" that she was denied twice the sanction of the church to preach. Bishop Richard Allen denied her because AMEC polity did not allow for the ordination of women. However, Bishop Allen encouraged her to continue in the work of exhorting and speaking at prayer meetings. He invited her to travel with him to conferences. Upon hearing her preach a creditable sermon on impulse from the biblical text originally chosen by the male preacher who suddenly floundered and could not speak, the bishop confessed that, eight years prior, Jarena Lee had asked him to sanction her. Bishop Allen made known to those present she was clearly one called by God to preach.[16]

As the black church evolved, the traditional inequality of the genders was built into role descriptions of *pastors* and *preachers* within the various denominations. A survey conducted by Lincoln and Mamiya revealed that the *pastor* was the officially ordained leader of a church, but a *preacher* may have been anyone who preached with or without denomi-

---

Church Beginnings: The Long Hidden Realities of the First Years (Grand Rapids: Eerdmans, 2004), 176.

15. Lincoln and Mamiya, *The Black Church,* 279.

16. Lincoln and Mamiya, *The Black Church,* 279. Also see McMickle, *An Encylcopedia,* 70–71, and Mitchell, *Black Church Beginnings,* 78. All three resources differ in the exact two dates pertaining to Jarena Lee's twice being denied an AMEC sanction to preach or receive full ordination, e.g., 1809, 1811, 1816, 1822.

national ordination or recognition as a pastor.[17] The first exceptions to the rule were those women ordained and not given pastoral appointments, but who taught in seminaries or served as executives and administrators. The other exceptions to the rule were women who were preachers or exhorters who were granted the privilege of preaching from the pulpit but restricted from carrying out any other pastoral duties.[18]

Women, however, continued to persevere. The earliest official example of gender equality making headway and the "stained glass ceiling" being removed for the ordination of women in ministry had its beginnings in the African Methodist Episcopal Zion Church (AMEZC) in 1898–1900. The AMEZC is documented as being the first of any Methodist denomination to grant women the rights of full ordination, whether they were black or white.[19] At the Seventy-Third Session of the New York Annual Conference held at the Catharine Street AME Zion Church in Poughkeepsie, New York, on May 20, 1894, Bishop Hood ordained Mrs. Julia A. Foote "deacon," and, on May 19, 1895, Mrs. Mary J. Small was ordained deacon by Bishop Alexander Walters.[20] The other two Methodist denominations that followed suit in ordaining women were the AMEC in 1948 and the CMEC in 1954.[21] On the other hand, the other four mainline denominations' histories of women's preaching and pastoring roles are undocumented and difficult to trace (three Baptists and one Pentecostal, the Church of God in Christ, or COGIC).[22]

In the 1990s, as Lincoln and Mamiya point out in their book, *The Black Church in the African American Experience*, a nationwide survey they conducted with 2,150 churches identified 3.7 percent black female clergy despite an overt attempt to include more women.[23] Therefore, the best estimate is that fewer than 5 percent within the historically black denominations were female clergy. The vast majority of black female clergy were found in storefront churches or independent churches. Still, their number is greater than that of their white female clergy counterparts. The

17. Lincoln and Mamiya, *The Black Church*, 292.
18. Lincoln and Mamiya, *The Black Church*, 293.
19. Lincoln and Mamiya, *The Black Church*, 285.
20. Lincoln and Mamiya, *The Black Church*, 285.
21. Lincoln and Mamiya, *The Black Church*, 286.
22. Lincoln and Mamiya, *The Black Church*, 286–87.
23. Lincoln and Mamiya, *The Black Church*, 289.

survey asked whether the clergy approved or disapproved of women as preachers or pastors of a church. The Likert scale (a numerical measure of agreement or disagreement) was used to measure the strength of the variable responses.[24] Of the women interviewed, 81.5 percent approved of women pastors and the remaining 18.5 percent disapproved. Of the men interviewed, 50.8 percent approved and 49.2 percent disapproved of women pastors. Lincoln and Mamiya noted, "what seemed a curious phenomenon [was] to have clergywomen who strongly disapproved of women as pastors, that these may have become ministers after their husband's death, often reluctantly taking over their ministries."[25] Lincoln and Mamiya also noted another possibility: "despite their own roles as clergy, they may also be reflecting the official policies of their denominations against ordaining women as pastors, particularly, in COGIC and some Baptist conventions."[26]

Secondly, the survey results of those thirty years old or younger found that 69.2 percent approved and 30.8 percent disapproved of women as pastors, and that among those sixty-five years old or older, 40.6 percent approved and 58.4 percent disapproved.[27] Thirdly, of those surveyed with less than a high school education, 43.2 percent approved of women as pastors and 56.8 percent disapproved.[28] However, of those surveyed who had a college education or higher, 66.8 percent approved of women pastors and 33.2 percent disapproved.[29]

Finally, of the seven mainline denominations, four were highly negative toward women as pastors (three Baptists and COGIC). For example, the Progressive National Baptist Convention's (PNBC) approval rate was 42.7 percent with a 57.3 percent disapproval rate.[30] The National Baptist Convention, USA, Incorporated (NBC, USA) is the largest black Baptist body and very strongly opposed to women pastors, with a total

---

24. Lincoln and Mamiya, *The Black Church,* 289.

25. Lincoln and Mamiya, *The Black Church,* 290.

26. Lincoln and Mamiya, *The Black Church,* 290–91.

27. Lincoln and Mamiya, *The Black Church,* 290, table 31, "Women as Pastors by Sex, Age and Education."

28. Lincoln and Mamiya, *The Black Church,* 290, table 31, "Women as Pastors by Sex, Age and Education."

29. Lincoln and Mamiya, *The Black Church,* 290, table 31, "Women as Pastors by Sex, Age and Education."

30. Lincoln and Mamiya, *The Black Church,* 291–92.

73.6 percent of the clergy disapproving and 26.5 percent approving.[31] The National Baptist Convention of America Unincorporated (NBCA, Uninc.) was a close third, with a total disapproval rate of 74.6 percent and approval of 25.4 percent.[32] However, the three Methodist denominations were more favorable: AMEZC led with 94.2 percent approval, the CMEC with 92 percent, and the AMEC with 88 percent.[33]

Some survey respondents also amplified their feelings and personal views with biblical support about women in church leadership roles. For those clergy respondents opposing women pastors, the frequently cited examples included: (1) Jesus not having a female among his chosen twelve disciples, (2) Adam being made first and then Eve, and (3) the Apostle Paul's injunction for women in the church to keep silent.[34] Similarly, clergy respondents who favored women being pastors cited biblical support using the following theological arguments: (1) God is all-powerful and can do anything, (2) Mary Magdalene and Mary the mother of James were called to be the bearers of the resurrection good news (Luke 24:10), (3) on Pentecost, the Holy Spirit did not discriminate against anointing both males and females in the Upper Room, (4) a woman minister "may" show greater care for her flock, (5) in Christ there is neither male nor female (Gal 3:28), and (6) "the call" is a divine call of God. An example of one paradigm shift comes from the surveyor's field interview with Rev. Dr. Gardner C. Taylor, former president of the PNBC and pastor of Brooklyn's Concord Baptist Church—in 1990, the largest black church in the United States. During his teaching on women, he admitted that he has observed women having an inkling of spiritual and religious leadership in them and, if they are properly trained in the ministry, he is open to women pastors.[35]

CONTEMPORARY VOICES

What are the contemporary views of gender equality among African Americans? Do African Americans believe that females have equal access to positions of leadership? In a survey conducted in the summer of

31. Lincoln and Mamiya, *The Black Church*, 292.
32. Lincoln and Mamiya, *The Black Church*, 292.
33. Lincoln and Mamiya, *The Black Church*, 291.
34. Lincoln and Mamiya, *The Black Church*, 294–95.
35. Lincoln and Mamiya, *The Black Church*, 296.

2007 at Fort Washington Baptist Church, in Fort Washington, Maryland, forty-six congregants, fifteen males and thirty-one females from the age of eighteen through those over sixty-five, responded to questions on gender equality.[36] The first series of questions asked whether or not the respondents believed that men and women received equal opportunities for leadership in the home, in the workplace, in the church, and in the government. The second series of questions focused on the receptivity of men and women in the church to women in leadership. The last series of questions asked respondents whether or not they believed that the Bible teaches that women are to be excluded from the highest levels of leadership.

On the question of leadership in the home, more than half of the women, 56 percent, believed that they had equal opportunities for leadership, but 69 percent of the men did not believe women received equal opportunities for leadership in the home. What men perceived was significantly different than women. Some of the women believed that there are equal opportunities for leadership in the home because of the diversity of needs within a family, offering both males and females numerous opportunities to lead. Some women commented that, in their experience, the mother was in charge of the house while the father took care of the financial burdens.

All of the respondents believed inequities exist in the workplace and in government. Seventy-nine percent of the men and 87 percent of the women believed that women do not have equal access to positions of leadership in the workplace. Sixty-four percent of the men and 71 percent of the women believed the same conditions exist in government. Some of the men commented that women are excluded from leadership positions because of their gender and not because of a lack of ability. Some women commented that they had to work much harder than their male counterparts who held the same positions, and they had to prove themselves continually in the workplace, in government, and even in the church. Of the respondents, more than 50 percent of the males and females held positions of leadership within their companies. The female respondents expressed sentiments from personal experience.

All of the respondents believed that inequities not only exist in the home, the workplace, and government, but also in the church. On the

36. Survey conducted by Darin Poullard.

question of whether men in the church were receptive to women serving in all areas of leadership, 71 percent of the women and 67 percent of the men responded "no." Male respondents believed that, even though there have been capable female leaders in the past, men are resistant to women serving in many leadership roles. Some women believed that most men have no desire to hear a woman teach or preach. Other women believed that men do not value the opinions of women as much as they value the opinions of other men, irrespective of the position a woman may hold.

In regard to women being receptive of other women serving in all areas of church leadership, males and females were evenly split. Forty-eight percent of the women and 50 percent of the men did not believe that females are receptive to women serving in all areas of leadership. Male respondents did not comment on the reasons they believed women do not welcome other women to positions of leadership. However, female respondents commented that "women are sometimes jealous of other women and therefore do not support them," "many women look for the role of pastor to be filled by a male," and "women are not receptive to female preachers because the Bible forbids women from teaching men."

Are there other reasons that women are not afforded equal access to positions of leadership? According to our respondents, there are! Thirty-six percent of men and 46 percent of women believed that African American women are denied access to leadership because they are not respected as leaders in the African American community. Indoctrination was mentioned as another possible cause of inequity. Fifty-three percent of the male and female respondents grew up hearing that women are to follow men and not lead men. Respondents commented that this was not their belief, but it is what they had been taught. Respondents believed that church leaders have misinterpreted passages that command women to submit to men; 68 percent of the women and 47 percent of the men felt this way. Roughly one-third of respondents also believed that fear of losing power and prestige caused men to deny women access to positions of leadership.[37] Thirty-two percent of the women and 27 percent of the men believed that men are threatened by women who are gifted and assertive. A final reason suggested by the respondents was the influence of tradition. Forty-five percent of the women and 40 percent of the men simply believe that congregants are more willing to follow male leadership out of tradition. Only 7 percent of the men and 3 percent of the women believe that the Bible forbids women from serving in positions such as deacon, preacher, or pastor and not one respondent believes that women did not have the abilities or gifts to serve in all areas of leadership. When questioned on whether they would support women being ordained to positions of leadership, only 21 percent of the men said they would not. Seventy-nine percent of the males and 100 percent of the females responded that they would support women being ordained to the positions of deacon, preacher, or pastor.[38]

37. Only the black preacher achieved a modicum of recognizable status in a society where all African Americans (whatever their attainment) were presumed to be incurably defective. In the limbo of a caste society, as Albert Raboteau has pointed out, the slave "preacherman" was "relatively mobile and privileged. . . . Hence the roadblocks to preaching for black women were further compounded by the complex problem of black male identity in a racist society. If the ministry was the only route to even a shadow of masculinity, the inclusion of women seemed very much like a gratuitous defeat for everybody." Lincoln and Mamiya, *The Black Church,* 278.

38. Among the many denominations, some have been out front in the ordination of women. Citing works written by Susie Cunningham Stanley, Cheryl J. Sanders writes, "By the turn of the century, the ordination of women was accepted virtually throughout the Holiness movement. And when Pentecostalism emerged shortly thereafter, 'it was carried through this theme and was perhaps even more consistent in the practice of the ministry and ordination of women.' Compared to mainline denominations that began ordaining women only in recent years, the Holiness movement has a 'usable past.' Women in five Wesleyan-Holiness denominations—Church of God (Anderson, Indiana), Church of the Nazarene, Free Methodist Church, The Salvation Army, and the Wesleyan Church—currently constitute twenty-five percent of the clergy in their denominations, whereas women comprise only seven percent of the clergy in thirty-nine other denominations that now ordain women." Quoting Cheryl Towsend Gilkes, Sanders writes, "The largest denomination of the Holiness-Pentecostal tradition, the Church of God in Christ (COGIC), does not permit the ordination of women but has the most powerful Women's Department of any black denomination." See Cheryl J. Sanders, *Empowerment Ethics for a Liberated People: A Path to African American Social Transformation* (Minneapolis: Fortress, 1995), 63, 74. According to Lincoln and Mamiya, none of the national *Black Baptist* conventions (National Baptist Convention, U.S.A., Inc., National Baptist Convention of America, Progressive National Baptist Convention, Inc.) has taken a formal stand either for or against the ordination of women (p. 44). They write further, "Women are eligible in all four Methodist denominations to hold

Based on the results of this survey, the respondents believe that women encounter resistance to being leaders from males and females, in the workplace, in government, and in the church. Inequities in leadership can be attributed to males not respecting the abilities and gifts of females, to indoctrination and a misinterpretation of the Scriptures, and to a refusal by men to share power with women out of fear of losing power and prestige. Even though 21 percent of the men would not agree to ordaining women to the offices of deacon or pastor, all of the respondents believed that women do possess the gifts and abilities to serve as a deacon, preacher, or pastor.

Like many of the respondents to the questionnaire given at Fort Washington Baptist Church, Cleophus J. Larue was indoctrinated with the belief that the role of preacher was exclusive to men. In *This is My Story: Testimonies and Sermons of Black Women in Ministry,* he writes that he came to faith in a congregation where it was absolutely unacceptable for a woman to claim that she had been called by God to preach.[39] As a result, he reports,

> I accepted this stance toward women as gospel truth and established fact. Those few women who insisted that they had been called by God to preach were thought by the rest of us to be eccentric to a fault or just downright "kooky." What woman in her right mind would knowingly subject herself to the wrath of God—we thought—and most assuredly to the wrath of the male pastors by insisting she had been called to preach?[40]

While serving on the Texas Baptist scholarship committee and doing all that was within his power to see that women who professed a call

---

any office at the local church, district, annual conference, and national levels. In recent years they have increasingly moved beyond the traditional women's organizations to become trustees and stewards, offices traditionally held by males. The A.M.E. Church began ordaining women as elders in 1948. Today there are an estimated five hundred to six hundred women elders in that denomination. A woman is currently the editor of the A.M.E Review. The C.M.E. Church voted to ordain women in 1954 and they were extended full clergy rights in 1966. . . . The first female presiding elder was appointed in 1985. . . . Women have been ordained deacons in the A.M.E. Zion Church since 1948, and elders since 1898. . . . Women are regularly ordained in the United Methodist Church and have achieved the office of bishop." Lincoln and Mamiya, *The Black Church,* 73–74.

39. Cleophus J. Larue, ed., *This Is My Story: Testimonies and Sermons of Black Women in Ministry* (Lousiville: Westminster John Knox, 2005), 1.

40. Larue, *This Is My Story,* 2.

to preach were denied a scholarship, Larue had a "Damascus road experience."[41] One woman who had been denied a scholarship confronted him outside the building. He writes,

> In a calm voice devoid of any venom or mean-spiritedness she said to me, "Who are you to get in the way of what God has called me to do?" She assured me that even though she had been denied financial assistance, if God was indeed for her, she would ultimately prevail. No more words were spoken between us, but I drove home that day a changed person. She had been denied the funds to further her education, but my stern opposition to women preachers had been dealt a lethal blow by the only thing that woman walked away with that day—her integrity.[42]

Larue's perspective on preaching women was changed by one woman's "integrity" to her call, and not through a systematic study of the Scriptures. He later writes that he was convinced that opponents of women in ministry, even those who are well intentioned, are on the wrong side of history, Scripture, Christian practice, and the unfolding revelatory will of God.[43] When one's view of preaching women changes as a result of a personal experience or sentiment, and not as the result of the sound interpretation and witness of the Scriptures, how does one defend one's view when challenged by opponents of preaching women? This is the very argument raised by Daphne C. Wiggins, who discovered that those who favor women clergy appeal to equality, justice, and pragmatism more than to biblical authority.[44] Proponents of women serving in leadership roles that have historically been dominated by men must be able to contend with opponents not on the basis of personal sentiment, but on the basis of a sound interpretation of the Scriptures.

---

41. Larue, *This Is My Story,* 2.

42. Larue, *This Is My Story,* 3.

43. Larue, *This Is My Story,* 8.

44. The case for women clergy is argued by appeals to equality, justice, and pragmatism more often than by appeals to biblical authority. The reasons given include the disproportionate representation of women in the church; the absence of a clear, convincing biblical basis for preventing women's ordination; the need for young children to see models of male and female leadership; and the belief that women's abilities and talents bring different strengths to the clergy role. See Daphne C. Wiggins, *Righteous Content: Black Women's Perspectives of Church and Faith* (New York: New York University Press, 2005), 124.

THE SCRIPTURES AND GENDER EQUALITY

Do the Scriptures teach that women are approved by God to serve in all areas of leadership in the Christian faith, or are there leadership roles that are exclusive for men? Based on the numerous contributions of women that have sustained churches, history bears witness that ability is not the question.[45] Cheryl Sanders analyzed and compared sermons preached by men and women and observed "that women and men preach the same types of sermons, from the biblical texts, but differ slightly in their choices of themes and tasks, and differ greatly in their talk about God and persons in inclusive terms. . . . Women tend to emphasize the personal and men the prophetic."[46] Again, ability is not the question. The question is one of biblical liberty and God's sovereignty. Does God call women to occupy the highest leadership roles within the Christian faith just as he calls men, or are women excluded from these leadership roles?

In the beginning, the first man and woman were created to share leadership equally. God created the male and the female in his image and likeness (Gen 1:26–27). Individually and together, the male and the female were created to reflect the image of God (Gen 5:2). As God creates, the male and female in his image procreate, thus reflecting God's image. Individually and together, they were blessed with the responsibility to be fruitful, to multiply, and to fill the earth with God's people (Gen 1:28). God has authority over his creation (1 Chr 29:12; Ps 89:8–9). Individually and together, the male and the female were given authority over the creation, thus reflecting his image (Gen 1:26–28; Ps 8:4–8). Together they were to rule over the beasts, and together they were to subdue the land. What was true for the male was also true for the female. God blessed them individually and together, and, in their togetherness, they reflected

---

45. African American women of Brooklyn initiated the creation of clubs and organizations in their churches and communities for social, charitable, educational, and political purposes. These organizations helped them to address issues and problems plaguing their community and to dispute racist images of African Americans. These organizations gave women the opportunity to come together and unite in a common cause exclusive of male influence. Under their own supervision, women addressed their concerns, raised and managed money, and decided their organization's direction. In many cases, they provided care and assistance to one another and to members of their church and community. See Clarence Taylor, *Black Churches*, 172.

46. Cheryl J. Sanders, "The Woman as Preacher," in *African American Religious Studies: An Interdisciplinary Anthology*, ed. Gayraud S. Wilmore (1989; repr. Durham, N.C.: Duke University Press, 1992), 388–89.

God's image of more than one Person in complete unity and cooperation with one another. Within the Godhead, there is equality, unity, and
complete cooperation among the Persons (John 8:29; 14:7, 16, 23; 17:21).
God created the male and the female in equality, thus enabling there to be
unity. It is through equality that one realizes unity with others.

Unity is not predicated upon all persons being the same. However,
for unity to exist, all persons must have equal value and worth. At creation,
the male and the female had equal value and worth. Without the female,
the male could not fulfill the purposes of God (Gen 1:28).[47] Equality was
necessary for unity. Jesus' desire was for unity to exist among those who
have faith in him (John 17:21), not just unity of doctrine (17:18–20) or
unity of sanctification, but unity as a result of equality even as it exists
among the Persons in the Godhead (17:21). The Apostle Paul alludes to
unity as a result of equality when he writes, "And if they were all one
member, where would the body be? But now there are many members,
but one body. And the eye cannot say to the hand, 'I have no need of you';
or again the head to the feet, 'I have no need of you'" (1 Cor 12:19–20
NASB). Every member of the body of Christ, while being different, has
equal worth and value. Unity that reflects the image of God is predicated
upon equality. Therefore, for unity to exist within the African American
church and community, African American women cannot be treated as
though they have less value or worth than men. Unity is dependent upon
women being treated as equals by having equal access to leadership roles
that carry decision making authority.[48]

John Chrysostom wrote, "For the woman taught the man once,
and made him guilty of disobedience and wrought our ruin. Therefore
because she made a bad use of her power over the man, or rather her

---

47. To marry and rear a family was a religious command—indeed, the first of all
the commands addressed by God to humans (Gen 1:28), and the Talmud stresses that
view: "The unmarried person lives without joy, without blessing, and without good" (Jeb
62b); "An unmarried man is not a man in the full sense; as it is said, 'Male and female
created He them, and blessed them and called their name man'" (Gen 5:2) (Jeb 63a). See
Abraham Cohen, *Everyman's Talmud: The Major Teachings of the Rabbinic Sages* (New
York: Schocken, 1949), 162.

48. Daphne C. Wiggins defined leadership roles as those that carry decision-making
authority or that involve heading an auxiliary or ministry. Persons with responsibility for
implementing tasks were considered *not to be leaders,* but to fill a supportive role. See
Wiggins, *Righteous Content,* 118.

equality with him, God made her subject to her husband."[49] He further argued, "The woman not the man saw that the tree was good for food and she ate and gave it to her husband. The woman taught once and ruined all."[50] Chrysostom believed that Paul wrote the instruction for women not to teach men (1 Tim 2:11–15) because of what happened in the garden (Gen 3:1–7).[51] Did the Apostle Paul forbid women from teaching men? Yes, he did! However, he only forbade women who taught doctrines that contradicted truth (1 Tim 4:7; 2 Tim 3:6–7). The Kroegers write,

> If 1 Timothy 2:12 is translated as prohibiting women from claim-
> ing the power of origin, it fits with the refutation which follows.
> Women are forbidden to teach that female activity brought man
> into existence because, according to the Scriptures, Adam was cre-
> ated first.[52]

Not only women, but all those who taught false doctrines were pro-hibited from teaching (1 Tim 1:3, 2 Tim 1:10–16), and all persons whose behavior was disruptive were to keep silent (1 Cor 14:27–28). Whereas, faithful *anthropois*—people, males and females—who were able to teach were to be entrusted with the stewardship of teaching others (2 Tim 2:2). The Apostle Paul does not use the masculine noun *aner*, which may be translated "male, man, or husband" depending on the context and is used to distinguish a male from a female. Instead, the Apostle uses the noun *anthropos*, which is used universally of a human being, whether male or female.[53] In the body of Christ, teachers of others are to be selected by their faithfulness to sound doctrine (2 Tim 2:2) and by their giftedness (1 Cor 12:28; 1 Pet 4:11), but never by their gender. Women were among those with the gift of prophecy (1 Cor 11:5). Those possessing the gift of prophecy prophesied to all *anthropois* (people) for the edification of the church (1 Cor 14:3–5).

---

49. John Chrysostom, Works of St. Chrysostom, "Homily IX, 1 Timothy 2:11–15," *Nicene and Post-Nicene Fathers First Series* (1889, repr. Peabody, Mass.: Hendrickson, 2004), 435.

50. Chrysostom, "Homily IX," 435.

51. Chrysostom, "Homily IX," 435.

52. Richard Clark Kroeger and Catherine Clark Kroeger, *I Suffer Not a Woman: Rethinking 1 Timothy 2:11–15 in Light of Ancient Evidence* (Grand Rapids: Baker, 1992), 113.

53. Joseph H. Thayer, *Thayer's Greek-English Lexicon of the New Testament* (1896, repr. Peabody, Mass.: Hendrickson, 1997), *s.v.* "aner."

Opponents of women occupying the highest leadership roles within the Christian faith contend that Jesus was a man, and, therefore, the biological distinctiveness of women makes them unsuitable for ministry.[54] Some also argue that leadership functions are based on social convention and custom. Ordained ministry does not fall within the socially defined roles and functions that make women subservient to men and devoted exclusively to the care of home and hearth.[55] Fifty percent of the male and 25 percent of the female respondents to the survey given at Fort Washington Baptist Church believed that the offices of pastor and deacon were reserved for men. In her interview with women, Daphne C. Wiggins wrote,

> The exclusion of women from the leadership roles of preacher and pastor has been so pervasive that it was not a significant source of discomfort or frustration for the majority of the group. They accepted the exclusion of women preachers as normal when they were growing up, even if they didn't agree with the mandate for the exclusion. Rosalind, now in her fifties, thought back to her early years in Wisconsin. She remembers learning the lesson that women weren't supposed to preach. It was told and modeled. Women didn't even go in the pulpit in her former church.[56]

Do the Scriptures teach that the roles of preacher, pastor, or deacon are exclusive to men? The Apostle Paul writes, "This is a trustworthy word. If someone desires the office of bishop/overseer, a good work that one desires" (1 Tim 3:1). Paul does not write, "If any *aner* (male or man) desires the office of overseer."[57] Instead, Paul uses the indefinite pronoun *tis*, which may be translated "a certain one or someone."[58] Paul's emphasis is not on gender. His emphasis is on the office of bishop or overseer. Those who desire to serve as an overseer desire a "good work."

Further, Paul writes, "Therefore, the overseer must be above reproach, the husband of one wife, temperate, self-controlled, well behaved, hospitable, able to teach" (1 Tim 3:2).[59] In this passage, Paul's concern

---

54. James H. Evans, Jr., *We Have Been Believers: An African-American Systematic Theology* (Minneapolis: Fortress, 1992), 138.

55. Evans, *We Have Been Believers*, 139.

56. Wiggins, *Righteous Content*, 120.

57. Poullard's translation.

58. *Thayer's Lexicon, s.v. "tis."*

59. Poullard's translation.

is not gender. Paul's concern is character. Anyone who desires the office of bishop must have character that is above reproach. He or she must be blameless. No one should be able to raise a credible accusation of sin against the overseer. The overseer must have self-control. The overseer must be a one-woman man (one-spouse person), temperate, having self-control, not addicted to wine, not always ready to fight, and not a lover of money (1 Tim 3:2–3). He or she must exercise self-restraint (1 Tim 3:2–3). The overseer is to have a good reputation with those inside and outside of the church (1 Tim 3:7). Like every member of the church, the overseer must know how to conduct himself/herself (1 Tim 3:15). Paul's concern is not with gender. His concern is with character. If someone, male or female, desires the office of overseer and lacks self-control, that same one will fail miserably as a parent, a spouse, and as an overseer (1 Tim 3:4–5).

Concerning deacons (or ministers), Paul writes, "In the same way *diakonous* (deacons)[60] must be dignified, not double tongued, not giving attention to much wine, not fond of dishonest gain" (1 Tim 3:8).[61] Not only did males occupy the role of *diakonos* (1 Cor 3:5; Eph 6:21), but Phoebe, a female, was also a *diakonos* (Rom 16:1). In regard to women, Paul wrote, "Women, in the same way must be dignified, not slanderers, temperate, faithful in all things" (1 Tim 3:11). The noun *gunē* may be translated "woman" or "wife" depending on the context (Matt 1:20, 5:28). If one translates *gunē* "wife," then the assumption is that Paul is referring to the wives of male deacons in 1 Timothy 3:11. Chrysostom called these women not wives, but deaconesses, and argues that we should not assume that Paul is speaking of women in general, for Paul would not have changed the subject in the middle of his argument.[62] We agree with

---

60. The noun *diakonos* is understood as one who executes the commands of another, especially of a master. The noun may be translated "servant, attendant, minister, or deacon." See *Thayer's Lexicon, s.v. "diakonos."*

61. Poullard's translation.

62. "Some have thought that this is said of women generally, but it is not so, for why should he introduce anything about women to interfere with his subject? He is speaking of those who hold the rank of Deaconesses." In reference to 1 Tim 3:12, Chrysostom believed, "This must be understood therefore to relate to Deaconesses. For that order is necessary and useful and honorable in the Church. Observe how he requires the same virtue from the Deacons, as from the Bishops, for though they were not of equal rank, they must equally be blameless; equally pure." John Chrysostom, Works of St. Chrysostom, "Homily XI, 1 Timothy 3:8–10, *Nicene and Post-Nicene Fathers First Series,* 441.

Chrysostom that Paul would not have changed the subject. The subject is not deaconesses, but deacons. Male deacons were to be *semnos* ("dignified," 1 Tim 3:8). Female deacons were to be *semnas* ("dignified," 1 Tim 3:11). Both male and female deacons were to have character that was beyond reproach.

Paul did not exclude females from the highest positions of leadership within the Christian faith. In fact, he acknowledged their gifts (1 Cor 11:5), their partnership and faithfulness to ministry (Rom 16:1–3, 6, 15), and their equality with males (Gal 3:28). He did not exclude persons from occupying roles of leadership because of gender. He excluded those whose character was not beyond reproach and whose doctrine was not consistent with truth. The Apostle's emphasis for those who serve as leaders was not gender. Leaders are to be selected because of their character, their faithfulness, and their giftedness, regardless of gender. Therefore, there must be a paradigm shift in the mindset of African American males and females who deny women opportunities for leadership based solely on physiological differences from men.

African Americans who exclude females from sharing decision-making leadership roles with males either intentionally or unconsciously truncate the image of God that is to be revealed in humanity (i.e., more than one Person functioning in unity and equality), maintain a practice that fails to appreciate the full worth of the covenant partner God gave to males when he made Eve (i.e., Adam and Eve shared authority equally), and dishonors the desire of Christ for unity and equality in his church. To conclude that the Apostle Paul excluded women from leadership based on gender is to misinterpret Paul's criteria for selecting leaders. Leaders were chosen based on giftedness, faithfulness, and character, but never gender. This misinterpretation perpetuates male dominance, results in called and gifted women being denied positions of leadership, and continues the oppression of African American women, who, while being liberated from bondage in society, are still not free to live out the full expression of God's call on their lives!

PRACTICAL BENEFITS TO A BIBLICAL VIEW ON GENDER EQUALITY

How can the church help to promote gender equality within leadership? This question was asked on the survey that was conducted at Fort

Washington Baptist Church in the summer of 2007. Respondents suggested the following:

1. Place gifted women of God in positions of leadership that enable them to fulfill their purpose in Christ.

2. Offer classes that review and discuss passages that appear to teach the exclusion of females from leadership roles.

3. Preach more often on the subject of gender equality.

4. Be willing to set aside traditions that promote male dominance.

As church leaders, the authors also realize that pastors must not embrace equality in private and reject equality in public. Pastors must not yield to pressures within clergy circles to treat the ministry as an exclusive boys' or girls' club. Male pastors must be willing to speak out on behalf of women of God who cannot speak out for themselves even as Israel could not deliver itself from Egypt. Moses was needed to intercede on its behalf. In addition, church leaders must seek to reeducate members who have been taught the doctrine of inequality.

If the church reeducates its members to understand and embrace gender equality accurately, there are so many possibilities for the African American community to flourish. Marriages can flourish as husbands and wives no longer compete for power, but allow the other to operate in each's areas of giftedness. As wives are encouraged to lead and to utilize their abilities and talents, it is possible that they will develop a greater sense of self-worth and confidence. Women rising up to the full measure of their potential can become partners with their husbands in making the wisest decisions for their families.

If congregations are reeducated to have a biblical view on gender equality, can you imagine the gifts for ministry that God can bring forth in places of worship? Those congregations will have the possibility of flourishing and thriving in ways yet to be experienced as women who had been denied opportunities to use speaking and serving gifts will be encouraged to use those gifts for the common good of God's people and his kingdom. Male leaders, who had expended far too much time and energies oppressing women, will be able to use those same energies to equip every saint for the work of the ministry to the building up of the body of Christ (Eph 4:11–12). No longer will pastors and clergy leaders feel compelled to waste time maintaining traditions and positions that eventually will be discarded because they do not reflect the image of God for males and females! Women and men have innumerable possibilities of flourishing individually and together as they each obey the call of God to serve in the offices of preacher, pastor, deacon, or any other leadership roles within the church.

If African American families teach and live out gender equality in the home, children will be impacted. Young women will learn that God made males and females to share authority equally. From an early age, sons and daughters can be instructed that males and females who labor together in unity and equality reflect the image of God and the heart of Christ for his church. Through this instruction, parents will be able to teach young males to respect and appreciate the talents and gifts of females, to treat them as equals, to acknowledge their abilities to lead, and to discontinue inequities in leadership because of gender. If and when these practices become normative, African American communities and congregations have the potential of becoming partnering communities utilizing all the gifts and talents that God has bestowed upon his people, communities that develop male and female leaders to reach their full potential in the church and in the workplace, and communities that liberate men and convert their fear of losing power to gifted women to an appreciation of gaining a partner to fulfill the will of God and Christ. Every aspect of the African American community has the possibility of flourishing in new and dynamic ways when each member of the community has equal worth and value in the eyes of every member of the community.

CONCLUSION

The historical and contemporary attitude toward gender equality in the black church has made some significant strides to encourage females in a historically male-dominated society. The AME Church today is the first to have three female bishops. They were elected and consecrated in 2000 and 2004. Rev. Dr. Henry Mitchell's wish is "that more and more African American congregations and denominations accept the full ordination of women to the itinerant ministry or senior pastorate."[63] However, he further notes that within those denominations women are still the minority

---

63. Henry H. Mitchell, *Black Church Beginnings*, 177.

of those being ordained.[64] There is also evidence that more than half of the student populations in seminaries are women.[65] More often than not, talented women are still typically appointed and assigned to the smallest churches in denominations, then appointed to larger established churches after serving their first pastoral charge in rural and small marginal urban churches.[66] Such outstanding women of faith have been steadfast, immovable, and abounding in the work of the Lord. They persevere and weather many challenges to answer their calls to ministry.

Henry Mitchell attests that some educated women have been forced to be bivocational in order to subsidize and even "resurrect" weaker congregations. He notes that only in the last few years has an AME bishop assigned a woman to a congregation of 1,300 members or more. Bishop McKenzie was able to build her last flock to that number. She, along with other outstanding female preachers like Rev. Dr. Ella Pearson Mitchell, who has been called "the dean of black preachers,"[67] has left an indelible mark upon the lives of so many of God's people.

In summary, this chapter examined reasons African American women have been denied access to positions of leadership in the black church. Among those reasons are that Jesus was male and, therefore, the biological distinctiveness of women makes them unsuitable for ministry. A second reason was that ordained ministry does not fall within the socially defined roles and functions of women to be subservient to men and devoted exclusively to the care of the home. A third reason women have been denied access to positions of leadership was due to teaching the Scriptures erroneously. And, finally, a fourth reason was that some men feared losing power and prestige to women. We have noted in the survey conducted at Fort Washington Baptist Church (and also historically) that many women have still evidenced and employed all the gifts required for the offices of pastor, preacher, or deacon. Neither ability nor a passion for the ministry has ever been in question when considering women for leadership, and, through a careful study of the Scriptures, it is also abundantly clear that gender is not a question. God made males and females to partner in leadership over his creation. Equality was and is God's plan for

64. Mitchell, *Black Church Beginnings*, 177.

65. Mitchell, *Black Church Beginnings*, 177.

66. Lincoln and Mamiya, *The Black Church*, 299.

67. McMickle, *Encyclopedia*, 74.

male and female relationships. The Apostle Paul never introduced gender as a means to exclude gifted women from positions of leadership. Many faithful, gifted women were his partners. All leaders were and are to be selected by the same standards: excellence in character, a commitment to proclaiming sound doctrine, faithfulness to Christ, and gifts for the area of ministry—but never one's gender!

7

Equality and Native Americans in North America

William David Spencer

I N 1758, A SHAWNEE raiding party abducted a fifteen-year-old girl
named Mary Jemison. Several months prior to this raid, a young warrior of their tribe had died in the battle called Washington's War. The
subsequent raid was ordered, among other reasons, as vengeance for the
loss suffered by two sisters of the young warrior. Their goal was to restore balance by either being brought a scalp or a replacement captive.[1] In

1. Mary Jemison's account was recorded by James Everett Seaver in *A Narrative of
the Life of Mrs. Mary Jemison* (New York: J. D. Bemis, 1824). John Demos notes that her
experience, as she feared, could have started "a mourning war. And when the battle was
over, the same woman might decide the fate of any captives—whether to 'send them to
the flames' (a common European description of ritual torture and execution by burning)
or to adopt them into her own or another village family. Women participated even in the
torture process itself. They were part of the gauntlets (armed groups arranged in a line)
of aroused villagers who taunted and beat newly arrived captives. And they were also in
the crowds that carried out decrees of full-scale immolation" *(The Tried and the True:
Native American Women Confronting Colonization* [vol. 1 of *The Young Oxford History of
Women in the United States of America*, ed. Nancy F. Cott; New York: Oxford, 1995], 48).
A direct example can be found in Charles Johnston, *A Narrative of the Incidents Attending the Capture, Detention, and Ransom of Charles Johnston, etc.* (New York: J&J Harper,
1827; repr., Cleveland: Burrows Brothers, 1905) in his report of Jacob Skyles, who encountered both responses from women. After he "experienced much kindness from the
wife of his surly sentinel, whose temper was altogether unlike that of her husband," he
was warned by her of his impending execution and, feigning sleep, he heard the woman
discussing his fate with a younger one: "The elder squaw lamented the event which was
next day to befall the white prisoner, and spoke in terms of compassion for the sufferings
which he was to endure; while the girl exulted in the prospect of his torments, which in
her opinion every white man justly deserved" (122–25). As soon as they all fell asleep, he
fled. Charles Johnston, who was captured some thirty-two years after Mary Jemison but
who published his account around the same time in 1827, experienced both kindness
and abuse from his captors, identifying various among them as "my humane friend" (85)
or as "merciless savages, ingenious in the invention and practice of torture" (94).

many Amerindian tribes, as in the five primary nations that made up the Iroquois confederation (the Mohawk, Oneida, Onondaga, Cayuga, and Seneca), women exercised influence and power great enough to determine even war actions such as this one. The French Canadian Jesuit priest often credited with founding "scientific ethnology," Joseph Lafitau, who served as a missionary among the Mohawks in Quebec from 1712–1717, observed:

> There is nothing more real than this superiority of women. . . . All real authority is vested in them. The land, the fields, and their harvest all belong to them. They are the souls of the councils, the arbiters of peace and of war. They have charge of the public treasury. To them are given the slaves. They arrange marriages. The children are their domain, and it is through their blood that the order of succession is transmitted.[2]

Archaeologist Susan C. Prezzano adds:

> Women wielded political power. Senior women selected and removed the hereditary peace chiefs of their lineage. . . . Women, although they did not speak at councils, could select an orator to speak on their behalf. They urged or prohibited raids by providing or withholding supplies, or by controlling the actions of the young warriors of their lineage. They often controlled the fate of captives.[3]

In Mary Jemison's case, she was the payment exacted. For the remaining seventy-five years of her life, she would live as an Amerindian, dying at the age of ninety at Buffalo Creek Reservation in upstate New York. In 1824, in her eighty-first year of life, nine years before she died and sixty-six years after she was first taken captive, she published her autobiography of her life as a Native American. Her story is remarkable within the genre of what are called "captivity narratives." Rather than suffering the death, tortures, or deprivations she expected, she reports:

---

2. The title of founder of "scientific ethnology" is noted in Arlene Hirschfelder and Paulette Molin, *Encyclopedia of Native American Religions*, 2nd ed. (New York: Facts on File, 2000), 154. The statement is quoted in Lydia Bjornlund, *Women of Colonial America*, Women in History (New York: Thomson/Gale, 2004), 12.

3. Susan C. Prezzano, "Warfare, Women, and Households: The Development of Iroquois Culture" in *Women in Prehistory: North American and Mesoamerica*, Regendering the Past, eds. Cheryl Claassen and Rosemary A. Joyce (Philadelphia: University of Pennsylvania, 1997), 90.

> It was my happy lot to be accepted for adoption; and at the time
> of the ceremony I was received by the two squaws, to supply the
> place of their brother in the family; and I was ever considered and
> treated by them as a real sister, the same as though I had been
> born of their mother.[4]

She soon discovered her captors were "kind good natured women; peace-
able and mild in their dispositions; temperate and decent in their habits,
and very tender and gentle toward me. I have great reason to respect
them.[5] Eventually, she married a Lenni Lenape (Delaware) "according to
Indian custom," and discovered:

> Sheninjee was a noble man; large in stature; elegant in his ap-
> pearance; generous in his conduct; courageous in war; a friend to
> peace, and a great lover of justice. He supported a degree of dignity
> far above his rank, and merited and received the confidence and
> friendship of all the tribes with whom he was acquainted. Yet,
> Sheninjee was an Indian. The idea of spending my days with him,
> at first seemed perfectly irreconcilable to my feelings; but his good
> nature, generosity, tenderness, and friendship towards me, soon
> gained my affection; and, strange as it may seem, I loved him!
> To me he was ever kind in sickness, and always treated me with
> gentleness; in fact, he was an agreeable husband, and a comfort-
> able companion. We lived happily together.[6]

As we consider this sensitive account of how kindness overcame prejudice
and fostered a happy marriage, we should factor it in with the realization
that the Iroquois, within whose sphere Mary Jemison now lived, were
matrilocal in practice. Lydia Bjornlund explains what this means for married life:

> According to what is known as a matrilineal system, many Native
> American nations traced their lineage on their mother's side of the
> family. When a man married, he became part of his wife's family.
> A new husband moved into his wife's abode, where he might live
> with her parents and other members of her extended family.[7]

---

4. Mary Jemison, "Mary Jemison Becomes an Iroquois," in *Native American Testimony: A Chronicle of Indian-White Relations from Prophecy to the Present, 1492–1992,*
ed. Peter Nabokov, 2nd ed. (New York: Viking, 1991), 75.

5. Jemison, "Mary Jemison Becomes an Iroquois," 76.

6. Jemison, "Mary Jemison Becomes an Iroquois," 78.

7. Bjornlund, *Women of Colonial America,* 11.

In this sense, the matrilocal practice is in a similar spirit to the biblical ideal in Genesis 2:24, where "a man leaves his father and mother and clings to his wife." In the case of Amerindians, extended families related through women lived in longhouses—a practice that stretched up from the Caribbean, where Columbus and his marauders first discovered the Tainos living in large multifamily structures, as the priest who accompanied them, Bartolomé de Las Casas explained: "They live in large communal bell-shaped buildings—housing up to 600 people at one time, and eight of the buildings have a capacity of 10,000 people."[8]

Such revelations beg the question: Were the original Native American bands egalitarian or patriarchal? Much controversy has centered around the answer to this question. For example, anthropologist Dean R. Snow comments:

> The central role of Iroquois women in food production and in the appointment of sachems has long attracted both popular attention and scholarly research. It has also been used to support arguments that would have mystified the Iroquois of four centuries ago. Iroquois matriliny was used by nineteenth-century advocates for women's suffrage to support their demands for equality, and has attracted the attention of modern feminists as well. Unfortunately, the cultural biases and political motivations of men and women alike have tended to misrepresent Iroquois matriliny as often as not. Iroquois women were not matriarchs, or Amazons, or drudges. They were Iroquois women, who lived in a nonhierarchical society in which their role as food producers was properly appreciated and in which the elevation of some aspects of kinship to political significance gave them influence that they might not otherwise have had.[9]

Susan Prezzano responds: "Several authors have suggested that female political power and prestige have been overstated, perhaps because of a lack of understanding of the concept of gender reciprocity in Iroquois society." She sees this differing understanding as "the classic debate over women's status in non-Western societies." But, she contends, "In the case

8. Bartolomé de Las Casas, *History of the Indies*, trans. and ed. Andrée Collard (New York, Harper, 1971), 1:164.

9. Dean R. Snow, *The Iroquois,* The Peoples of America (Cambridge, Mass.: Blackwell, 1994), 65.

of Iroquois women, however, access to public power and prestige are clearly evident in their role of selecting chiefs."[10]

In the case of Mary Jemison, one explanation for the gentle treatment she received may very well be the particular matrix into which she was brought. Her capture was instigated by women for familial concerns—she replaced a fallen family member—so she completed the family circle and was treated accordingly.

Clearly, apprehending the nuanced balance of power between women and men in an area as varied and vast as the Native American population in all its tribal configurations is extremely challenging. Adding to that the introduction of Christianity either as end or as means by people who would use the faith to liberate or subjugate, and the varied perspectives on women's place and power that divided even the most selfless among them, heightens that challenge even more. To glimpse some of what the issues are, this chapter will look at the current devaluation sensed by many Native women since colonization, examine some of the reasons for that drop in status, and ascertain if the use or the misuse of Christianity contributed to that devaluation. We will then look briefly at the political and religious tasks of various tribal women and men before Christianity and the adjustments made both among authentic Christians as well as among true Amerindian converts as the faith became Native. Finally, we will survey representative examples of the cooperation between North American Christian women and men through history into today, with attention to issues of identity, and draw out conclusions ultimately applicable to all of us who consider ourselves true followers of Jesus Christ.

WHAT WAS LOST?

Recently in an internet discussion ("Discussing im so proud to be native in Beautiful Native American Women"), one correspondent posted a statement thanking the "creator" for "native women" who "keep the tradition alive." A woman responded:

> I wish my husband thought that way about me. He says back in the days our fathers sold us for shells or objects. I don't think that is true. The feelings of how a father feels towards their daughters is so strong. Fathers protect their love ones. A man must prove he

10. Prezzano, "Warfare, Women, and Households," 90–91.

could support his daughter. why do so many of our men think this
way. It makes me want to grab him by his man-hood![11]

Indeed, in stark contrast to the "nonhierarchical" and truly complementary model that groups like the Iroquois practiced and Mary Jemison
experienced, today professors at Colorado State University's Center
for Applied Studies in American Ethnicity, Roe W. Bubar and Irene S.
Vernon, report:

> Rates of violence against women are higher for Native women than
> for any other women in the country. In fact, Native women experi-
> ence a rate of violent crime 50 percent higher than that experienced
> by African American men. U.S. Census estimates indicate that on
> reservations, households that do not have telephones—which can
> be an indication of both social isolation and economic depriva-
> tion—can have a rate of violence as high as 60 percent. Most of the
> data available on intimate partner or domestic violence in Native
> communities is not tribally specific, and given the great diversity
> of tribal populations it is difficult to get an accurate picture of
> violence against Native women. And perhaps most striking in the
> report is the race of offenders in intimate partner violence. Among
> Native women who are victims of intimate partner violence, 75
> percent of the victimizations involve an offender of a different
> race. Within families, 25 percent of family victimizations involve
> an offender of a different race. Among violence victims of all races
> those rates are 11 percent and 5 percent, respectively. We now
> know Native women are victimized in intimate partner relation-
> ships more than other women and the offenders are most often
> non-Native men.[12]

How is it that Native American women are more at risk than women
of other races in the United States? One can speculate numerous reasons.
With no data available to assess pre-colonial violence, we cannot assess
how prevalent domestic abuse may have been, but Roe and Vernon note
that "many would agree violence was addressed quickly, sanctioned severely, and that some tribal communities would banish offenders, which
resulted in their own demise because they were left without the protection

---

11. tamit44, "tamit44 [deleted] says," n.p. Accessed 21 January 2008. Online: http://
www.flickr.com/groups/nativeamericanwomen/discuss/72157594335059579/.

12. Rowe W. Bubar and Irene S. Vernon, *Social Life and Issues*, Contemporary Native
American Issues (Broomall, Pa.: Chelsea House, 2006), 51.

and support of the tribe."[13] With colonization, however, tribal structures were broken down, which "resulted in greater oppression and less protection for Native women and their children."[14] The fact that most offenders are non-Native American reveals that the destruction of traditional societal structures has removed the protections that safeguarded women.

Nonhierarchical tribal structures were dismantled during colonization and restructured along patriarchal lines to match European patriarchy apparently with the degree of cultural sensitivity with which democracy has been introduced to Afghanistan and Iraq. One such means was by forcing men to do farming in place of hunting. Crop provision had been women's contribution and basis of influence and power. But, "in the late nineteenth and early twentieth centuries," as Molly Mullin explains, "government programs attempted to teach men to farm," therefore "federal education policies" were "designed to train native women as domestic servants and housekeepers," concentrating them on "domestic skills as cooking and sewing."[15] With men now restricted to being reluctant farmers so that tribal range land could be swiftly cordoned off by non-Native settlers and business interests, women's sphere was curtailed and relegated to second-class assistance. Women's work reduplicated that assigned by the dominant culture to men, and thus was diminished in power and honor. Such second-class status swiftly degenerated into the revisionist view of women as chattel that we saw in the lament that opened this subsection. Changing status also exposed Native women to be targets for abuse to a greater extent than women of other ethnicities. Further, poverty and lack of attention by authorities that isolated women on tracts of reservation land opened up opportunity for victimization. Motive lies in the twisted mind of the abuser, opportunity in the drop-in status and the isolation that forces a woman to seek her livelihood unprotected in the larger culture or leaves her unprotected in the empty plains or hills of the reservation, and means can simply be the misuse of power by a man she meets who looks capable of providing for her and her dependents.

13. Bubar and Vernon, *Social Life,* 49.

14. Bubar and Vernon, *Social Life,* 50.

15. Molly H. Mullin, "Women," *American Indians,* vol. 3 (Englewood Cliffs, N.J.: Salem Press, 1995), 867.

HOW WAS EQUALITY LOST?

That colonization itself destroyed the infrastructure of Native American tribal culture on a continuum with the way slavery destroyed the societal and familial structures of Africans kidnapped to America seems indisputable. Institutions like the Carlisle Indian Industrial School, to which many children were required to go, were set up solely to transform Native Americans culturally into European-type North Americans in attitude and appearance.[16] That is just one example of an inexorable trend that began with the conquest itself. Often, among the arguments used to justify such cultural transformation was the claim that such transformation would improve the status of Native women. Jacqui Popick of the University of Lethbridge, Alberta, Canada, building on the work of P. K. Buffalohead and C. J. Voyaguer, observes:

> [European historians] reported that the women were exploited and mistreated which they used to justify policies forcing Natives to adopt the religion and life style of Euro-American society. . . . An elitist attitude prevailed that Indians were savages in need of fixing and Native women were particularly invisible as European men viewed all women as inferior. . . . The attitude that European culture was superior to that of the Native people led to bias in the observers so that they failed to comprehend the full range of women's economic roles or their political and social power within their societies.[17]

Is such an assessment accurate? Did past scholarship misreport the status of women and the sophistication of Amerindian society either because of male prejudice or imperialistic goals? Arguing against such a premise seems self-defeating, given the history of provocation of Native populations to precipitate large-scale appropriation of Amerindian territory by

16. Native American responses to such forced education can be found in Peter Nabokov, ed., *Native American Testimony: A Chronicle of Indian-White Relations from Prophecy to the Present, 1492–1992*, 2nd ed. (New York: Viking, 1991), 213–24.

17. Jacqui Popick, "Native American Women, Past, Present and Future," *Lethbridge Undergraduate Research Journal* 1:1 (2006), n.p. Accessed 21 January 2008. Online: http://www.lurj.org/article.php/vol1n1/running.xml. See also P. K. Buffalohead, "Farmers Warriors Traders: A Fresh Look at Ojibway Women" (Document No. 28), *Minnesota History: The Quarterly of the Minnesota Historical Society* 48:6, St. Paul: Minnesota Historical Society, 1983), 236–44; and C. J. Voyageur, "Contemporary Aboriginal Women in Canada," in *Visions of the Heart: Canadian Aboriginal Issues,* eds. D. Long and O.P. Dickason (Thompson, Canada: Nelson, 2000), 81–106.

gun or law. But, germane to our topic are the more focused questions: Were women essentially disenfranchised in Native American religious practices and did Christians free them to greater participation? Or, were women fully involved in all levels of society, the secular and the sacred, prior to the interference of Europeans, and did Christian missionaries curtail their activities and ensure them their new second-class status?

DID THE INTRODUCTION OF CHRISTIANITY STRENGTHEN OR THREATEN THE COMPLEMENTARY STATUS OF WOMEN AND MEN?

The temptation on either side of the discussion appears to be to demonize or aggrandize either Native cultures or missionaries. The truth, however, seems to lie more in the middle. The data suggest that Native American religious cultures ranged between being patriarchal to egalitarian to matriarchal, while Christianity could be freeing or restrictive, depending on the liberating quality of the faith and practice of the Christians seeking to introduce or implement it.

For example, while women did at times lead Taino communities in secular government, only the men appeared to be involved in the religious ceremonies, including the inhaling of the hallucinatory drug *cohoba* that produced the trance with which they believed they could communicate with the *cemies* (gods) who lived in *Turey* (heaven). While the Taino were gentle and were not known for domestic violence (Las Casas reports, "They treat women so decently no one in the world would mind seeing them together"), the few abusive practices they had, as handing their virgin daughters around like party favors to all and sundry to show friendship and seal alliances, casting off spouses as soon as they tired of them, the women giving "themselves abortions with herbs that force stillbirths" "if they tire of their men,"[18] and burying the wife of a *cacique* (chief) alive with his corpse so that she died of asphyxiation, were soon terminated with the arrival of the conquistadores.[19] This is not saying much, however, since the conquistadores virtually destroyed nearly

18. Las Casas, *History*, I.164.

19. Information on live wife burial gleaned at the Museo del Hombre in Santo Domingo, Dominican Republic. Contorted skulls of asphyxiating wives are on display in large display cases, their skeletons in taut fetal curls beside their more peacefully appearing husbands.

everything in Taino civilization (and nearly everyone in the population). Only those Tainos who escaped to safe harbors like the fortified camp of the great and devout Christian warrior chief Enrique, who successfully held the conquistadores at bay, survived to preserve the remnant which is today rebuilding the great Taino nation.

Among the Pueblo tribes (including the Hopi, Zuni, Tewa, Tano, Piro, and others), "the position of women was notably strong." As John Demos notes, the "senior women . . . owned most family property and controlled its use," so that "a newly married man would typically move into his wife's family's house," "men, by contrast, predominated in local politics and in communication with the gods."[20]

Molly H. Mullin observes:

> Among many Indian communities, past and present, women have been as likely as men to serve as spiritual leaders and doctors. Women have been powerful members of religious societies—some composed of women only, others including both women and men—within tribal communities. Many Indian communities have also held their most powerful and sacred ceremonies centering around female rites of passage, such as a girl's first menstruation.[21]

She observes that, even when religious practices were male-oriented, "beliefs about power, deities, and the nature of the universe have tended to emphasize and venerate women."[22]

Many women who led in traditional Amerindian religions were medicine women as the Cahuilla shaman Ruby Nesha ("Woman of Mystery") Modesto; Pretty-Shield of the Crow, whose story, *Red Mother*, was published by Frank Linderman; the Apache Ola Cassadore Davis; among countless others.[23]

What is usually absent in the literature when discussing the impact of Christian conversion is the distinction between being forced to become European and culturally or nominally Christian (by oppressors misusing this faith to mandate submission) and being given the opportunity to consider becoming authentically Christian (as shared by those attempting to

20. Demos, *The Tried and the True*, 27, 29.

21. Mullin, "Women," 867.

22. Mullin, "Women," 867.

23. See Hirschfelder and Molin, *Encyclopedia of Native American Religions*, 184, 231–32, 66.

incarnate Jesus' others-oriented Golden Rule in their conduct, by living under the daily Lordship of Christ). For example, in Columbus's journal of his travels, the adventurers, soldiers of fortune, and former prison inmates who comprised his crew are regularly referred to as "Christians." The well-meaning but initially clueless priest Bartolomé de Las Casas, whose bumbling attempt to rescue the Tainos from annihilation helped instigate African slavery, swiftly raised in consciousness and reported in his own journal the often blasphemous atrocities done by these so-called "Christians." In my chapter in our book *The Global God*, I have detailed many of these crimes against the Tainos, and therefore crimes against God, so I shall only mention a few here. First, about the dedication to sharing their faith with the Tainos of these reputed "Christians," Las Casas reports that "falseness applies to the statement about indoctrination into the holy Catholic Faith, for, upon my oath, the truth is that in those days and many years later there was no more concern for their Christianization than if they had been horses or working beasts."[24] In fact, "sin leads to sin, and for many years they lived unscrupulously, not observing Lent or other fasts."[25] Dominican friars who protested Taino slavery and such unspeakable acts as disemboweling women captives had their residences stormed and their removal demanded. In their wanton bloodlust to slaughter for amusement, Columbus's so-called "Christians" would set up thirteen nooses on a scaffold, hanging thirteen Tainos at a time, while jesting they were executing that number for Christ and the apostles. They would also "plant" crosses in the ground and "induce" Tainos to worship them, so that "Indians think that they are given an idol that represents the Christian God and they can be made to worship a stick."[26] As a result, many Tainos misunderstood the nature of Christianity itself. One responded, "Yes, Sir, I am a bit Christian because I have learned to lie a bit; another day I will lie big, and I will be big Christian."[27] Las Casas lamented:

> I left Christ in the Indies not once but a thousand times beaten, afflicted, insulted and crucified by those Spaniards who destroy and

24. Las Casas, *History*, 2:11. For my previous discussion of the conquest and its effect, please see my chapter "God of Power Versus God of Love: The United States of America" in *The Global God: Multicultural Evangelical Views of God*, eds. Aída Besançon Spencer and William David Spencer (Grand Rapids, Mich.: Baker, 1998), 37–62.

25. Las Casas, *History*, 2:1.

26. Las Casas, *History*, 3:117.

27. Las Casas, *History*, 3:145.

ravage the Indians. They die untimely deaths, having neither the Faith nor the sacraments. I pleaded with the royal council many times to have the obstacles to their salvation removed, namely, their enslavement to the Spaniards. Where the soil is untouched, I have asked that Spaniards be not allowed where missionaries have begun preaching the Gospels, for Spanish violence and the bad example they set make the Indians curse the name of Christ.[28]

He himself realized, "God did not want Christianity at that cost; God takes no pleasure in a good deed, no matter its magnitude, if sin against one's fellow man is the price of it, no matter how minuscule that sin may be,"[29] adding, "When Christians merely pass through infidel territory—but even if they should stay—the safest and surest rule is to set a good example of virtue so that, as Our Redeemer says, the sight of it will prompt men to praise and glorify the God and Father of Christians: they would see that such believers can only worship a good and true God."[30] And, returning to Spain, he railed against the Spanish jurist who wrote the injunctions that allowed raids, slavery, and the takeover of land:

> How could he think that Indians would believe a mere statement unsubstantiated by proof, read by men held to be infamous and cruel evildoers, purporting that God in Heaven had given the government of the world to a man called the Pope who in turn had given all the kingdoms of the Indies to the Castilian kings, and that should they fail within two months to swear obedience to the Castilian King, it was lawful to declare war upon them? How could the president of that Audiencia even believe that Indians were under the obligation to obey the kings of Castile, when they had their own rulers . . . ?[31]

28. Las Casas, *History*, 3:138. Las Casas' heartrending pleas are as much indictment as intercession, as in this poignant example, presented to counteract what he claims to be exaggerations "in order to justify Spanish tyranny and accuse the poor and forsaken Indians": "Endless testimonies . . . prove the mild and pacific temperament of the natives, as well as the fact that we surpassed them in arms so that, had we lived among them as Christians, we would have had no need of weapons, horses or fierce dogs to attract them to us. But our work was to exasperate, ravage, kill, mangle and destroy; small wonder, then, if they tried to kill one of us now and then" (2:1).

29. Las Casas, *History*, 2:43.

30. Las Casas, *History*, 3:117.

31. Las Casas, *History*, 3:167.

Such "raids," he declared, "were unjust, loathsome, and worthy of eternal damnation; that the injunction scorned truth and justice as well as our Christian religion and the charity of Christ who had suffered so much for the salvation of these souls."[32]

To call the people who would do such actions "Christians" is inaccurate. It disgraces the gospel of Christ and misrepresents the truth almost as effectively as the calumnies devised against the Native Americans in order to justify stealing their land distorted the truth. But what about those we would recognize in conviction and temperament and caring action as true Christians? Were they help or hindrance to the Amerindians? Even the best intended sometimes err and do so with grave consequences. Bartolomé de Las Casas mourned his own misguided attempt to exchange freeing the Tainos from slavery for his support of the "sins committed by the Africans and the Portuguese" in initiating the black slave trade ("not to mention our own sin of buying the slaves"). He wrote of himself, "The clergyman soon repented and judged himself guilty of ignorance. He came to realize that black slavery was as unjust as Indian slavery and was no remedy at all, even though he had acted on good faith, and he was not sure that his ignorance and good faith would excuse him in the eyes of God."[33]

On the mainland, perhaps the best test case to address this question would be that of John Eliot, "the apostle to the Indians," whose missionary work to the villages that surrounded his meeting house in Roxbury, Massachusetts, gave rise to the "Praying Indians." John Eliot was clearly a man of deep, sincere, steadfast, virtue-producing faith. A scholar with the compassionate heart of a pastor, the dedicated zeal of an evangelist, and the unflagging conviction of a social activist, he had seen in the Amerindians not bestial savages but lost children of God. Learning the Algonquian language from Cockenoe, a Pequot boy serving a sergeant in the Army, Eliot traveled from Roxbury to the wigwam of Waban, Chief of Justice of the Massachuset tribe on October 28, 1646. Eliot's sincerity was manifested as he catechized the children and preached to the adults on Ezekiel 37:9 (a sermon that pleased the gathering since the passage reads, "Then said he unto me, prophesy unto the wind"—the Algonquian term for wind being "Waban," so the gathering naturally assumed that this message was placed

---

32. Las Casas, *History*, 3:167.
33. Las Casas, *History*, 3:129.

in Eliot's holy book specifically for them.)[34] The practical dimension of his sincerity was confirmed when, after he had handed out tobacco to the men, sweetmeats and apples to the children and other gifts, Waban asked for a much larger and more difficult bestowal: "We need more ground to build our town on."[35] Only twenty-seven years after the first Puritans took up residence on their shores, the English had already proliferated in number and extended their culture of one law over all so that Waban, who wanted to keep the peace, had to ask for what had formally been assumed: enough land upon which a village could thrive. This is not to suggest that Native Americans had not struggled with each other in long-seated tribal battles for land and control of trade back beyond memory. But, the new technologically advanced encroachers had the power to enforce their law's peculiar views of exclusive possession, and Eliot looked like a means to navigate these rules. Eliot replied, "I will speak to the General Court about that,"[36] and he did. He petitioned and won the concession of more land. Waban's village spread and so did Puritan discontent as the wigwams multiplied. The Algonquian language encompasses tribes as diverse as the Cree, Montagnais, Naskapi of Canada; the Abnaki, Chickahominy, Lenni Lenape (Delaware), Lumbee, Mahican, Malecite, Massachuset, Mattapony, Micmac, Mohegan, Nanticoke, Narraganset, Nipmuc, Pamlico, Pamunkey, Passamaquoddy, Pennacook, Penobscot, Pequot, Powhatan, Shawnee, Wampanoag, and Wappinger, who together spread from Nova Scotia down through the Carolinas; the Illinois, Kickapoo, Menominee, Miami, Ojibwa (Chippewa), Ottawa, Peoria, Pottawatomi, Sauk, and Fox, out around the Great Lakes; the Arapaho, Atsina (Gros Ventre), Blackfoot (Blood, Piegan, Siksika), Cheyenne, and Plains Cree in the plains; and connects these to tribes as well who speak the related Ritwan and Kutenai dialects.[37] Barring the intratribal animosities that might keep them apart, John Eliot had a potentially huge constituency to address, and Native Americans did regularly sojourn as guests within each other's tribes. Suffice it to say, the Pilgrims were unnerved by the daily proliferation of warriors in Waban's village, so the leaders of the village and Eliot decided to seek a new location at a sufficient distance.

34. Ola Elizabeth Winslow, *John Eliot: "Apostle to the Indians"* (Boston: Houghton Mifflin, 1968), 98.

35. Winslow, *John Eliot*, 101.

36. Winslow, *John Eliot*, 101.

37. Alvin M. Josephy, Jr., "American Indians," *Collier's Encyclopedia*: 12:648.

Natick, which at seventeen miles away seemed west enough of Boston, became the first of fourteen "Praying Indian" towns. But how were these towns to be set up and governed, now that the leaders had converted to faith in Christ? As Eliot explained,

> it pleased the Lord of his free mercy to me (in my self being no way fitted for such a work) to put me on, to instruct our poor, blind, and dark Indians, in the good knowledge of the Lord: who when (through grace) they tasted of the knowledge of God, of themselves, of Christ and redemption by him; they desired to leave their wild and scattered manner of life, and come under Civil Government and Order; which did put me upon search, after the mind of the Lord in that respect. And this VOW I did solemnly make unto the Lord concerning them; that they being a people without any forme of Government, and now to chuse; I would endeavour with all my might, to bring them under the Government of the Lord only. Namely, that I would instruct them to embrace such Government, both Civil and Ecclesiastical, as the Lord hath commanded in the holy Scriptures; and to deduce all their Laws from the holy Scriptures, that so they may be the Lords people, ruled by him alone in all things. Which accordingly they have begun to do through grace, covenanting with the Lord, in a day of fasting and prayer, to be the Lords people; and to receive that forme of Government, which they learned to be a Divine institution in the holy Scripture. This occasion did first put me upon this Study, who am no Statesman, nor acquainted with matters of that nature; but only spend my time in the Study of the holy Book of God.[38]

As he reports, Waban and the other tribal leaders did indeed embrace his pious vision of selecting their new Christian government from the "holy Book of God" and, in fact, appeared to enforce it with a vigilance and severity that exceeded even Eliot's view.

At first glance, a casual reader might be tempted to lump in Eliot's recommendations with all the British's usual imperialistic ignoring of tribal laws and governing structures in favor of the custom of law they had brought with them. And it is true that Eliot appeared to be afflicted somewhat with the myopia of his age, not recognizing that these Native Americans were certainly not without "government" and "order." But, to

---

38. John Eliot, *The Christian Commonwealth: or, The Civil Policy of The Rising Kingdom of Jesus Christ* (London: Livewell Chapman, 1659; repr. in facsimile, Research Library of Colonial America, New York: Arno, 1972), ix–x.

conclude that he wanted to institute British law and order would be a complete misjudgment. In fact, quite the opposite was true.

Having helped the Amerindians adopt a biblical order, Eliot now wrote up his findings and sent them back to England for publication, urging the British as well,

> in the name of the Lord Jesus Christ, the King of Saints (whose Kingdom I desire to advance, with all my might and heart) I do beseech those chosen, and holy and faithful Saints, who by Councils at Home, or by Wars in the Field, have fought the Lords Battels against Antichrist, and have carried on the Cause of Christ hitherunto, That you would now set the Crown of England upon the head of Christ, whose only true inheritance it is, by the gift of his Father (a): Let him be your JUDGE, Let him be your LAW-GIVER, Let him be your KING! Take the pattern and form of your Government, from the Word of his Mouth.[39]

In other words, Eliot was suggesting a theonomy to replace the civil law of England. His book, *The Christian Commonwealth: or, The Civil Policy of The Rising Kingdom of Jesus Christ*, had to wait until the death of Oliver Cromwell, the resignation of Cromwell's son Richard, and the collapse of Cromwell's commonwealth to be published in 1659 (and even then the title page noted cautiously: "Written Before the Interruption of the Government"). Obviously, the British were less enthusiastic than the Praying Indians and did not adopt Eliot's vision. What exactly did it look like? As Eliot explained, referencing Deuteronomy 1:18 in a side note, which repeats what Moses' father-in-law Jethro had suggested to Moses in Exodus 18, he was recommending governance by "Rulers of thousands, of hundreds, of fifties and of tens, who shall govern according to the pure, holy, righteous, perfect and good Law of God, written in the Scriptures of the Old and New Testament."[40]

So, what was the impact of this system on any previous equality of men and women and what were the implications for any nonhierarchical structures that may have previously existed? First of all, whether actual full equality existed in any of the matrilocal and matrilineal societies when women did not sit in political meetings but made recommendations is still in question, namely, does influence completely equal decision making power? Second, men already held political positions of power in

39. Eliot, *Christian Commonwealth*, xiv.
40. Eliot, *Christian Commonwealth*, 4.

the tribe, so Eliot's proposal simply appeared to suggest that the tribe(s) reassign the men already in power to the biblical positions. Twenty-nine families of one hundred and forty-five people composed the settlement at Natick, and they chose Waban as a ruler of fifty, Totherswamp[e], an aged and respected man became the highest chief, and in this manner they proceeded to select their leadership most probably on August 6, 1651.[41] In his book, Eliot had written, "The Child is implicitely comprehended in the Fathers Covenant, the Wife is explicitely comprehended in her Husbands, insomuch that in her Widowhood she and her Family are one, under the order of the Government of God." He prooftexts his claim by citing a version of Deuteronomy 29:14–15: "Neither with you onely do I make this Covenant this day, but with him that standeth here this day before the Lord our God, and with him that is not here with us this day,"[42] although verses 10–11 specifically state that everyone was present to make the covenant: "Ye stand this day all of you before the Lord your God; your captains of your tribes, your elders, and your officers, with all the men of Israel, your little ones, your wives, and thy stranger that is in thy camp, from the hewer of thy wood unto the drawer of thy water" (KJV). Apparently, the tribal mothers were not convinced that they had been subsumed entirely under their husbands, since they had already begun to participate from the outset. As early as March 3, 1647, Thomas Shepherd records one such adjustment required of those who would preach to the Amerindians:

> On which day . . . perceiving divers of the Indian women well af-
> fected, and considering that their soules might stand in need of
> answer to their scruples as well as the mens, and yet because we
> knew how unfit it was for women so much as to ask questions
> publicly immediately by themselves, wee did therefore desire them
> to propound any questions they would be resolved about by first
> acquainting either their Husbands or the Interpreter privately
> therewith; whereupon we heard two questions orderly propound-
> ed; which because they are the first ever propounded by Indian
> women in such an ordinance that ever wee heard of, and because
> they may bee otherwise useful, I shall therefore set them down.[43]

41. Winslow, *John Eliot*, 128.

42. Eliot, *Christian Commonwealth*, 3. Women were certainly allowed to make vows in Israel, even those underage (see Num 30:3–4 of a woman vowing while "in her youth").

43. Nehemiah Adams, *The Life of John Eliot: With an Account of the Early Missionary Efforts among the Indians of New England*, vol. 3 of *The Lives of the Church Fathers of New*

Of the first by the wife of Wampooas, "a serious Indian," ("Do I pray when my husband prays, if I speak nothing as he doth, yet if I like what he says, and my heart goes with it?") and the second by the wife of Totherswampe, probably the same who would become the highest chief, ("Whether a husband should do well to pray with his wife, and yet continue in his passions and be angry with his wife?"), Shepherd remarks he had "heard few Christians when they begin to look towards God, make more searching questions than these Indians."[44] In fact, so zealous were the women to enforce the law, that a group reported the sachem's wife to the "native Indian preacher" one Sabbath for what they considered to be "worldly conversation" as she fetched water. He adjusted his sermon to preach upon "the sanctification of the Sabbath." Not to be so easily reproved, the sachem's wife insisted her conversation was private, therefore harmless, while the preacher had sinned even more greatly for overemphasizing such a topic on the Sabbath. The debate extended until "by common consent" the gathering decided to refer it all to John Eliot for "arbitration."[45] Clearly, the women were maintaining their rule of influence, the men were adjusting Eliot's system to their tribal style, and those missionaries like Thomas Shepherd who would participate were finding it necessary to adjust to these Native cultural realities as well.

Richard W. Cogley in an even-handed assessment of Eliot's effect on the Praying Indians observes three areas of chief cultural concern to John Eliot, while the rest was apparently negotiable. The first was in "grooming": "'most' Natick residents wore English clothing" and he cites an observer who supposes "the Christian and civilized Indians . . . follow the English mode in their habit." But, he also notes that this style change served the "Christians Indians to advertise their connections with English power," pointing out the Massachusetts government issued an edict to protect those "clothed in English apparel," with hairstyles "in the manner of the English."[46] The second was sexual behavior. Though extramarital sex was previously common, polygamy was not and domestic abuse, as we noted, already punishable. The third of the earliest laws the Praying Indians put into effect before they even established Natick and the other

---

England (Boston: Massachusetts Sabbath School Society, 1847), 112.

44. Nehemiah Adams, *The Life of John Eliot*, 112–13.

45. Adams, *The Life of John Eliot*, 128.

46. Richard W. Cogley, *John Eliot's Mission to the Indians before King Philip's War* (Cambridge, Mass.: Harvard University, 1999), 241.

towns had been "If any man shall beat his wife, his hands shall be tied behind him, and he shall be carried to the place of justice to be severely punished."[47] Nehemiah Adams notes, "A great improvement was soon visible among them in their treatment of their wives."[48] The third was to settle in the Praying towns and not keep moving about. In response, the Praying Indians built their first public structure in the center of Natick for Eliot to stay in when he sojourned among them—and also, ever practical, to store "furs, clothing and provisions,"[49] and began building their wigwams larger to accommodate a cordoning off of rooms for the purpose of affording more modesty for the residents.

Part of Eliot's concern for this last point was no doubt possession being the proverbial nine-tenths of the law. In that he was justified, for the subsequent conflict, termed King Philip's War, devastated the Praying towns. Cogley concludes "the natives' progress in religion was similarly uneven. Many 'praying Indians' wore the Christian faith loosely, and others not at all," observing Eliot himself complained about "profane" and "unsound" residents in Natick in the 1650s,[50] but this war two decades later not only devastated the Praying Indians who had not bought completely into Christianity, but also those who had, while polarizing everyone involved. A white woman captured by King Philip's group was told by her captors: "Those seven that were killed at Lancaster the summer before upon a Sabbath day, and the one that was afterward killed upon a week day, were slain and mangled in a barbarous manner, by one-ey'd John, and Marlborough's Praying Indians, which Capt. Mosely brought to Boston, as the Indians told me."[51] She also lists various "Praying Indians" she encountered on King Philip's side, one who wrote her letter of ransom to her husband, another who explained to her how he convinced

---

47. Adams, *The Life of John Eliot*, 100. Despite the severe ruling and the zeal of the Praying Indians to enforce their rules, they also "kindly admonished and instructed," as in the case of an offender who "made no defence, but confessed his sin, and . . . turned his face to the wall and wept," and as a result was let off with a fine, Nehemiah Adams explaining, "all did forgive him; onely this remained, that they executed their law notwithstanding his repentance, and required his fine, to which he willingly submitted, and paid it" (130).

48. Adams, *The Life of John Eliot*, 129.

49. Winslow, *John Eliot*, 125–26.

50. Cogley, *John Eliot's Mission*, 242.

51. Mary Rowlandson, "The Captivity of Mary Rowlandson," in *The Portable North American Indian Reader*, ed. Frederick W. Turner III (New York, Viking, 1974), 315.

his brother to eat horse by expounding 2 Kings 6:25 to him, a third who saved his own life by betraying his father to the English, a fourth who fought in the battle of Sudbury and was hanged for it, a fifth "so wicked and cruel, as to wear a string about his neck, strung with Christian fingers," and a sixth who decided "to Powaw" with the spirits and was guided to join in the "Sudbury-fight."[52] But, staying neutral also did not spare the Praying Indians, as the British were committing their own atrocities even against noncombatants. Soon they interned the peaceful Praying Indians to bleak Deer Island, ostensibly to keep them from being slaughtered, but under such restrictions that a great proportion died. When the English began crying, "Let us go to Deer Island and kill every Praying Indian," they were stopped only by the General Court insisting they honor the "covenant of allegiance," made back at the outset in 1643–44.[53] As it was, of the estimated 1,100 Praying Indians who lived in the fourteen towns at the onset of the war in 1675, only about 300 remained at the end. The Praying towns were eventually taken over and most ceased to exist. By 1682, only four were left. Of the 2,500 Christians estimated from all tribes, many were killed by both sides. Some of those who survived Deer Island did so only by becoming scouts and spies for the English army, for whom, Ola Winslow notes, they "removed their clothing, painted their bodies and became savage Indians again." Industrious, as Christians are, their military supervisor Major Thomas Savage reported they "approved themselves courageous soldiers, and faithful to the English interest." Captain Daniel Richardson observed, "I had experience of the sobriety, courage and fidelity of the generality of those Indians." Samuel Hunting, who sent out eighty as volunteers, explained they "behaved themselves courageously and faithfully to the English interest," so that Daniel Gookin praised them for "turning ye balance to ye English side, so that ye enemy went down ye wind amain.[54]

Eliot himself was subjected to "continuing abuse" and "personal danger" throughout the conflict, but steadfastly spoke against selling captive warriors (whether Praying Indians or not) into West Indian slavery, ceaselessly interceding for those accused of participating in the Indian

---

52. Rowlandson, "*The Captivity*," 344–45.
53. Winslow, *John Eliot*, 176.
54. Winslow, *John Eliot*, 176–77.

victory at Sudbury, and even accompanying them to the gallows when he lost a case.[55]

WHAT IS CHRISTIANITY'S LEGACY TODAY?

Almost four hundred years have passed since the Praying Indians were caught between two cultures. What has endured of the legacy of John Eliot, Chief Waban, the strong women, and the rest of the devout Christians? Today, Praying Indians still thrive in Natick. The structure of John Eliot's Christian commonwealth along with the proclivity by the Wampanoag Amerindians to appoint men as political leaders has passed. Today's Praying Indians have turned to the leadership of two strong Christian women: Grand Squaw Sachem Silva and Clan Mother Caring Hands. These are contemporary representatives of a long line of Christian women whose work for Jesus Christ has endured, such as Way-johnie-ma-son (Sister M. Sirilla Larush), the Ojibwa Roman Catholic Nun who, with the Ojibwa priest Ti-Bish-Ko-Gi-Jik (Fr. Philip Gordon), restored and rebuilt a reservation mission before extending her ministry to serve missions in Chicago and in Mississippi;[56] or Sophia Thomas Mann, the Cree educator and translator, who with her husband translated the entire Bible into Cree.[57] Three generations of Mohegan women (Lucy Occum Tantaquidgeon, Lucy Tantaguidgeon Teecomwas, and Cynthia Teecomwas Hoscott) in 1827 founded the Mohegan Congregational Church, which also provided the site of the first Mohegan school, and still exists today in Uncasville, Connecticut.[58] Gay Head Community Baptist Church of Aquinnah, Massachusetts, was also founded by devout Wampanoag men and women in 1693 and today "is the oldest native Baptist church in continuous existence in the country," according to Boston's Emmanuel Gospel Center Senior Researcher Rudy Mitchell.[59] Non-Native female missionaries also worked beside Native Christians, as did the Presbyterian missionary Ann Eliza Worcester Robertson, who with Creek Baptist

---

55. Winslow, *John Eliot*, 175.

56. Hirschfelder and Molin, *Encyclopedia*, 156, 105.

57. Hirschfelder and Molin, *Encyclopedia*, 172.

58. Rudy Mitchell, "New England's Native Americans," *Emmanuel Research Review* 32 (Nov. 2007), n.p. Accessed 12 Jan. 2008. Online:http:/www.egc.org/research/issue_32.html.

59. Mitchell, "New England's Native Americans."

minister Pahos Harjo (James Perryman) and his nephew Presbyterian minister Thomas Perryman translated the New Testament, Genesis, and the Psalms into Creek. Born at a Cherokee mission, the daughter of a Congregational missionary who was arrested and sentenced to hard labor for opposing the state of Georgia's usurpation of jurisdiction over Cherokee land, Ann Robertson taught for a school sponsored jointly by the Creek Nation and the Presbyterian Board of Foreign Missions, was awarded an honorary doctorate by the University of Wooster, and was the mother of the second woman elected to the United States Congress.[60] The controversial, partially paralyzed Susan Law McBeth, called "little mother" by the Nez Perce, took over a mission and was so popular a teacher that her students followed her to a new location when she had to relocate for her health. She fought to eliminate poverty, worked on a Nez Perce dictionary, and trained numerous pastors, while her sister set up a school for women.[61] Congregational missionary Laura Wright, with her husband Asher, opened her home to orphans of a typhoid epidemic (and was concerned for so many she eventually established an orphanage), founded the Iroquois Temperance League, and published bilingual textbooks for the Seneca.[62]

Among the many Native Christian men who worked diligently beside exemplary Christian women to champion the gospel and the wellbeing of the tribes was the Dakota Christian Napeshneeduta (Joseph Napeshnee), whose name means "Red Man Who Flees Not." On February 21, 1840, he was baptized as the first full-blooded Dakota man to become a Christian. After his first wife died and his second abandoned him, he married a staunch Christian woman. Together they were ostracized for their new faith, but they persevered through suffering, illness, and deprivation. Eventually, he became a Presbyterian ruling elder and his locale's leading farmer, helping both Amerindians and whites and winning great respect from all.[63] The devout Unaduti (Jesse Bushyhead), the first ordained Cherokee Baptist minister, was elected to represent his tribe as a delegate to Washington and became a justice of the Cherokee Supreme Court. So compassionate were he and his wife that, in the face

60. Hirschfelder and Molin, *Encyclopedia*, 248.

61. Hirschfelder and Molin, *Encyclopedia*, 165.

62. Hirschfelder and Molin, *Encyclopedia*, 339.

63. Hirschfelder and Molin, *Encyclopedia*, 195.

of misunderstandings and accusations, he bought a black slave family in order to set them free, and his wife freed a slave she inherited.[64] Choctaw Presbyterian minister Kiliahote (Allen Wright) married the missionary Harriet Newell Mitchell with whom he had eight children, including noted Presbyterian minister Dr. Frank Hall Wright. Among his accomplishments, Kiliahote suggested the name for Oklahoma, became principal chief of the Choctaw Nation and its delegate to Washington, D.C., was renowned as a linguist of Choctaw, English, Latin, Greek, Hebrew, among other languages, translated Choctaw and Chikasaw legal documents and hymnals, and the Psalms from Hebrew to Choctaw, and compiled a Choctaw dictionary.[65] Shahwahnegezhik (Henry Bird Steinhauer), the Ojibwa Wesleyan Methodist missionary, was a translator, educator, and establisher of missions and schools for which he secured United States government financial support. He was married to a Cree, Jessie Mamanuwartum, and at least three of their children were involved in missionary work.[66] The Lenni Lenape (Delaware) Baptist minister Neshapanacumin (Charles Journeycake), whose mother had been an interpreter for Methodist missionaries, was the first Lenni Lenape to give his life to Christ west of the Mississippi. He helped found the Delaware and Mohegan Baptist Mission Church. He was a gifted linguist who preached in Lenape, Shawnee, Wyandot, Seneca, Ottawa, and other languages and was delegated to Washington and then chosen principal chief by the Lenni Lenapes. He also pastored, translated hymns and religious documents, and he and his wife, Jane Socia, a Lenni Lenape, had fourteen children.[67] Ojibwa Methodist missionary, renowned author, preacher, translator, defender of tribal lands, establisher of schools and Christian communities, and husband of Eliza Field, Kahkewaquonaby (Peter Jones) was a delegate who represented Ojibwa concerns before Queen Victoria.[68] William Apes[s], a Pequot whose wife was non-Native American, served the Mashpee tribe as an ordained Methodist minister and was sentenced to jail for reclaiming wood stolen from Mashpee land, but sued and won,

---

64. Hirschfelder and Molin, *Encyclopedia*, 34–35.

65. Hirschfelder and Molin, *Encyclopedia*, 338.

66. Hirschfelder and Molin, *Encyclopedia*, 284–85.

67. Hirschfelder and Molin, *Encyclopedia*, 139.

68. Hirschfelder and Molin, *Encyclopedia*, 292, 138–39.

including gaining concessions from the government.[69] Honored for his forty years of ecumenical ministry, Cherokee Baptist pastor and educator David W. Owl, who married the Seneca Janie Crow, served an Episcopal school, a Presbyterian Church among the Pima people, a Baptist church on the Cattaraugus Reservation, and various calls from other denominations, receiving awards from Chicago's Indian Council Fire, the Iroquois Temperance Society, and the State of New York.[70]

With a five hundred year history stretching from Enrique to today, replete with countless Native American Christians working with parallel attention to advocate for the tribes while advancing the life-enhancing message of Christ, for such leaders to hear continual doubt expressed that their dual commitment is authentic or even possible is discouraging. As James Treat wrote in the introduction to his important collection of thought-provoking essays *Native and Christian: Indigenous Voices on Religious Identity in the United States and Canada*, "To dismiss all native Christians as acculturated, anachronistic traces of religious colonialism, is to miss innumerable demonstrations of their insightful historical and social analysis, their complex and sophisticated religious creativity, and their powerful devotion to personal and communal survival."[71]

So, in answering whether Christianity limited or liberated Native peoples, improved or destroyed their cultures, fostered or impeded equality of service between women and men, we have to take into account a number of factors. First, to demonize Native cultures and suggest that they were all bestial and abusive before Christianity arrived is absurd. Kindness and cruelty alternated as it does in all cultures. Certainly, William Apes[s] was brutalized by his grandparents, having his arm broken when he was only five by his grandmother, before he was rescued by his uncle and a neighbor,[72] but, on the other hand, Mary Jemison,

---

69. Hirschfelder and Molin, *Encyclopedia*, 8.

70. Hirschfelder and Molin, *Encyclopedia*, 208–9.

71. James Treat, *Native and Christian: Indigenous Voices on Religious Identity in the United States and Canada* (New York: Routledge, 1996), 10. Professor Treat adds, "Native Christians have been called heretical, inauthentic, assimilated, and uncommitted; they have long endured intrusive definitions of personal identity and have quietly pursued their own religious visions, often under the very noses of unsuspecting missionaries, anthropologists, agents, and activists. . . . To disregard Indian Christians, either as Indians or as Christians, is to deny their human agency, their religious independence, and—ultimately—their very lives" (9–10).

72. Hirschfelder and Molin, *Encyclopedia*, 8.

who expected to be brutalized, was treated tenderly.[73] The same is true of outsiders as of Native Americans. Spanish conquistadores brutalized Amerindians while friars tried to champion them. Second, we do note the balance of influence and power between males and females did seem to shift toward men when Europeans imperialistically restructured Native American societies. But, when Christians were involved, as in the case of John Eliot, Native American men already holding political positions simply seemed to shift over to the new structure while women continued to assert their power and the missionaries apparently learned to adjust. The dominant secular society, however, did not adjust and was more than willing to jail both Native and non-Native clergy if they opposed its self-serving, greed-impelled legislation. To champion women, Christians regularly fought against domestic abuse and any vestiges of polygamy. That Amerindians could see the difference between counterfeit use of the faith to serve greed and true self sacrificial incarnating love and justice reaching out in a caring human life is clear by all the examples of Native Americans who embraced the Christian faith, often against opposition from both sides. The great and brilliant statesman Ohiyesa (Dr. Charles Eastman) put it so well:

> From the time I first accepted the Christ ideal it has grown upon me steadily, but I also see more and more plainly our modern divergence from that ideal. I confess I have wondered much that Christianity is not practiced by the very people who vouch for that wonderful conception of exemplary living.[74]

So, third, perhaps the most compelling factor is found in the enduring presence of true Christianity among Native American women and men today. This is a lasting affirmation that would not have been maintained some five hundred years later if true Christianity had not enhanced life. The people are wise and not foolish. They did not let it die out as they did so many other movements both foreign and Native.

---

73. Jemison, *Mary Jemison Becomes an Iroquois*, 75–76. She reports, "During my adoption, I sat motionless, nearly terrified to death at the appearance and actions of the company, expecting every moment to feel their vengeance, and suffer death on the spot. I was, however, happily disappointed, when at the close of the ceremony the company retired, and my sisters went about employing every means for my consolation and comfort."

74. Treat, *Native and Christian*, 4.

In summary, as we observed earlier, when people truly take on the Lordship of Jesus Christ so as to incarnate his life-enhancing message of wholeness in God's love within his Golden Rule of treating others as well as one would have themselves treated, their message is fully liberating. Residual cultural biases, as preferring male hegemony, as we have seen in Thomas Shepherd's example, begin to melt away. The final result as the Natick Praying Indians reveal is that God raises up the right leaders, women as well as men, to lead God's church. Compulsion lasts for a time, but only liberation can endure the years. Sydney Byrd, an ordained Presbyterian minister, put it well: "I am a Dakota and I freely chose to be a Christian. I agree that force was used to convert Indian people, but the loving example of my grandparents who were Presbyterian missionaries to our people, made me want very much to be like them, to be a Christian."[75] The Rev. William Apes[s] in his autobiography, *A Son of the Forest*, which appeared in 1829 as the earliest autobiography by a Native American, declares, as James Treat notes, he "found in Christian teachings the rationale for an egalitarian social order, becoming convinced that 'age, sect, color, country, or situation made no difference.'"[76] I would add gender to that list, since it is an egalitarian component Native Americans have regularly valued from the evidence of female chiefs in the history of the tribes encountered by the Jamestown Settlement in what has become Virginia to today's female rulers such as Anne Richardson, chief of the Rappahonnock Tribe, and Wilma Mankiller, chief of the Cherokee Nation, to name just two.[77] Particularly significant in uniting spiritual and social concern have been Hawaii's many ruling Christian Queens. Aída Besançon Spencer notes that "between 1823 and 1825 Queen Kaahumanu, Chief(ess) Keopuolani, King Liholiho, Queen Kamehamaru, and Chief(ess) Kapiolani had all converted to Christianity," and notes, "many chiefs and chief(esses) led

---

75. Treat, *Native and Christian*, 18.

76. Treat, *Native and Christian*, 8.

77. Mullin, "Women," 868–69. Wilma Mankiller, who was chosen in 1985, is specifically highlighted by Molly Mullin, who also points out that women took part in the occupation of Alcatraz and the protest at Wounded Knee and are increasingly elected to tribal councils. Many have become lawyers and judges, raising consciousness on "issues that pertain to both men and women in Indian communities." Organizations like Women of All Red Nations (WARN) deal with "health care, in particular women's health matters and the misuse of sterilization practices on Indian women . . . children's foster care, adoption, political imprisonment, and juvenile justice," and even "inequities resulting from abuses of energy resources development on Indian-owned land."

significant lives for Christ. Queen Kaahumanu, Chief(ess) Keopuolani, and Chief(ess) Kapiolani are extolled again and again for their advancement of God's reign in the political and spiritual arenas."[78] James Treat in *Native and Christian* specifically highlights Queen Liliuokalani, a contemporary of Ohiyesa, who, he points out, "was not the first native Christian to wrestle with the problem of identity." The Queen, too, was "a devout Christian," who "directed church choirs" and authored a history of Hawaii while struggling against a group of American merchants seeking to overthrow her government. She was jailed and even betrayed by the missionaries, but "remained a Christian throughout her life."[79] As Barry O'Connell observes, rather than becoming less Native American, Queen Liliuokalani, Ohiyesa, and so many others shared a consciousness similar to that of Rev. William Apes[s], who "employed his Christian identity so as to assert, more forcibly and coherently, his identity as a Native American . . . for a Pequot to convert to Christianity is not . . . to take on white ways but only to claim one of her rights as a human being."[80]

The message that comes through to us is clear: The good news of Jesus is a gift given by God to Native American women and men to enhance the best human values that are already present in their cultures and assist them to serve together in bringing Christ's reign of love and justice to earth. Those who would seek to help them do so should serve under their leadership. For all of us, Native or not, we should constantly remind ourselves and each other that, if we wish to represent Christ, we must represent Christ and not our culture, our prejudices, our personal desires for power, renown, gain, sacrifice, salvation, or anything else. Only Christ can truly liberate. Anything less is a danger to the safety of the populations we profess to love, a disgrace to the mission of our Lord, and a betrayal of our word.

78. Aída Besançon Spencer, "How God's Spirit Worked a Revolution in Hawaii in 1819–1825," *Priscilla Papers* 19:3 (Summer 2005), 8.

79. Treat, *Native and Christian*, 6–7.

80. Treat, *Native and Christian*, 8.

8

Biblical Equality and United States Latino Churches

Awilda González-Tejera

IMAGINE ALL THE WORK that is involved in presenting a play. We have to consider not only the actors and actresses, but also the people who work behind the stage. The audience only sees and applauds those who appear on stage; but, without the hard work of the entire group of men and women, the play cannot be presented. In the same manner, in Latino churches, many women work very hard in the church alongside men, being often behind the stage.

This essay reflects on biblical equality in United States Latino churches as addressed through the study of how Paul considers working hard for the gospel as one of the main qualities of his male or female coworkers.[1] In Paul's letters, a coworker (*sunergos*) is a "helper, fellow-worker,"[2] someone who helps him as his colleague. The letters of the Apostle Paul provide social and historical insights to support the understanding of the place God has given to men and women in serving the church together.

In this chapter, I first discuss how, in Paul's letters, some of the most important qualities of Paul's coworkers are their service and hard labor for the gospel. My discussion is enlightened by the study of some social practices and understandings of Paul's times. Second, I analyze how those in the Latino church are similar or different from Paul's coworkers. I examine how, as in Paul's churches, some of the most important qualifications

---

1. This essay seeks to present a general picture of the gender issue in U.S. Latino churches in relation to what qualifies Paul's coworkers; it does not pretend to present a broader discussion of the gender issues topic.

2. Walter Bauer, *A Greek-English Lexicon of the New Testament and other Early Christian Literature*, translated, adapted, revised, and augmented by W. F. Arndt, F. W. Gingrich, and F. W. Danker (Chicago: University Press, 1979), hereafter BAGD, s.v. "*sunergos*."

of those in leadership in United States Latino churches are used in service and work on behalf of God's church. I give special emphasis to the work of women in the church. I intend to draw an overall picture of how Latino theological reflection and practice on gender issues have developed over the last two decades in regard to working hard for the gospel, and, finally, I speculate where they might be going in the future.

WORKING HARD FOR THE GOSPEL AND THE CHURCH[3]

In his letters, the Apostle Paul describes himself as one who believes that sharing the gospel with his coworkers implies preaching, teaching, laboring, and even struggling on behalf of God's churches (1 Cor 4:1–14, 6:3–10, 11:23–33; 2 Cor 1:8, 6:4–10).

Consequently, serving and working hard for the gospel are some of the qualities Paul values most in his coworkers. In fact, Paul uses his letters as a way of commending his coworkers,[4] as we shall see in two commendation passages (1 Cor 16:15–18; Rom 16:1–2) and one appeal passage (Phil 4:2–3). These passages, directly or indirectly, attest to the inclusion of women among these coworkers.[5]

The Household of Stephana(s), Fortunatus, and Achaicus:[6] *1 Corinthians 16:15–18*

In 1 Corinthians 16:15–18, Paul commends the members of the household of Stephana(s), Fortunatus, and Achaicus. Stephana "could be a woman's or a man's name."[7] If it is a male name, we can assume that,

---

3. The discussion on Paul's coworkers and their laboring for the gospel is mostly from my dissertation work. See Awilda González-Tejera, *Intercession in Paul's Letters in Light of Greco-Roman Practices of Intercession* (Ann Arbor: Pro-Quest, 2002).

4. The Apostle Paul follows the social conventions of his times; his practice of commendation was "representative of widespread customs and understandings available to him and his audience." See González-Tejera, *Intercession,* ix. For the investigation on Greco-Roman conventions of commendation and how patron-client relations promoted leadership advancement in the Greco-Roman world see Efraín Agosto, "Paul's Use of Greco-Roman Conventions of Commendation" (Ph.D. diss., Boston University, 1996).

5. For a broader discussion on Paul's coworkers, their identity, and designation, see E. Earle Ellis, "Co-workers," *Dictionary of Paul and his Letters* (Downers Grove, Ill.: InterVarsity, 1993), 183–88.

6. See González-Tejera, *Intercession,* 135.

7. Aída Besançon Spencer, *Beyond the Curse: Women Called to Ministry* (Nashville: Thomas Nelson, 1985), 119. Spencer says that Stephana(s) "might very well have been a

even though only men are mentioned, there were also women in the household. The members of Stephanas's household (16:15) "have devoted themselves to the service [*diakonia*] of the saints."[8] Paul points to the work that Stephanas's household had already done: "Their authority is legitimated through their service."[9] They set themselves aside for this work. Paul describes the service of Stephanas's household using one of the terms (*diakonia*) he customarily used for those who worked on behalf of the churches of God. Paul urges the Corinthians to submit themselves to them and reciprocate by service (16:16).

The Corinthians should submit and serve "everyone who works [*sunergeō*] and toils [*kopiaō*] with them [Stephanas's household]" (16:16). The verb *sunergeō* and the noun *sunergos* are other terms Paul uses to refer to his coworkers. As I mentioned earlier, *sunergos* means "helper, fellow-worker," "working together with, helping."[10] Paul uses this term to refer to those who help him as his fellow workers in spreading the gospel (Rom 16:3, 9, 21; Phil 2:25; 4:3; 1 Thess 3:2; Phlm 1).

Paul introduces *kopiaō*, which means "become weary, tired, work hard, toil, strive, [and] struggle."[11] The apostle's use of the term *kopiaō* shows that his coworkers' labor is a severe and exhausting work like Paul's own work. He uses *kopiaō* for himself in 1 Corinthians 15:10 and Galatians 4:11. Paul's description of his coworkers' labor functions to enhance their reputation. Service entails hard toil, which in turn deserves respect and honor.[12]

In Greco-Roman commendation, enhancing the moral status or reputation of the person recommended was important for the result of the commendation. The recommender appeals to the ties or connection with the person recommended and to what this person has done. Cicero

---

woman" because *Stephana* is a woman's name; the male counterpart is *Stephanos*, 119. She also says that "*Stephana* might possibly be a diminutive of *Stephanos* or *Stephanephoros*," 119. See also "'El Hogar' as Ministry Team: Stephana(s)'s Household" in *Hispanic Christian Thought at the Dawn of the 21st Century: Apuntes in Honor of Justo L. González*, ed. Alvin Padilla, Roberto Goizueta, and Eldin Villafañe (Nashville: Abingdon, 2005), 71.

8. I will regularly cite from the New Revised Standard Version.

9. Richard B. Hays, *First Corinthians* (Louisville: John Knox, 1997), 290.

10. BAGD, s.v. "*sunergos.*"

11. BAGD, s.v. "*kopaiō.*"

12. Anthony C. Thiselton, *The First Epistle to the Corinthians*, The New International Greek Testament Commentary (Grand Rapids: Eerdmans, 2000), 1339.

wrote many letters of recommendation.[13] In recommending his friend Aemilius to Sulpicius, Cicero also recommends a freedman client called Hammonius. Cicero says:

> M. Aemilius Avianius has always regarded me with respect and esteem from his earliest youth. He is a [good man], and at the same time an exceedingly courteous man, and in the performance of every kind of duty worthy of esteem. If I thought he was at Sicycon and were not informed that he is still staying at Cibyra, where I left him, there would have been no necessity for my writing to you about him at any greater length. For I feel sure that he would succeed by his own character and culture, unaided by anybody's recommendation, in winning your esteem no less than mine, and that of all his other intimate friends.
>
> But, believing him [Aemilius] to be away, I commend to you with more than customary earnestness his family (they live in Sicyon) and his private property, and particularly Gaius Avianius Hammonius, his freedman, whom I also commend to you on his own account. For not only has he won my approval by his remarkable sense of duty and loyalty to his patron, but he has also conferred great obligations upon myself, and in the days of my greatest trouble he stood by me as faithfully and affectionately as though it were I who had manumitted him. I therefore beg of you to give that Hammonius not only your support in his patron's business, as being the agent of the man I am recommending to you, but also your regard on his own account, and put him on the list of your friends. You will find him a modest and obliging person, and worthy of your regard.[14]

Cicero intends to support his commendation on the merits of the freedman. He emphasizes Hammonius's own values, especially those related to his service and faithfulness to him. Cicero is in great obligation to the freedman because, in the days of his greatest trouble, this man stood by his side.

---

13. My discussion of Cicero's commendation is from my dissertation. See González-Tejera, *Intercession*, 45–46. Literary letters dominate the commendation collection. Because the volume of literary letters is large, I investigate intercession in material roughly contemporary to Paul, such as the letters of Cicero (106–43 B.C.) and Pliny (c. A.D. 61–c. 120).

14. *Epistulae ad familiares* 13.21.

In the same manner, Paul points out his coworkers' values, especially those related to their serving together with him. Stephanas, Fortunatus, Achaicus, and the male and female members of that household have served together with Paul. They exemplify the service and behavior that Paul is seeking to inculcate among the Corinthians. Paul follows the pattern of Greco-Roman commendations of enhancing status and the common literary device of exemplification (mentioning someone as a model or example) to encourage his audience to imitate his coworkers' behavior, their laboring hard for the gospel.

Euodia and Syntyche:[15] Philippians 4:2–3

Philippians 4:2–3 includes two occurrences of intercession through petition, a plea to Euodia and Syntyche and to one of the apostle's coworkers.[16] Paul writes to the Philippians because he is concerned, among other things, about the harmony of the community (Phil 1:10, 3:18–19; 4:1–2).[17] In this context, Paul petitions Euodia and Syntyche, who were in conflict about some matter, to be united.[18] He also asks one of his coworkers to intercede between these women.

It has been suggested that Euodia and Syntyche were prominent and influential members of the church.[19] In Greco-Roman culture, women

15. See González-Tejera, *Intercession*, 187–89, 192–95.

16. Even though Paul's tone of exhortation is present in this passage, Paul is petitioning these women to be unified. For a classification of Phil 4:1–3, see Fred O. Francis and J. Paul Sampley, *Pauline Parallels* (Minneapolis: Fortress, 1992), 81. Francis and Sampley classified Phil 4:1–3 as a primary passage of appealing. See also Nils A. Dahl, "Euodia and Syntyche and Paul's Letter to the Philippians," *The Social World of the First Christians: Essays in Honor of Wayne A. Meeks* (Minneapolis: Fortress, 1995), 3.

17. Carolyn Osiek, *Philippians, Philemon,* Abingdon New Testament Commentaries (Nashville: Abingdon, 2000), 31.

18. The disagreement of these important leaders must have been serious, because Paul petitions and addresses them publicly. Paul introduces his petition with two appeals (4:2). Paul gives a separate appeal to each woman as a way of strengthening his petition. The nature of their disagreement is not stated.

19. See Wayne A. Meeks, *The First Urban Christians* (New Haven: Yale University Press, 1983), 57; Nils A. Dahl, "Euodia and Syntyche," 4; Davorin Peterlin, *Paul's Letter to the Philippians in the Light of Disunity in the Church* (New York: Brill, 1995), 104; Maxie D. Dunnam, *Galatians, Ephesians, Philippians, Colossians, Philemon,* Communicator's Commentary (Waco, Tex.: Word, 1982), 310–11; Moisés Silva, *Philippians,* Baker Exegetical Commentary of the New Testament (Grand Rapids: Baker, 1992), 221; Wendy Cotter, "Women's Authority Roles in Paul's Churches," *Novum Testamentum* 36, no. 4 (1994): 353; Francis X. Malinowski, "The Brave Women of Philippi," *Biblical Theology*

were not mentioned by name "unless they were either very notable or very notorious."[20] That Paul follows this practice suggests that Euodia and Syntyche "were women of status and of great importance for the congregation."[21] In the Hellenistic world, many women had prominence and were involved in social organizations.[22] Women also owned provincial estates, and the wives of Roman officials were often honored in inscriptions.[23]

Paul describes Euodia and Syntyche as believers who have bravely worked for the advancement of the gospel. Paul shows respect toward each woman.[24] In his request, Paul exhibits these women's "proven bravery"[25] and counts them among his coworkers. Paul enhances their reputation by showing how they have labored for the gospel. Euodia and Syntyche "struggled [*sunathleō*] beside [Paul] in the work of the gospel, together with Clement and the rest of [his] co-workers [*sunergos*]" (4:3). Paul uses the same term (*sunathleō*) in 1:27b in regard to the Philippians' struggling for the gospel: "I will know that you are standing firm in one spirit, striving [*sunathleō*] side by side with one mind for the faith of the gospel." *Sunathleō* translates as "to strive together" or "labour with others."[26] One of the emphases of the term stresses the "commonality of suffering" between Paul and the women.[27] In describing Euodia and Syntyche, Paul probably had in mind the Romans' athletic contests in the arena or the contest of war.[28] Paul anticipates the metaphor of athletic contest in his introduction to his appeal (4:1); the Philippians are his "joy and crown," and he calls on them to "stand firm in the Lord" (4:1).[29] Only in the letter

Bulletin 15 (1985): 62–63.

20. Ben Witherington III, *Friendship and Finances in Philippi*, The New Testament in Context (Valley Forge, Pa.: Trinity, 1994), 108.

21. Witherington, *Friendship and Finances*, 108.

22. Witherington, *Friendship and Finances*, 107.

23. Tacitus *Agr.* 6.3, 45.4. *Inscriptiones Graecae* 329 (1898) 12:3, 80. See A. J. Marshall, "Roman Women and the Provinces," *Ancient Society* 6 (1975): 108–27.

24. Cotter, "Women's Authority," 353.

25. Malinowski, "Brave Women," 63.

26. H. G. Liddell and R. Scott, *An Intermediate Greek-English Lexicon* (Oxford: Clarendon, 1997), s.v. "*sunathleō*."

27. Peterlin, *Paul's Letter to the Philippians*, 126.

28. See Malinowski, "Brave Women," 62; Dahl, *Social World*, 6; Morna D. Hooker, "The Letter to the Philippians," *The New Interpreter's Bible*, vol. XI (Nashville: Abingdon, 2000), 540.

29. Dahl, *Social World*, 6.

to the Philippians does Paul use the term *sunathleō* (1:27, 2:3) to picture these women and the Philippians as brave coworkers in their struggling for the gospel.[30]

Paul also uses another word, *sunergos*, to describe Euodia and Syntyche (4:3). Philippians 4:3 suggests that Paul "has a close personal friendship with both women based on their previous collaboration in the gospel."[31] As mentioned before, *sunergos* is one of the terms Paul uses to refer to those who work beside him for the gospel (Phil 2:25, 4:3; Rom 16:3, 9, 21; 1 Thess 3:2). This is the terminology of equality.[32] As in Greco-Roman practices, Paul depicts his relationship with them as a friendship of equals (see, for example, Aristotle, *Ethica eudemia* 7.6.9).

Paul petitions one of his coworkers at Philippi to intercede between Euodia and Syntyche and help them to overcome their differences (Phil 4:3). On the side, Paul describes his loyal companion as *syzygos*;[33] this term translates as fellow-soldier, yoke-fellow, and comrade.[34] Such a description denotes a mutual sharing in the gospel. John T. Fitzgerald asserts that "the word 'yoke' was one of the metaphors used" in the classical and Hellenistic world to describe the relationship of friends (e.g., Cicero, *De officiis* 1.58; Plutarch, *De amicitia* 93E).[35] Moisés Silva states that Paul may strengthen his appeal "by linking Euodia and Syntyche with a promi-

---

30. Malinowski, "Brave Women," 62.

31. John T. Fitzgerald, "Philippians in the Light of Ancient Discussions of Friendship," *Friendship, Flattery, and Frankness of Speech* (Leiden: Brill, 1996), 156.

32. Pheme Perkins, "Christology, Friendship and Status: The Rhetoric of Philippians," *Society of Biblical Literature Seminar Papers* 26 (1987): 512.

33. Paul's use of *syzyge* in this verse is vague; the text does not identify who is Paul's loyal companion. See also Gordon Fee, *Paul's Letter to the Philippians* (Grand Rapids: Eerdmans, 1995), 389, 393–95; Witherington, *Friendship and Finances*, 106. Witherington says that "unprovable but just barely possible is the suggestion that the Greek word *syzygos* is a proper name rather than a term meaning yokefellow. There is no evidence in the relevant sources of such a name. What is clearer is that this third party, who has been asked to intercede, is a male, as the gender of the word 'loyal' makes apparent." Compare with Hooker, "The Letter to the Philippians," 540; Hooker stands with Lightfoot; Hooker's main argument is that "Paul is referring to Epaphroditus" because he was still with Paul when he wrote this letter, 540. See also J. B. Lightfoot, *St. Paul's Epistle to the Philippians* (London: Macmillan, 1894), 158–59.

34. Liddell and Scott, s.v. *syzygos*; BAGD, s.v. *syzygos*. Even though Paul's use of *syzyge* in this verse is vague, my interpretation is that Paul uses this word as a way to call his coworkers to harmony.

35. Fitzgerald, *Friendship, Flattery*, 149.

nent leader in the community."[36] This coworker might have substantial standing with the Philippians and with these women. Paul also mentions Clement, who had struggled with him and with Euodia and Syntyche in their laboring for the gospel (v. 3). By exemplification of his coworker, Clement, and Paul's use of his own example, the apostle calls these women to unity. In antiquity, such "calls to imitation often assumed a very special and close relationship between the mentor and his followers."[37] The relationship between Paul's coworker and these women must have been a close one. Paul requests reconciliation, and this coworker would be an appropriate mediator between Euodia and Syntyche.

Paul stresses mutual friendship to move these women to resolve their disagreement, to ask his coworker to help them, and to stimulate unity among the Philippians. In doing this, the apostle enhances Euodia's and Syntyche's and other coworkers' reputations through direct references to their work for the gospel.

Similar to the practice in Roman society, Paul uses commendation as a significant factor in social interchanges. But, Paul differs from the Roman's convention on the basis of reputation since, for him, reputation is enhanced through working hard for the gospel. In Roman pyramidal society, reputation was enhanced through advancement in social status (Cicero, *De officiis* 1.45, 1.50; Seneca, *De beneficiies* 1.11.5).

Paul's Other Coworkers: Romans 16:3–12

In Romans 16:3–16, the Apostle Paul greets his coworkers and brothers and sisters.[38] In particular, Romans 16:3–12 records greetings that describe Paul's coworkers and their labor using the same terminology of *sunergos* and *kopiaō*. It is significant that in this list women are prominent.

Paul describes Andronicus and Junia as those who are outstanding among the apostles. He refers to them as "my relatives who were in prison with me; they are prominent among the apostles" (16:7). He also says they believed in Christ before he did. This man (Andronicus) and this woman (Junia) are known for their apostleship.[39] In his letters, Paul

---

36. Silva, *Philippians*, 221.

37. Witherington, *Friendship and Finances*, 96.

38. In this section, I only discuss those who are mentioned as coworkers in Rom 16:3–12.

39. Junia was a female Latin name. The "name Junia occurs over 250 times among

describes what it means to be an apostle as one who endures a ministry of hard labor, troubles, dangers, and many other struggles (1 Cor 4:1–14, 6:3-10, 11:23–33; 2 Cor 6:4–10). Like Paul's ministry, Andronicus's and Junia's apostleship might be one of laboring and struggling. They were imprisoned, very probably because of conflicts about their work for the sake of the gospel.

A letter addressed to Servilius explains Cicero's intervention in favor of a member of his own household, T. Agusius, who had shared with Cicero times of misfortune.[40] Cicero writes:

> Now that our intimacy and your goodwill towards me is a matter of common knowledge, I find myself obliged to recommend ever so many people to you. But although all whom I recommend ought to have my best wishes, I have not the same reason for such wishes in every case. T. Agusius was not only my companion during the most miserable period of my life, but also shared with me all my journeys, voyages, troubles, and dangers; nor would he have left my side at the present time, had I not given him permission. That is the reason I recommend him to you as being one of my own household, and one of those most closely attached to me. You will do me a very great favor by also treating him as to convince him that this recommendation has been of material service and assistance to him.[41]

Cicero's intercession expresses the ties of his feelings toward Agusius. When Cicero was in extreme circumstances, Agusius helped him, comforting him during a miserable period of his life. Now, Cicero asks for assistance and intercedes on behalf of Agusius.

Even though Paul's description of Andronicus and Junia is part of a greeting passage, some features of Cicero's commendation are comparable with Paul's description of his relationship with his coworkers. They were

---

inscriptions from ancient Rome alone," see Bernadette J. Brooten, "Junia," *Women in Scripture* (Grand Rapids: Eerdmans, 2000), 107. For a history of interpretation of Rom 16:7, see Brooten, "Junia," *Women Priests*, eds. Arlene Swidler and Leonard Swidler (New York: Paulist, 1977), 141–44. See also Craig. S. Keener, "Man and Woman," *Dictionary of Paul and his Letters*, 589; Peter Lampe, "The Roman Christians of Romans 16," *The Romans Debate*, ed. Karl P. Donfried (Peabody, Mass.: Hendrickson, 1995), 223.

40. My discussion of Cicero's commendation of Agusius is from my dissertation. See González-Tejera, *Intercession*, 50–51.

41. Cicero, *Epistulae ad familiares* 13.71.

in prison with Paul, and they shared with him the troubles and dangers that characterize apostleship.

Paul also refers to Prisca (the diminutive form is Priscilla) and Aquila as his fellow workers (vv. 3–4) "who work [*sunergos*] with me in Christ Jesus, and who risked their necks for my life" (16:3–4). The fact that Prisca is mentioned first attests to her playing the more important part in church work.[42] Paul mentions that Prisca and Aquila risked their lives for him; such effort works to enhance their reputation.[43]

Another letter from Cicero indicates how he interceded for a freedman who served and risked his life for him. Cicero wrote to Munatius in order to help L. Livinieus Trypho (one of his friend's freedmen) to whom Cicero was in debt.[44] Cicero says:

> L. Livinieus Trypho is, in any case, the freedman of my very intimate friend L. Regulus, whose misfortune makes me more ready than ever to serve him; more friendly in my feeling for him than I always have been I cannot be. But I esteem this freedman of his [Regulus] for his own sake; his services to me were conspicuous at that crisis in my life when I was able most easily to appraise the goodwill and loyalty of my fellow-men.

> I therefore commend him to you as men who are grateful and not forgetful are bound to commend those who have deserved well of them. You will have done me a great kindness if he is led to believe that by frequently risking his own safety for mine, and often taking ship in the depth of winter, he did what was acceptable to you also, since you wish me well.[45]

In this letter, Cicero pointed out the freedman's services to him. It is interesting that, even when Cicero mentioned his friend Regulus, it is the name of the freedman (Trypho) that stands at the very beginning of the letter. This is a sign of great esteem based on the freedman's own merits. This freedman helped Cicero under circumstances that led the freedman to risk his own safety. Having been favored by his help and

---

42. See also 1 Cor 16:19; Rom 16:3; 2 Tim. 4:19; Acts 18:18, 26.

43. Also Epaphroditus, another of Paul's coworkers, risked his life for Paul. He suffered an almost fatal illness in his determination to serve Paul (Phil 2:27, 30).

44. The discussion of Cicero's commendation of Trypho is from my dissertation; see González-Tejera, *Intercession*, 51.

45. *Epistulae ad familiares* 13.60.

services, now Cicero is bound to him and shows his gratitude through this recommendation.

In the same manner, risking their lives for the apostle attests to Prisca and Aquila's bonding to Paul. In Paul's writings, Prisca, as well as Aquila, "can be recognized as a highly esteemed missionary who is understood as Paul's 'co-worker' and who stands as an equal not only alongside Aquila, but also in the company of Paul and other missionaries."[46]

Paul also describes Mary, Urbanus, Tryphanea and Tryphosa, and Persis as those who expended much labor for the church: Mary, "who has worked [kopiaō] very hard among you" (16:6); Urbanus, "our coworker [sunergos] in Christ" (16:9); Tryphanea and Tryphosa who are "workers [kopiaō] in the Lord" (16:12a); and the beloved Persis, "who has worked [kopiaō] hard in the Lord" (16:12b). Paul singles out each one of them among other brothers and sisters in Rome. Without the labor of these devout workers, the gospel would not have spread.

In his list, Paul uses the terms sunergos and kopiaō for both males and females. In doing so, he stresses his coworkers' equality to him, and he recognizes the kind of work they have done. Like Paul, the women in his list have worked equally hard for the gospel. Beverly Roberts Gaventa states, "Nothing in Paul's comments justifies the conclusion that these women worked in ways that differed either in kind or in quantity from the ways in which men worked."[47]

Paul opens the door for women in his churches.[48] For him, gender is a "matter of indifference."[49] Wendy Cotter asserts that Paul "provided women with an open avenue for their involvement and, unlike the andro-centric organizations of his day, encouraged and praised women for their exercise of leadership in his communities."[50]

We should not underestimate the role of early Christian women. In the same manner, we should not diminish the work of Latina Christian

---

46. Beverly Roberts Gaventa, "Romans," *Women's Bible Commentary* (Louisville, Ky.: Westminster John Knox, 1998), 219.

47. Gaventa, "Romans," 410.

48. J. Paul Sampley, *Walking Between the Times* (Minneapolis: Fortress, 1991), 115.

49. Sampley, *Walking*, 79. See also James L. Jaquette, *Discerning What Counts*, SBLDS 146 (Atlanta: Scholars, 1995), 214; Antoinette Clark Wire, *The Corinthian Women Prophets* (Minneapolis: Fortress, 1990), 184; Victor Paul Furnish, *The Moral Teaching of Paul* (Nashville: Abingdon, 1985), 111.

50. Cotter, "Women's Authority," 354.

women. In the next section of this chapter, we shall assess similarities and differences between Paul's leadership and his coworker and the Latina woman's role of coworker.

GENDER ISSUES IN UNITED STATES LATINO CHURCHES

In this section, I present a brief understanding of where United States Latino theology and practice on gender issues has been over the last two decades, and where it might be going. This is a descriptive and general understanding, not an exhaustive one.[51] We shall see how the experience of the Latina woman as coworker is both similar and different from that of Paul's coworkers. We shall also assess how Latino churches recognize the Latina Christian woman's role as compared to Paul's recognition of his female coworkers' role.

Where Have We Been?

For decades, Latina women have been laboring in the church behind the scenes. Latina women were hidden, although not before God. Their participation and work in the church has been meaningful in the advancement of God's gospel, but their work has not been appreciated properly, especially the efforts of those women in leadership. The experiences and stories presented in this section shall illustrate how, like Paul's coworkers, Latina women have served and struggled; they have done severe and exhausting work. Their work can be described with the same terminology Paul used for his coworkers (*sunergos, kopiaō, diakonia*). But, unlike Paul, many Latino churches have diminished the role of women. In this section, I first discuss the hard work of the Latina women and their commitment to be trained to do church work. Then, I assess how many women have experienced acceptance and rejection of their leadership role.

The hard work of the Latina Christian woman is evident in different ministries and services in the church and communities.[52] In most Latino

---

51. This description cannot be exhaustive; a broader discussion is beyond the scope of this essay. I am making evaluative observations on the place of women in the church that will help in assessing the past and the future of U.S. Latino theology and practice in gender issues. I base my arguments on my own observations and on the observations of other people who have studied gender trends in Latino churches. The lack of statistical data about gender issues in Latino churches limits any attempt to be more specific in my discussion.

52. By no means do I intend to deny the successful work of Latino Christian men.

churches, women are involved in children's ministry; they are the ones expected to do it. Women's ministries at the church bring new believers to Christ, and, of course, new members to the church. Many Latina Christian women are involved in dealing with social issues. Jeanette Rodríguez studied the relationship between service and spirituality among the Latina Christian women.[53] She conducted many interviews and concludes that "Latinas have become increasingly aware of the social injustices sustained and suffered."[54] Rodríguez also tells several stories of Latina women that show their "efforts to improve the quality of life in their communities."[55]

Luis Benavides studied the role of Latina women in the Methodist church in New England and concluded: "The hard work and commitment of women in the local church has been precisely what has allowed many congregations to survive, grow, and move ahead in ministry."[56] In many evangelical churches, the women are the ones who "not only carry out the day to day operations of the church, but also hold many of the leadership positions."[57] Similar to that of Paul's coworkers, Latina Christian women in the United States have exhibited their "proven bravery"; they have served, worked, and even struggled together with men on behalf of God's churches.

Many Latina women are also committed to be trained to do church work. In 2003, the Centro Educativo de Estudios Bíblicos conducted a survey in the Dallas metropolitan area of Texas to see the interest of Latino/a leaders in theological education.[58] From a total of 100 persons

---

But, in general, the participation of Latina women in the church is less recognized than the participation of men.

53. Jeannette Rodríguez, "Latina Activist: Toward an Inclusive Spirituality of Being in the World," *A Reader in Latina Feminist Theology: Religion and Justice* (Austin, Tex.: University of Texas Press, 2002), 114–30.

54. Rodríguez, "Latina Activist," 120.

55. Rodríguez, "Latina Activist," 119.

56. Luis E. Benavides, *Latino Christianity: History, Ministry, and Theology (The New England Methodist Situation)* (General Commission on Archives and History, Conference Commission on Archives and History, Conference Committee on Hispanic/Latino Ministry, 2005), 193.

57. Loida Martell, "Women Doing Theology: Una Perspectiva Evangélica," *Apuntes* (Fall 1994): 84.

58. The Centro Educativo de Estudios Bíblicos (Educational Center for Biblical Studies) was founded in 2002. It is located in Dallas, and its mission is to train and equip

who were interviewed, 95 percent were interested in doing theological studies, and 66 percent were women. This survey shows how women of the Dallas area are often self-motivated to be trained to do church work. The women who were interviewed enjoyed being instructed in the word of God and also teaching others. In my past pastoral experience in Boston and Texas, I noted that women were even more interested in leadership training than were men. Also, I have conducted many leadership seminars and workshops, and, most of the time, women's attendance has surpassed men's, even in some workshops I presented together with my husband.

Different from Paul who welcomes and engages the gifts of women coworkers, some fundamentalist Latino churches have not properly and consistently recognized the role of their women as coworkers. Apparently, Latino women have experienced both acceptance and rejection of their leadership role. For example, María was a very committed Christian leader in her Pentecostal church.[59] She was a qualified leader to start what Latinos/as call *una misión* (a new church that is opened hoping for growth), and her pastor called her to do it. Like Paul's coworkers who were faithful to God and the apostle, this woman was faithful to God and her pastor. María stood by her pastor's side in his project of starting a *misión*. María had to struggle and work very hard, almost taking care of every aspect of church planting: outreach, teaching, preaching, implementing programs, administering, giving encouragement and counseling to the new believers, reaching their families, and doing many other tasks. But, after she did a great job and the membership of the new *misión* grew, she had to return to her former church because a male pastor was appointed to the new church. The reason for this decision was that the denomination does not allow women to be pastors. This is an example of what happened in the past and is still happening in the present in some Pentecostal churches. María's leadership was accepted and recognized for starting a new church, but her leadership and "proven bravery" were rejected for being pastor in the church she planted. Based on María's hard work and commitment, I could give her a different name: Junia, Priscilla, or any other female name of Paul's coworkers.

The assertion that Latina Christian women experience acceptance and rejection of their leadership can be also illustrated with the work

---

Latino/a leaders for ministry.

59. This is an actual incident. I changed the name of the woman involved.

of Anna Adams, who studied the role of women in Latino Pentecostal churches in Allentown, Pennsylvania. [60] She says that "Pentecostalism is a Patriarchal religion" that "presupposes the superiority of men."[61] But Adams also asserts, "Although generally there are no women pastors in Allentown's churches, women play an active role in church governance and leadership."[62] She mentions the participation of women in missionary work, evangelism, serving as deacons, leading the services, and how some women "have attended Bible institutes to prepare for a role in church leadership."[63] Adams studied four oral histories of women and concludes that these "women's words and experiences support and contradict their perceptions of equality."[64]

Other non-fundamentalist denominations allow women's participation in positions of authority. But some of these women are still experiencing rejection. Luis E. Benavides, when he studied Latino Christianity in the United Methodist Church in New England, asserted, "Latina women have been permeating all aspects of the life of the United Methodist Church; from general boards to superintendences, to pulpits, to staff/pastor-parish chairs, missioners, to positions of lay leaders, and the like."[65] Benavides also says that, despite these facts, Latina women experience "the rejection of their ministerial roles by the structural hierarchy or by some members at the local church."[66] These women have been experiencing acceptance and rejection.

The experiences and stories presented illustrate how, similar to Paul's female coworkers, Latino women are hardworking leaders. They also illustrate how Latina Christian women's experiences affirm and negate the

60. See Anna Adams, "Perception Matters: Pentecostal Latinas in Allentown, Pennsylvania," *A Reader in Latina Feminist Theology: Religion and Justice* (Austin, Tex.: University of Texas Press, 2002), 102. Adams recognizes that the growth of Pentecostalism has "prompted scholarly examination of women and the status and influence they hold in this very patriarchal church whose doctrine holds that women are naturally inferior to men," 99.

61. Adams, "Perception Matters," 99.

62. Adams, "Perception Matters," 102.

63. Adams, "Perception Matters," 102.

64. Adams, "Perception Matters," 104.

65. Benavides, *Latino Christianity*, 194.

66. Benavides, *Latino Christianity*, 194. See also, Minerva Garza Carcaño, "Una perspectiva bíblico-teológica sobre la mujer en el ministerio ordenado," *Apuntes* (Summer 1990): 27.

idea of biblical equality as practiced and presented by Paul in his writings. I perceive two main reasons for the diminished role of Latina women in church leadership: theological positions and cultural trends. I will explain them briefly.

Theological Issues

In the Scripture, the role of women has a place that for centuries was ignored among many Latino churches. María Pilar Aquino says: "If today Latina feminist theologians are still few in number, we were 'invisible' thirty years ago!"[67] The secular feminist movement has helped in the recognition of the role of women in society and in the church.[68] Orlando O. Espin states: "There is no question in my mind that one significant dynamic within Latino/a theology, over the last decade or so, has been the ever increasing reception and incorporation of methodological concerns and issues raised by feminist critical theory."[69] Espin recognizes that the growing interest in gender roles and in many other critical issues was "originally raised by Latina feminists outside the theological academy."[70] This interest in gender issues has impacted Latino theology.[71] The feminist movement has helped to redefine the focus of doing biblical exegesis.[72]

67. María Pilar Aquino, "Latina Feminist Theology," *A Reader in Latina Feminist Theology: Religion and Justice* (Austin, Tex.: University of Texas Press, 2002), 138.

68. Gretchen G. Hull asserts that "the first U.S. women's rights convention, held in 1848 in Seneca Falls, New York, was an outgrowth of both the religious revivalist and abolitionist movement." See G. G. Hull, "Biblical Feminist: A Christian Response to Sexism," *ESA Advocate* (Oct. 1990): 14. I agree with some concerns characterized as feminist. I think that feminist issues that have biblical bases demand the support of all Christians.

69. Orlando O. Espin, "The State of U. S. Latino/a Theology: An Understanding," *Perspectivas* (Fall 2000): 28.

70. Espin, "The State of U. S. Latino/a Theology," 28.

71. For an introduction to Latina feminist theology, see María Pilar Aquino, Daisy L. Machado, and Jeanette Rodríguez, eds., *Religion, Feminism and Justice: An Introduction to Latina Feminist Theology* (Austin, Tex.: University of Texas Press, 2002). See also Linda A Moody, *Women Encounter God: Theology across the Boundaries of Difference* (New York: Orbis, 1996); María Pilar Aquino, "Directions and Foundations of Hispanic/Latino Theology: Toward a *Mestiza* Theology of Liberation," *Journal of Hispanic/Latino Theology* (Nov. 1993): 5–21; Jeanette Rodríguez, "Experience as a Resource for Feminist Thought," *Journal of Hispanic/Latino Theology* (Nov. 1993): 68–76; Ada María Isasi-Díaz, "'Apuntes' for a Hispanic Woman Theology of Liberation," *Apuntes* (Fall 1986): 61–71.

72. Aquiles Ernesto Martínez, "Imágenes Feministas en Santiago: Óptica de género y destellos de liberación," *Apuntes* (Fall 1998): 67 (translation is mine).

Cultural Issues

Latino culture is mostly a *machista* culture. The term *machismo* is associated with the oppression of women. *Machismo* is the way of thinking and resultant behavior based on men's superiority over women and the exaltation of masculinity. Being *macho* "implies both domination and protection of those under you, especially women."[73] Miguel De La Torre suggests that "within the marginalized space of the Latino/a community intra-structures of oppression along gender, race and class lines exists."[74] We have to realize that religion is culturally influenced, but we cannot perpetuate forms of oppression either in Latino churches or in theology. Paul's society was a patriarchal one, but he recognized the role of his female coworkers as equal to his and to that of other male coworkers.

Where Are We Going?

The Latino church needs to overcome cultural and theological issues in word and in action. We have seen how Paul chose to work with coworkers of both genders and how he acknowledged them in his letters. Paul followed practices of his times and, similar to Cicero, who wrote letters of commendation in favor of those who helped him, Paul commended his coworkers on the basis of their working hard for the gospel. In the same way, Christian men need to make public commendations of Latina women who have been working and struggling alongside them in ministry. Our Latino churches must recognize equally the participation of men and women in different ministries and leadership positions. It could be done, for example, by nominating Latina women who have worked hard to positions such as regional area minister, bishop, superintendent, or any other position of authority in the church and paraecclesiastical organizations. We also need to consider other models of church leadership, for example, a model where a couple can serve together as pastors. I know a few independent Latino churches in the state of Texas where a couple has been recognized as ministers on an equal basis. One of these churches is Centro Internacional de Alabanza located in La Feria, Texas. Pastors Ronaldo and Juanita Ortíz are husband and wife and have been serving

---

73. Miguel A. De La Torre, "Confesiones de un Macho Cubano," *Perspectivas* (Summer 2001): 66. De La Torre explores the multidimensional aspects of intra-Hispanic oppression by unmasking the socio-historical construction of *machismo*.

74. De La Torre, "Confesiones," 66.

this church for almost thirty years. It is important to mention that Pastor Juanita Ortíz was the founder of this church, which she started in 1979. She worked very hard since the very beginning, and this church has an actual membership of more than five hundred persons. This congregation is a model of a church where men and women can serve together in authoritative positions, as did Prisca and Aquila and Junia and Andronicus.

Equal acknowledgement of the work of men and women will empower us to bring transformation in our churches and society. We need to break the pattern of acceptance and rejection of women in leadership, and follow Paul's model of leadership by recognizing and supporting the work of women consistently.

Certainly, we are not back where we were two decades ago, but we still have a long journey ahead of us. In the last two decades, social struggles have influenced many sociocultural aspects of Latino American churches. The reception of Latinas in theology and ministry has increased. A good sign that this is taking place is that more women have been ordained to ministry in mainstream denominations. Latina women have come out onto the stage, not only in the church, but also in academia. Academia is more open to Latinos/as in teaching positions.[75] According to the statistics of the Association of Theological Schools, in 2002, there were twenty Latinas in full-time faculty positions in the United States and Canada; in 2006, that number increased to twenty-seven.[76] Latina feminist theologians are developing theology that "arises from the experience of yesterday's and today's" Latinas.[77] It is a theology that is consistent with the global reality of "poverty, inequality, social exclusion, and social insecurity."[78] The church needs to be more receptive to recognize the par-

75. We thank those who were pioneers in the struggle for the presence of Latinos/as in the academia, Dr. Justo González, Cecilio Arrastía, The Hispanic Summer Program, The Asociacón para la Educación Teológica Hispana (Association for Hispanic Theological Education), Hispanic Theological Initiative, and many other scholars and organizations. For the work of Latino/a scholars in gender issues and other topics, see Paul Barton and David Maldonado, Jr., eds., *Hispanic Christianity within Mainline Protestant Traditions: A Bibliography* (Decatur, Ga.: AETH Books, 1998). This bibliography has more than two thousand references in five categories: theology, biblical studies, history, the church and its ministry, and social science.

76. See The Association of Theological Schools 2006–2007 Annual Data, 64.

77. Gloria Inés Loya, "The Hispanic Women: *Pasionaria* and *Pastora* of the Hispanic Community," *Frontiers of Hispanic Theology in the United States* (New York: Orbis, 1992), 133.

78. María Pilar Aquino, "Latina Feminist Theology," 140. See also Aquino, Machado,

ticipation of women in ministry. In the past, many women went through long and painful struggles, but they kept their hope. Because they did not give up, Christian contemporary women are in a better position than they were two decades ago.

The fact that, in our times, the theological foundation for women in ministry is a topic more openly discussed than it was decades ago does not deny that some churches, denominations, and theologians are still in entrenched positions. Zaida Maldonado, speaking about exercising "a healthy dose of self criticism," says that we Latinos/as are increasingly aware of our "sins against our women, that hinder the development of their God-given potential and ministries, and therefore, also, the development of the body of Christ."[79] Like the Apostle Paul, Latino male leaders and churches need to respect and appreciate the work of women, especially of those in leadership, and publicly highlight the contribution of these coworkers who labor alongside them.

In the present as in the past, the Latina Christian woman works hard and continues struggling not only for the benefit of the church, but also for equality. It is an ongoing struggle that demands courage, tolerance, and hope: courage to continue fighting against a *machista* understanding of the role of women in the church, tolerance for those who are still in entrenched theological positions, and hope because the struggle continues.

CONCLUSION

Both Latino men and women need to free themselves from culturally and religiously extreme positions and follow Paul's example of working with both women and men and recognizing publicly their contributions. That will not happen by accident. The challenge for both men and women in Latino churches is to redefine theological and cultural understandings that serve to exclude and marginalize and to make Latino theology truly inclusive, not only in word, but also in practice. It can be done only if we overcome the patriarchal framework that has been present in our churches and society.

Whether we are Latinos/as or not, all of us Christians across the globe need to restore the ties that make us neither male nor female, but

---

and Rodríguez, eds., *A Reader in Latina Feminist Theology.*

79. Zaida Maldonado, "U.S. Hispanic/Latino Identity and Protestant Experience: A Brief Introduction for the Seminarian," *Perspectivas* (Fall 2003): 105.

all one in Christ (Gal 3:28)—believers who work together on behalf of the gospel. The believers' identity is their unity in Christ. Because all believers participate equally in this unity, they should firmly reject the gender prejudice that diminishes the ministry and work of women in the church. This new millennium demands that, like Paul's coworkers, Latina women be recognized along with men fully in God's partnership.

9

Biblical Equality among Pastoring Couples in the New England Portuguese District of the International Church of the Foursquare Gospel

John Runyon and Eliana Marques Runyon

A HISTORY OF WOMEN IN LEADERSHIP

THE INTERNATIONAL CHURCH OF the Foursquare Gospel (ICFG) has a long history of affirming women in ministry, both as individual ministers and ministers who minister alongside their husbands. The denomination, started by Aimee Semple McPherson in 1926, has since seen mostly male leadership, particularly in high leadership positions, although the wives of these leaders often do maintain strong roles alongside their husbands. Women were very encouraged in the early years to pursue callings of ministry, and, in fact, the first graduating class of the Foursquare Training Institute saw only two men out of the sixteen graduates.[1] During those first twenty-five years until shortly after the death of Aimee McPherson, women comprised up to 60 percent of all the credentialed ministers in the Foursquare movement.[2] But by 1986, the minutes of the annual convention indicated that 41 percent of all ordained[3] min-

1. Nathaniel M. Van Cleave, "The First Branches of the Vine," *The Vine and the Branches: A History of the International Church of the Foursquare Gospel* (Los Angeles: International Church of the Foursquare Gospel, 1992), 41.

2. Steve Schell, ed., *Women in Leadership Ministry* (Los Angeles: Foursquare Media, 2007), 69.

3. "Licensing" in the Foursquare credentialing process qualifies a person to hold an official pastoral or leadership position in a Foursquare church, whereas ordination is the final step in which the person has received full approval and commissioning by the denomination for the vocational ministry to which he or she is called. Through the vari-

isters in the Foursquare were women,[4] although, as Nathaniel Van Cleave points out, this percentage does not reflect how many women were actually actively engaged in "public ministries such as pastoring, evangelizing and church planting."[5]

The decline continued, from 1986 with 41 percent licensed women in the ICFG in the United States to a low in 1993 of 29 percent,[6] rebounding by 2006 to 36 percent, but with only 6 percent of total licensed or ordained female ministers as senior pastors in the 1,900 Foursquare churches of the United States.[7] This decrease reflects a general trend among Pentecostal and Holiness movement churches, which have seen fewer women in ministry over the course of the century, although the percentages in the Foursquare movement have held up well over the years in comparison to other similar denominations.[8]

The Foursquare (ICFG) came to Brazil in 1951 and has since become the largest Foursquare work in the world, expanding to more than 7,500 churches with national membership approaching 2.5 million.[9] In Brazil, 42 percent of all credentialed ministers are women. They are pastoring their

---

ous types of licenses, Foursquare polity recognizes and endorses the level of authority the minister can have. As the minister grows in knowledge and maturity, by upgrading the licenses (going through application processes again), the minister may receive approval to minister in a larger geographical area and more independently of the mentor's presence at the place and time of ministry. Ordination is the last step in the Foursquare ministerial licensing process, which requires that a candidate have at least four years of a combination of preparation for and practice of ministry (*Handbook for the Operation of Foursquare Churches*, International Church of the Foursquare Gospel, Los Angeles, Calif.).

4. Vinson Synan, *The Twentieth Century Pentecostal Explosion* (Altamonte Springs, Fla.: Creation House, 1987), 107.

5. Synan, *Pentecostal Explosion*, 43.

6. Schell, *Women in Leadership*, 69.

7. It should also be noted that Foursquare bylaws indicate that a local church must have one "senior pastor"; therefore, many men carry that title while their wives are listed as "associate pastor," even when they function as co-pastors. Article XIV of the *Corporate Bylaws of the International Church of the Foursquare Gospel*, 2007 Edition, Los Angeles, Calif.

8. Richard M. Riss, "Role of Women," *Dictionary of Pentecostal and Charismatic Movements*, ed. Stanley M. Burgess and Gary B. McGee (Grand Rapids: Regency Reference Library, 1989), 893.

9. Current information as of March 2008. See http://www.igrejaquadrangular.org.br for more information.

own churches or ministering as co-pastors, assistant pastors, Theological Institute directors, or in other roles within the Foursquare Church.

Foursquare missionaries readily passed on to the patriarchal Brazilian culture the value of the strong role of women in ministry. Although in the secular Brazilian culture gender roles have undergone major change in the last century from a predominately patriarchal structure to a more egalitarian one, patriarchal structure and traditional gender roles are still strong.[10] Traditional gender roles are characterized by two themes: gender-based division of labor within the home and "male dominance, commonly reflected in the belief that the husband should be head of the family and should take the lead in making decisions."[11]

In the church, then, one would assume a parallel social structure, and, indeed, many Brazilian denominations restrict women in their roles in the church. In at least one mainline (traditional) denomination in Brazil, women are allowed to minister to children and other women and to lead congregational worship in song, but cannot do so from the pulpit or the platform. Eliana experienced this firsthand when she was invited to minister at a non-Foursquare church and was instructed by the leadership to lead everything from the floor level and not from the pulpit. From this and further interaction with that particular denomination, Eliana learned that women were not allowed to be a part of the decision-making body (the church council) of that church according to denominational policy.

On another occasion, and from a broader Brazilian Christian cultural perspective, while still single and conversing with an older married woman (herself a minister), Eliana shared her plans to pursue further education and the potential ministry doors that were opening up for her. Her friend proceeded wholeheartedly to warn Eliana not to develop fully her skills and gifting before getting married, because in so doing she would be dramatically decreasing the number of eligible bachelors who might consider her for marriage. According to her friend, "Brazilian men feel threatened by powerful and well-defined women." Eliana valued her friend's opinion, but, upon consideration and reflection on the issue, she decided to go ahead in studies and ministries, trusting that God would provide her with a husband who would join her in ministry instead of feeling threatened, or else that God would give her grace to remain single

10. Sylvia Duarte Dantes DeBiaggi, *Changing Gender Roles: Brazilian Immigrant Families in the United States* (New York: LFB Scholarly Publishing, LLC, 2002), 50–60.

11. DeBiaggi, *Changing*, 45.

and unmarried. In either case, limiting herself to the general understanding that men have a need to feel stronger and more well prepared or well educated than their wives seemed wrong to Eliana, especially when God's calling is clear in a woman's life.

In some more recently established Brazilian Pentecostal denominations, women are allowed and expected to lead and take part in prayer ministries, social ministries, and children's ministries. If women in these denominations demonstrate undeniable preaching or teaching ministry, they are allowed to do so only under the title of "missionary," and never of "pastor" or "minister."

Within the Foursquare throughout the world, however, women are very much accepted in pastoral roles, and many couples are ministering together with both the man and the woman licensed or ordained. It is interesting to note, however, that while the Foursquare maintains a strong acceptance and encouragement of women in leadership roles in the church, it still maintains that this endorsement "in no way alters our convictions regarding the command of Christ to each married woman who is a believer. She is called to live and abide in full righteous acknowledgement of her husband's leadership, just as Sarah did; at the same time, her husband is to lovingly honor her as his wife (1 Peter 3:6)."[12] This position leaves room for a more traditional understanding of gender roles in the family while addressing the difference in the way gender roles are viewed in church leadership. In this way, it seems that the Foursquare has been able to fulfill cultural expectations of the traditional role of males in the home while releasing women into ministry at all levels of leadership within the church.

MINISTERING TO BRAZILIAN IMMIGRANTS IN NEW ENGLAND

How then, if at all, have the Brazilian immigrants to the United States been affected by the broader role of women in United States society? Research has shown that Brazilian immigrants encounter major paradigm shifts in their thinking and value patterns, and, as Sylvia DeBiaggi proved, these shifts often result in moving away from traditional gender role understandings they might have brought with them from Brazil.[13]

---

12. Jack Hayford, "A Pastoral Perspective," *Women in Leadership*, ed. Schell, 21.

13. DeBiaggi, *Changing*, 100.

How has the church been affected, particularly within a denomination like the Foursquare that so strongly supports women in ministry? The answer lies not only in doctrine and American practice, but also in the lives and example of the leaders who have pioneered the establishment of the Brazilian Foursquare churches in the United States.

The story of the Brazilian Foursquare churches here in the United States has a key ministering couple at its heart: Rev. Cairo and Rev. Iracy Marques. In 1962, Pastor Cairo Marques, youth pastor at the Foursquare Gospel Church in São Paulo, Brazil, married Iracy Godoy de Oliveira, who was also licensed in 1967. They ministered together as youth pastors for three years before taking the position of senior pastors at the Foursquare Gospel Church in São Vicente, state of São Paulo. Through the years, they pastored various churches together and were instrumental in bringing quantitative and qualitative growth to all of them. In 1986, Pastor Cairo was invited to pastor the "headquarters church" in São Paulo, which at that time numbered around four hundred. In this pastorate, for the first time in their ministry, Pastor Iracy functioned as one of three associate pastors with a very defined role. From 1986 through 1992, the church grew from four hundred to more than two thousand members.

During this period, Rev. Dale and Rev. Patricia Downs and their children were American Foursquare missionaries in Brazil. A close ministerial and personal relationship developed between the Downs and Marques families. When, in 1989, a Foursquare pastor in Brockton, Massachusetts, noticed the presence of Brazilians in the church's neighborhood, he called Rev. Downs in Brazil and asked him to come to Boston to conduct a firsthand assessment of the possibilities for home missions among the Brazilians in Massachusetts. Upon confirmation of the existence of a great number of Brazilians in Brockton, Somerville, and the greater Boston area, they immediately began looking for a Brazilian pastor to come from Brazil to plant a church in the heart of Somerville, as the Brazilian community was more concentrated in that area.

Their first choice was a Brazilian Foursquare couple who were pastors from the city and state of Rio de Janeiro in Brazil. They had grown children and were willing and able to come. Arriving in New England in the cold autumn weather right out of the hot climate of Brazil, they struggled together to adapt, but the wife had a particularly hard time because her arthritis was aggravated by the cold weather. After only three months in the planting effort, they were forced to call back to the American missionary in Brazil and communicate their decision to move back to Brazil due to the wife's health condition.

The Downs then decided to approach Pastors Cairo and Iracy Marques, Eliana's parents, and ask if they would be willing to come and help "hold the fort" while they tried to find someone else to continue the planting effort. They hesitated to call them because at that time Eliana's parents had many commitments in the local and regional church and also the national denomination, which might make it impossible for them to spend any longer than a couple of weeks away from their responsibilities. However, with a missionary heart and a willingness to dive into a cross-cultural adventure together for the first time, Cairo and Iracy made quick arrangements and took a three-month trip to Somerville in the winter of 1990. Eliana, then twenty years old, came to enjoy a two-week vacation with them in Massachusetts in February of 1990 and returned to Brazil.

At the end of their three-month stay, Eliana's parents returned to Brazil as changed people. Pastor Iracy had initially been resistant to a move to the States, even temporarily, but she came back to Brazil with her heart broken for the Brazilians in New England. Pastor Cairo arrived back in São Paulo with a strong leading of the Holy Spirit that indeed God was calling them to return to Massachusetts in his time for a longer commitment. Soon after, an official invitation came specifically to Eliana's parents from an American Foursquare pastor in Rockland, Massachusetts, another city where Brazilians were beginning to build community. After prayer, they accepted and started the long process of applying for their United States permanent residency visa while still in Brazil, as well as transitioning out of their Brazilian ministerial engagements.

It took some time for the visas to be approved, but, finally, in March of 1993, Pastors Cairo and Iracy arrived in Miami, duly documented. They left everything behind them—a church of more than two thousand members, a national leadership position in the denomination, friends, family, as well as a high salary and benefits—and came to the United States in response to God's call for them to embark on an "adventure of faith," as they called it.

At that time, Eliana was a young single woman living with her parents in São Paulo. Already a licensed minister, she worked with a worship team in the church her parents pastored, with no desire to leave Brazil permanently. During Cairo and Iracy's time of preparation to come to the United States, they asked God to give them three signs of confirmation (like Gideon) in order to be assured that it was really God calling them to leave Brazil. One of the signs they requested of God was that Eliana would agree to come and live in the United States with them, since she was very reluctant to do so. However, Eliana did agree to come ahead of them for a six-month period and make preparations for their arrival. In their private conversations, they used to call Eliana "Johanna the Baptist," because she was going to the United States before they arrived, in order to "prepare the way."

So, when Eliana's parents came in March of 1993, everything was prepared. The relationship between them and the pastor of the Rockland Foursquare Church in Massachusetts was established, an apartment in Weymouth was rented, and Eliana had oriented herself and polished her English enough to be ready to help her parents open a bank account, obtain driver's licenses, and furnish the apartment. By the time her parents were completely settled, Eliana's six-month commitment was complete, and she was ready to pack her bags and return to Brazil. However, during a retreat Eliana attended the weekend before her planned return date, God made it very clear to her that her ministry was to be developed initially among Brazilians in the United States and eventually spread to touch other cultures. Not knowing that one of the signs her parents had requested was that she would stay, Eliana responded to what she now understood to be God's calling for her own life and ministry in the context of the United States and made the decision to stay permanently.

The first years were difficult and very challenging. Adapting and adjusting to a new reality was not an easy endeavor. Moving from São Paulo (a city of seventeen million people) to Rockland (seventeen thousand people) was a shock. Leaving a church of two thousand to pioneer a new one in a town where the Marques family knew absolutely no one was stressful. Adjustments to the American culture and language, weather, food, and lifestyle were difficult while simultaneously trying to reach the Brazilian community in the South Shore of the Boston area. Soon, it was clear that the Brazilian community in Rockland was comprised of Brazilians from diverse roots, from different states in Brazil, and from a variety of social classes and religious backgrounds. In addition to their Brazilian cultural, religious, and class diversity, they were somewhat "Americanized," and it took some time to understand how all these elements worked together, how best to minister to them, and how to find acceptance among them.

Pastor Iracy found it particularly challenging to discover her scope of ministry in the new community. While Pastor Cairo has a strong preaching and teaching ministry, Pastor Iracy thrives in mentoring relationships, discipleship, women's gatherings, and ministry of helps, which were easily carried out in Brazil during weekdays with mothers and with women's groups. Brazilian women in the United States commonly work from the early hours into early evening and many times have barely any strength left to go to church during the week at all. This new situation caused Pastor Iracy to redirect her ministry to be more focused on the ministry of helps than public ministry.

This initial change in Pastor Iracy's ministry was also facilitated by the views of women in ministry by the then-forming Brazilian community in Rockland. For those who were familiar with the Foursquare Church in Brazil, the ministering couple idea was not new, and Pastor Iracy was immediately accepted as the co-pastor of the church. However, for those with Catholic backgrounds and those who came from other denominations, Pastor Cairo was "the" pastor, while Pastor Iracy was "the pastor's wife." With time, the new congregants were able to recognize the "wife's" gifting and calling, as she was continually recognized and affirmed in her ministry by Pastor Cairo.

Pastors Cairo and Iracy came with a goal in their minds and hearts to facilitate the planting of twelve churches and a Portuguese Language Bible Institute in five years. The Somerville Brazilian church they had helped start during their three-month visit was now pastored by another Brazilian minister, and the Rockland Brazilian church was the second official Brazilian Foursquare church in the United States. Later, as Pastor Cairo developed relationships with the Foursquare denominational leaders in the United States, he was instrumental in bringing to official status two other Brazilian congregations that were formed in New Rochelle and Queens, in New York State.

The five-year term commitment that Pastors Cairo and Iracy had with the American church was coming to an end. However, they were directed by the Lord to stay there longer, because God's work through them was not yet done. So, they remained in the United States, and, not long after, things started happening more expeditiously. Five years later, by 2003, seven more churches had been established: Brockton, Plymouth, and Worcester in Massachusetts; one in Newark, New Jersey; and two more in Danbury and Bridgeport, Connecticut.

In 2003, an ICFG initiative to multiply its districts led to the establishment of the New England Portuguese Foursquare District to minister specifically to the needs of the growing number of Brazilian churches, and Pastor Cairo was appointed as supervisor of the newly created district. With more freedom and decision-making authority, "explosion" came, and, from 2004 to 2008, twenty-two new churches were planted. In the same period, two churches were closed.

While it has taken longer than five years to reach the initial objective, a total of thirty-three Brazilian Foursquare Churches in the United States have been planted or officially organized from 1993 to 2008, with thirty-one remaining active: twenty in Massachusetts, two in New York, one in New Jersey, three in Florida, one in North Carolina, and four in Connecticut.[14] Out of the currently fifty-four ordained and licensed ministers in the Portuguese Language District of the ICFG, twenty-five are women. Four of them are senior pastors while the others are serving shoulder to shoulder with their husbands as co-pastors or associate pastors. They perform all the regular activities of a senior pastor, such as water baptisms, weddings, communion, preaching, and teaching in the church. In a time such as this with so many single mothers, separated and divorced women, women working full-time outside the home, and so on, they are indispensable in the ministry.

In practice, the Foursquare value of encouraging and accepting women in leadership roles is experienced at all levels of leadership in the Portuguese Language District. Women are encouraged to pursue their licenses and be a part of the ministry. Some of them are very enthusiastic preachers while others are more comfortable teaching in smaller groups and giving Bible counseling.

REMAINING BARRIERS TO EGALITARIAN MINISTRY

In spite of all acceptance and affirmation of women in ministry and leadership positions, there remains some hesitancy among ministers regarding various aspects of ministering together as husband and wife. The roles women assume in the church are taken for a variety of reasons, and not all based simply on gifting. Some of the women pastors do not feel comfortable preaching because they are still working through issues of what it means to have a more egalitarian ministerial relationship with

14. New England Portuguese District records, March 2008.

their husbands. Even those who have the full support of their husbands hesitate when it comes to public leadership alongside their husbands.

Some of these uncertainties of calling and gifting, as well as obstacles to ministry development, were highlighted at a recent district meeting. In January 2008, the first Portuguese Language District meeting of women pastors and pastor's wives was held. At that meeting, there was an open forum question and answer period with three women pastors on a panel to respond to questions that the participants had written on paper for anonymity. Five out of the seven recorded questions related to their role as women in ministry alongside their husbands:

1. Do you feel lesser than your husband?
2. To what degree do you feel fulfilled as a pastor today?
3. How many times were you introduced as a pastor's wife and not by name?
4. Sometimes I think that my husband does not accept me fully in the ministerial aspect. Sometimes I don't know how to act. What should I do?
5. Have you ever been chastised by your husband by him saying, "Watch what you're going to say; don't embarrass me!"

Although the three women pastors on the panel had only encouragement from their husbands to develop in their respective ministries, they responded as best they could to encourage the women to respect their husbands and at the same time to develop as much as possible for the calling they felt God was placing on their lives. The fact that these questions arose, however, indicates that even within a district where the ministry of women is encouraged, within the nuclear families, the understanding of egalitarian ministry is still being worked out.

In a recent informal survey conducted by the authors with about 50 percent participation from the licensed and ordained ministers in the Portuguese District, it was evident that some patriarchal church leadership concepts are present in the district, but that 78 percent of the respondents made decisions together in the ministry. Percentages show that the ratio of women in ministry within the Portuguese Language District is equal to those of all Foursquare Districts across the United States. The role of women in the Foursquare continues to be strong and continues to be greatly encouraged internationally.

Even within a patriarchal culture, the Foursquare denomination in Brazil (Igreja do Evangelho Quadrangular) has been able to uphold the strong value and tradition of women in ministry. Within the Brazilian community in the United States, and particularly within the New England Portuguese District of the Foursquare Church, these values have been upheld, and this has been made possible largely by the influence of Pastors Cairo and Iracy Marques, who have lived out a pattern for couples in ministry. The result is a vibrant, rapidly growing community of churches and ministries in which both men and women put their hands to the plow and work harmoniously side by side in the harvest field.

APPENDIX A

INTERNATIONAL CHURCH OF THE FOURSQUARE GOSPEL

Age and Gender of All Licensed Ministers and Senior Pastors for the
International Church of the Foursquare Gospel in the United States,
May 1, 2008

Age Level	Licensed Ministers	% Total	Men	% Age Level	Women	% Age Level
20–29	380	6%	238	63%	142	37%
30–39	1022	15%	704	69%	318	31%
40–49	1587	23%	1048	66%	539	34%
50–59	2005	29%	1321	66%	684	34%
60–69	1029	15%	620	60%	409	40%
70–79	498	7%	293	59%	205	41%
80–89	233	3%	103	44%	130	56%
90+	59	1%	20	34%	39	66%
Total	6813	100%	4347	64%	2466	36%

Age Level	Senior Pastors	% Total	Men	% Age Level	Women	% Age Level
20–29	20	1%	18	90%	2	10%
30–39	219	12%	215	98%	4	2%
40–49	520	28%	491	94%	29	6%
50–59	716	39%	672	94%	44	6%
60–69	292	16%	260	89%	32	11%
70–79	45	2%	37	82%	8	18%
80–89	14	1%	12	86%	2	14%
90+	1	0%	1	100%	0	0%
Total	1827	100%	1706	93%	121	7%

The Cause of the Gospel for Men and Women in Europe

Elke Werner and Roland Werner

HISTORICAL OVERVIEW

Europe is an old continent. The gospel has been preached in it for almost two thousand years, right from the time of the Apostles. Paul's mission in Macedonia and Greece and his final preaching in Rome are recorded in the Acts of the Apostles. Early church writings tell of Peter's sojourn and preaching in Rome. With the Christianization of the Roman Empire and the subsequent evangelization of the western, central, northern, and eastern European people—the Celtic, Germanic, Slavic, and Baltic tribes—almost all of Europe had become a Christian continent by the Middle Ages.

So, the gospel is not new to Europe. But just that might be part of our problem. Many questions remain. Yes, the gospel has been around in Europe. But in how far has it really been able to shape European society, or, rather, our various European societies? Yes, there are churches, which have been for centuries in every town and almost every village. But have they really portrayed the truth of the gospel? Or has their message been diluted and reshaped by the cultural, social, and religious traditions of the respective people groups? Yes, there have been revivals and mighty moves of the Holy Spirit. But have they been able to transform in depth all of European culture?

When we look at the history of Europe—or "Western Christendom," as it used to be called—we see that this is at best a can of "mixed pickles." Along with the Christianization first of the Roman Empire and then of the peoples of the North, as the gospel influenced European culture, in equal measure the cultures of traditional societies have exerted their influence on the church.

Christian Europe—European Christianity?

When Europe became a Christianized continent, Christianity also became Europeanized. Church and state coalesced, the life of the church was governed by canonic law, and human hierarchies took precedence over the spirit of communality that marked the early church. As clergy and laity became divided, relationships between men and women also started to change. The primitive Christian fellowship of brothers and sisters was soon changed into a hierarchical system of male dominance. Women were first relegated to lower positions and soon were excluded from church functions altogether.

As Christianity successively became the official religion of the Roman Empire in the centuries after Emperor Constantine stopped all persecutions and declared it as *religio licita* (a permitted or legitimate religion), the church was remodeled on the basis of the governmental principles of the Roman Empire. Subsequently, the church moved rapidly toward a highly developed patriarchal system of government identical in structure to the political empire. With this came the simultaneous stifling and subordination of women.[1] The priesthood and all other offices were now entirely in the hands of men. Only in the institution of the monasteries was there a defined place in society for women. As sisters—or nuns—they were able to take an alternative role in religion to that of housewife and mother—or maidservant, for that matter.

Women's Role in the Church

Although the monasteries were a safe and defined place of worship and service for women, they also limited their ministerial roles considerably. Firstly, the sacraments had to be administered by male priests in all women's convents. Thus, even the "dedicated" women who followed the "spiritual life" were not on an equal footing with men. Most women, housewives, maids, and others who were living in the secular world were

1. Susan Hyatt, *In the Spirit We're Equal: The Spirit, the Bible, and Women: A Revival Perspective* (Dallas: Hyatt Press, 1998), 40. See also the diagrams of corresponding offices of the church and the Empire in Lars Wualben's *A History of the Christian Church* (New York: Thomas Nelson, 1933), 99. We want to acknowledge being helped by Julietten Rautenberg, who made some helpful suggestions.

excluded from any ministry role in the church anyway. Secondly, the ministry of nuns was limited to serving other women, children, the sick, and the poor. Notable exceptions like Catherine of Siena, who was active in the political realm also—for example, she negotiated a diplomatic peace agreement between the warring city-states of Florence and Rome, as well as organizing nuns and monks into teams to nurse plague victims—are just that: exceptions to the rule. Overall, there was little room for teaching or direct pastoral work by women, and, of course, all women, including nuns, were excluded from leading congregations or celebrating the Eucharist (Lord's Supper). "Only that Eucharist which is under the bishop is to be considered valid," states Ignatius in *To the Trallians*. And the bishop, of course, had to be male.

Thirdly, there was a male "counselor" or "master" set over these female convents, indicating that women needed male spiritual guidance. In the middle of the sixteenth century, the Council of Trent ruled "that all of the women's and double monasteries ruled by abbesses had to either join with a male monastery and submit to the rule of a male abbot, or come under the direct control of the male bishop. This was the final stroke eliminating women from the leadership in the church up to that time."[2]

Of course, the female monastic movement also brought forth a number of outstanding Christian women with great leadership gifts, among them Teresa of Avila, Julian of Norwich, Hildegard of Bingen, and Elisabeth of Thüringen. But, it was mainly in renewal movements that the role of women in leadership was reaffirmed. Thus, the "Beghines" of the Lowlands (nowadays Belgium and the Netherlands) formed secular educated women into religious associations in the twelfth to fourteenth centuries. Originally, they started as houses for widows and destitute women. Over time, however, they became associated with the Waldenses, an evangelical pre-Reformation movement, and stood in opposition to proper convents that were subordinate to the papacy. They became a haven for new spiritual life and were often opposed and even persecuted by the Catholic Church, as, for example, in the Inquisition of Toulouse in 1307, when many gave their lives. Eventually, they had to submit to episcopal and papal authority and to accept the rule of St. Francis as binding. From then on, they were permitted again.

---

2. Maria Boccia, "Hidden History of Women Leaders," *Journal of Biblical Equality* (September 1990): 66.

In the Reformation, the two-tier system of spirituality—monks, priests, and nuns being in a higher, truly "spiritual" rank and laymen and laywomen being in the lower rank—was abolished. All states of life and all employments were to be regarded as "spiritual," if offered to God. This new emphasis on the sanctity of secular life reaffirmed the value of women and women's work in everyday occupations as pleasing to God. Still, in the mainline Protestant churches, as in the Catholic Church, women were excluded from actual leadership functions. Preaching and teaching theology continued to be men's work. The Reformation emphasis on the "priesthood of all believers" was more of a theoretical position in contrast to the Roman Catholic Church rather than an actual, real-life model for the ministry of the church. Laymen and laywomen continued to be only second-class Christians in the Lutheran and Reformed established churches. This is reflected by some of the theological underpinnings, which continued within the framework of traditional medieval Catholic theology. Thus, Susan Hyatt reflects on Martin Luther's "Lectures on Genesis" and concludes, "He believed that 'woman was more liable to superstition and occultism,' and he appealed to the apparent rule of female silence (1 Cor. 14:34; 1 Tim. 2:11). Furthermore, he held women responsible for the Fall, and therefore retained the concept of female subjugation."[3] John Calvin also takes a similar stance when he says, "Let the woman be satisfied with her state of subjection, and not take it amiss that she is made inferior to the more distinguished sex."[4]

Some more charismatic or free church movements such as the Quakers in England or the "prophetic" movement of the Camisards in France, which arose out of Protestant environments, carried the Reformation emphasis on all-member ministry to a more logical conclusion and can serve as an exception to this rule. So, Margaret Fell's 1666 treatise, "Women's Speaking Justified, Proved, and Allowed of by the Scriptures," was an apology by a Quaker woman defending the right to speak publicly, prophesy, teach, or preach.[5] As the pietist/evangelical

---

3. Hyatt, *In the Spirit*, 66.

4. John Calvin, *Commentary on the Epistles of Paul the Apostle to the Corinthians* (Edinburgh: Calvin Translation Society, 1848), 361.

5. Margaret Fell, "Women's Speaking Justified, Proved, and Allowed of by the Scriptures, All such as speak by the Spirit and Power of the Lord Jesus. And how Women were the first that Preached the Tidings of the Resurrection of Jesus, and were sent by Christ's own Command, before he Ascended to the Father, John 20:17," *A Brief Collection*

revival started to influence the mainline churches, women experienced greater freedom. Susannah Wesley, Lady Huntingdon, and, later, both Catherine Booth and her daughter Evangeline Booth, who became General of The Salvation Army, can serve as examples of such women liberated to preach, teach, and lead in England. John Wesley, who was heavily influenced by his erudite and fervently pious mother, Susannah, at first stated that women should "exhort" rather than "preach" and have "prayer meetings" rather than "congregations." However, Methodist women went on to "preach" and, faced with their success, Wesley later publicly affirmed and privately encouraged women who had a call to ministry to answer that call.[6] Women such as Erdmuthe Countess of Zinzendorf, Nikolaus Count of Zinzendorf's first wife; Anna Nitschmann, his second wife after Erdmuthe's death; and many others on the continent are also examples of women in leadership positions in evangelical revival movements in the eighteenth century.[7]

The deaconess orders, a Protestant movement of celibate women in organized groups reminiscent of Catholic nuns, arose in the middle of the nineteenth century and grew to include tens of thousands of women, mostly in Germany and other central European countries. This movement helped bring the possibility and rightness of women's ministry to the forefront. It served as an outlet for many gifted evangelical women who for various reasons were not able to marry and still sought a meaningful role in promoting the cause of Christ. Many of these deaconesses and also other women served as youth evangelists, missionaries to foreign countries, nurses, parish workers, and so forth.[8] The nascent nursing profession, for which Florence Nightingale must be mentioned as a pioneer, and missionary work often went hand in hand.

---

of Remarkable Passages and Occurrences Relating to the Birth, Education, Life, Conversion, Travels, Services, and Deep Suffering of the Ancient, Eminent, and Faithful Servant of the Lord, Margaret Fell, But by her Second Marriage, Margaret Fox Together with Sundry of her Epistles, Books, and Christian Testimonies to Friends and Others, and also to those in Supreme Authority, in the several late Revolutions of Government (London: J. Sowle, 1710), 331–50.

6. Stanley J. Grenz, *Women in the Church: A Biblical Theology of Women in Ministry* (Downers Grove, Ill.: InterVarsity, 1995), 43–44.

7. See Edward Langton, *History of the Moravian Church* (London: George Allen & Unwin, 1956).

8. Grenz, *Women*, 49.

The rise of the foreign missions movement, also from about the middle of the nineteenth century, provided another outlet for women determined to serve Christ with all of their lives. Ironically, some of the women who preached to "heathen" men, planted churches, built schools and hospitals, and trained and ordained pastors and bishops were not allowed to preach or teach publicly, and sometimes not even to report on their successful mission work to their sending churches back in their European home countries. Similarly, in the United States of America, as Stanley Grenz notes, the University of Chicago (Baptist), while admitting women to all degree programs, stated, "Women are to receive no encouragement to enter upon the work of public preaching, but on the contrary are distinctly taught that the New Testament nowhere recognizes the ordination of women to the Christian pastorate." This was further emphasized when a dean declared that "women in the divinity school were preparing for pagan pastorates. That is, women could prepare for foreign service among 'pagans' but could not prepare for similar work in North America."[9]

Altogether, however, it must be stressed that evangelical women were liberated for public service well before their mainline church sisters or, for that matter, women in the secular arena in Europe. In North America, five key movements helped to accelerate this process: the Holiness Movement, the Temperance Movement, the Missionary Movement, the Suffrage Movement, and the Healing Movement.[10] Of these, three had their counterparts in Europe; only the emphases of Holiness, Mission, and Suffrage had a major impact there. However, as stated above, the "deaconess movement," which included tens of thousands of women, served as a catalyst to show to the public, both church and general, that women were indeed capable of leadership and public preaching.[11] Often, this was combined with care for the sick at home as the nursing profession increasingly became acceptable. Over time, it was seen as a noble and respectful place that committed Christian women were able to occupy. But, the actual ministerial office did not become accessible for women till the middle of the twentieth century. From then on, most mainline Protestant denominations in Europe—with the exception of Roman Catholic and

---

9. Grenz, *Women*, 60.

10. Hyatt, *In the Spirit*, 145–206.

11. Emanuel Scholz, *Die Frau im Verkündigungs und Zeugendienst der Gemeinde* (Marburg an der Lahn: Verlag der Francke Buchhandlung, 1964).

Orthodox—started to ordain women to full ministry, with the Anglican Church still hesitant to allow women to the Episcopal ministry. In some of the smaller evangelical denominations, this development is still in process.

In spite of great opportunities for women to minister, full-member ministry is still an exception in many churches, and the European church is in need of discovering and affirming the variety of ministry gifts rather than adhering to an unbiblical, twofold or threefold hierarchy of ministries. (While most Reformation churches only differentiate between deacons and pastors, with the bishop being just a pastor with a specific function, the Anglicans and Roman Catholics have three steps: deacon, priest, and bishop). The future of the European church will depend on our capacity to mobilize all of our members to affirmative, positive, and joyful service and witness. The forces of secularization and atheism that arose in the wake of the so-called "Enlightenment" movement are nowhere as pronounced and influential as in Europe. The rise of new religious movements and the growth of Islam are further factors that should not be overlooked. Only a church where men and women, lay and full-time followers of Christ, rise up together to proclaim God's kingdom by life, word, and deed and in the power of the Holy Spirit (Rom 15:14ff) will be able even to attempt to win Europe fully to Christ and thereby complete the task of fully evangelizing this formerly "Christian" and now mostly post-Christian continent . Hope for Europe will not be in vain if the church will liberate the full potential of women and men working together for Christ.

WOMEN IN THE FUTURE CHURCH IN EUROPE

As we have tried to show, women have played an important role in the evangelization of Europe right from the beginning. When the merchant woman Lydia in the European city of Philippi accepted Christ, she opened her heart, her house, and her city for God—and also the continent of Europe. The author of the Book of Acts, the physician Luke, reports,

> On the Sabbath we went outside the city gate to the river, where we expected to find a place of prayer. We sat down and began to speak to the women who had gathered there. One of those listening was a woman named Lydia, a dealer in purple cloth from the city of Thyatira, who was a worshiper of God. The Lord opened her heart

to respond to Paul's message. When she and the members of her household were baptized, she invited us to her home. "If you consider me a believer in the Lord," she said, "come and stay at my house." And she persuaded us. (Acts 16:13–15 NIV)

The drive of evangelism is ever-present with women. They talk to other people about Christ, they raise their children in Christian homes, put up events, and host meetings to evangelize their friends and neighbors. Elke's book, *Frauen verändern ihre Welt (Women Change Their World)*, profiles twenty-two German Christian women and how their lives serve the Lord.[12] Rosie Nixson provides many wonderful examples of the daily lives of women in ministry in her book, *Liberating Women for the Gospel: Women in Evangelism.*[13]

Each generation of women in Europe faces new and different challenges. For our generation, it was the post–Second World War trauma, modernism, abortion, socialism, communism, moral decline, rising numbers of resident Muslims and immigrants, the rise of the esoteric "New Age" movement and alternative religions, and a pervasive liberal theology in mainline churches, feminism, and the sexual revolution, just to name the major ones. What challenges will the future bring for women in leadership? And who are these women of the current generation?

Women in Europe today have enjoyed a good education. Their thinking is often shaped by postmodernism, which claims the individual is the center of the universe. In her book, *Created or Constructed? The Great Gender Debate*, Elaine Storkey goes into great detail in examining women in postmodern reality.[14] More often than in times past, they come from broken families. They are faced with endless expectations and multiple choices in all aspects of life. They are on their way to become "Europeans" rather than just citizens of their own countries, and are well connected with the rest of the world by Internet and media. The European Union and the common Euro currency (since 2002) help to shape a European identity in addition to national and regional identities, which retain their value. Women today live in a world different from the one in which they

---

12. Elke Werner, *Frauen verändern ihre Welt: Wege zu verantwortlicher Mitarbeit und Leiterschaft* (Holzgerlingen: Hänssler, 1999).

13. Rosie Nixson, *Liberating Women for the Gospel: Women in Evangelism* (London: Hodder & Stoughton, 1973).

14. Elaine Storkey, *Created or Constructed? The Great Gender Debate* (Guildford: Paternoster, 2000).

grew up. In the same way, problems in the future will differ from our present problems. A number of factors have the potential to affect the lives of women in Europe.

Environmental Changes, Climate Changes

If global warming continues, the church will have to face doing a lot more work in relief after droughts, floods, or other changes of nature. The church needs to be prepared to help in relief work. It is largely the women who have to bear the brunt of these challenges, as men are often absent from the families by long working hours, work abroad, or also divorce. A large number of women in Europe are single mothers.

Broken Families

Inside and outside the church, many families break up. Single parents need help. Churches need to see this need and become a haven for broken hearts. Counseling, marriage seminars, education seminars, and practical help for single parents are very much needed. A new reconciliation between men and women is needed. Biblical models of communication between genders and biblical standards and counsel for married life, if heeded and applied, can start to make a difference in the lives of many. Teaching men and women what it means to be healthy males and females, and how to start living in stable, respectful, and creative relationships that express mutuality and love, certainly is an important task ahead of us.

Unchurched and Unreached People

In many areas of Europe, several generations have not yet heard the gospel even once presented to them. State-enforced ideologies like "National Socialism" and communism, both of which were anti-Christian, have left their mark on millions of Europeans. This means that, in many instances, evangelism has to start from zero. New forms of evangelism and new ways of explaining and living out the gospel message must be found.

It is a cause for joy that, in many European countries, women are at the forefront of evangelism. In Germany, for example, the women's breakfast movement ("Frühstückstreffen für Frauen") has in the past couple of decades rallied tens of thousands of women in locally organized, evangelistically oriented meetings. These breakfast meetings, often involving several hundred women each, meet in hotels, church halls, town halls, and other venues across the country and draw a very high percentage of unchurched and de-churched women.

Hope for Europe, a coalition of Christian ministries, holds European gatherings of women interested in reaching other women for Christ in their respective countries. In 2005, they organized a congress in Frankfurt, Germany, with ten thousand women present, which served as a tremendous source of encouragement and inspiration and was followed up by many national conferences and initiatives.

Islam and Fundamentalism

Islam has become a challenge in many parts of Europe. Muslim immigrants and European converts to Islam are in danger of being radicalized. The growing influence of Muslim fundamentalists poses a danger to peaceful coexistence and threatens to poison the social atmosphere. Future leaders in the church, men and women, will have to reach out to their Muslim neighbors and bring them the good news of a liberating gospel. Here again, a biblical view of the dignity of women, mutuality and commonality in service for God, and a healthy model for marriage are very much needed. Muslim women in Europe need to see the gospel as liberating for themselves. Men need to see that their identity and worth need not lie in dominance over women.

Intolerance and Media Propaganda

As governments and societies seek to protect themselves against fundamentalist religions, they are in danger of misunderstanding us Christians. Yes, as Christians, we believe in the existence of God and the authority of his word. Yes, we try to follow God's commands and seek to live a life of commitment to Christ. That means that we seek to follow moral and ethical standards that may differ from that of the majority who are informed by other worldviews. But, no, as Christians, we do not fight against those of differing beliefs or lifestyles, we do not kill or kidnap, and we do not hate and persecute. Our agenda is truth spoken and lived out in love. Such truth needs to be emphasized again and again both internally in the Christian church and in our relations with the larger public.

In a pluralistic society, which emphasizes tolerance to the exclusion of absolute truth and values, however, the challenge before us in the future will be to show the love of Christ for everyone and still be willing and able to confront sin and speak up against trends that are against God's will as shown in God's word. We need the courage to call injustice and sin what they are and, at the same time, the strength to love the sinner and the unjust, knowing that it is only the experience of God's grace that sets us apart from others.

In this context, it is only as we regain a truly biblical theology and practice of the place of men and women as equal partners in the kingdom of God that we will be able to be a prophetic voice in our society. Against the propagandistic misrepresentations of Christianity by media guided by anti-Christian values and worldviews, protests alone will not prevail. Only as we show by our love and respect of one another, and, indeed, of all human beings, that Christians are not intolerant, bigoted, or narrow-minded, but are imitators of Christ, captive to his truth and love, will we be able to start communicating with our culture again. Increasing intolerance toward Christianity, endemic in European culture, can only be countered by true humility, love of the truth, and a willingness to forgive even those who, in the guise of tolerance and liberty, tend to be intolerant toward Christians as people who hold to a given set of values and convictions.

The Politics of "Gender Mainstreaming"

Gender justice is in accordance with God's creation of men and women. God never intended one to rule the other. The challenge for the future will be to show that men and women are different, but still both of them reflect the image of God in a unique way. In this, we will have also to stand up against attempts at blurring gender differences. The European parliament ruled in 2008 that there is to be no legal difference whatsoever between heterosexual marriages and homosexual partnerships. This applies to all areas of life, such as the right to inherit, the right to adopt children, and so forth. The guidelines of gender mainstreaming are also to inform educators in schools and universities and are to be applied at all levels of society. The uniqueness of the male-female union in marriage is thus blurred. This both poses a problem to national governments that are forced to comply with European law and also increasingly will cause problems for churches and Christian organizations as it becomes illegal to refuse employment to self-asserting, practicing homosexual men and women, to uphold biblical standards, and to differentiate on the basis of sexual orientation.

While Christian men and women are called to stand for equality and equal opportunity for men and women, they will also need to uphold the differences in the genders, which alone make for meaningful complementarity. Also, they will stand against attempts to blur the image of God, which is reflected in men and women alike and in their complementarity (Gen 1:26ff).

Funding

Many Christian organizations face severe financial challenges. Young people tend to give less to Christian ministry. Because of unemployment and economic crisis, it might be harder in the future to find funds for Christian ministry. In Europe, there are very few women evangelists or itinerant female preachers. They find it even harder to support their ministries than do their male counterparts. On the other hand, there is a willingness on the part of women donors to fund special ministries directed toward women.

Biblical Basis for Women in Leadership

A lot of work needs to be done to explain the biblical foundation of women in leadership inside and outside the church. God has created men and women in his image, has redeemed them in Jesus Christ, has empowered them with his Holy Spirit, and has given them both the task of evangelism and the gifts of the Holy Spirit to use inside and outside the church. The Hope for Europe network, as mentioned before, provides a pan-European platform to encourage women in leadership. The Women's Breakfast movement, also mentioned before, has been used to bring women speakers to the forefront. Increasingly, they are invited to speak to general audiences, too, helping to break down prejudices. Mentoring younger women in leadership and evangelism is very crucial. Student movements such as the International Fellowship of Evangelical Students (IFES/InterVarsity) and their respective national member movements, and also Campus Crusade, are helping in developing women leaders. In some of the international immigrant churches—African and others—in Europe, women pastors are allowed. Often, however, the biblical basis for this biblical practice needs further elucidation and defending.

Opportunities for Growth

These are just a few challenges. But, there are also tremendous opportunities as the Christian church in Europe moves on into the twenty-first century. What is there to be said for the future of women serving in leadership roles in the church? A number of factors are working for a new, more biblical definition of the roles and responsibilities of men and women in the Christian church and in mission to the world.

Firstly, there is the reality of *global connections.* Access to almost immediate communication and the formation of relationships and partnerships around the world can help women to exchange experiences and ideas. Instead of working in isolation, we can learn to become and stay connected and develop working partnerships around the world. Resources can be shared more easily. This is especially possible for European Christians in the West as well as the East, who, after the fall of the "Iron Curtain," now have the opportunity to travel freely.

Secondly, we see a *new openness* for the gospel, especially among the women of Europe. Overall, people in Europe look for answers to the great questions of life. After the demise of traditional religions, the death of ideologies, the revolt against conservative moral standards, and the experience of the shallowness of materialism, men and women in Europe have become more open to the gospel. Yet, the problem remains. Because of the smallness of the evangelical church in many countries and the scarcity of Christian laborers, many have no real opportunity to hear the gospel. The Christian voice is too weak and often not heard. But, we should not become defeatist, but seize all opportunities that are available. In Europe, we still have the freedom to preach, to use the media, to build churches, and to evangelize.

Thirdly, we live in an era of *peace and stability.* Now that the horrible shadows of the two world wars of the twentieth century are beginning to vanish, and after the era of the so-called Cold War in Europe has come to an end, we now enjoy peace in all countries, along with open borders. The European Union is creating new possibilities of interchange and cooperation. This presents great opportunities to commit ourselves to evangelism and a missional lifestyle in which our preaching is fleshed out.

Fourthly, let us hold on to *Europe's Christian heritage,* which was the basis for freedom, tolerance, wellbeing, and stability. Our European Christian heritage continues to be our platform for evangelism and church life. Building on this foundation, European followers of Christ, women and men, can and should invest themselves in education, social work, professional work, politics, media, and all other realms of public life. As committed believers, we can influence trends and moral standards and can help to shape Europe's future. The challenge before us is clear. Therefore, let us cooperate, speak up, love, and work hard, men and women together, each of us using our spiritual gifts and giving our best to the Lord of the harvest, to Jesus Christ himself. He loves us. And he loves Europe—yesterday, today, and in the future. *Amen!*

11

A Long Hard Struggle: The Australian Story and the Australian Churches and Women

Kevin Giles

I N 2006, MY WIFE and I spent a month in England and a month in the United States, places where we have spent extended periods in previous years. What struck us this time was how unlike in quite different ways these two countries were to Australia and how alike in quite different ways they both were to Australia. This observation is foremost in my mind as I sit down to write this chapter. I see my challenge as finding some answers as to why women in Australian culture generally, and why women in the Australian churches in particular, are as they are at the beginning of the third millennium. In attempting to answer these two questions, I must say something about our unique history, our distinctive culture, and our present economic prosperity. It is my premise that the marginalization of women in leadership in Australian society in general, and in the Australian churches in particular, which will be documented in what follows, must be understood contextually.[1]

THE AUSTRALIAN STORY

Australia Today

Australia is a very prosperous nation. Our population has just reached 21 million, but we have the twelfth largest economy in the developed world, and this is expanding. Gross domestic product is increasing and unem-

---

1. I would like to thank three friends, Drs. Janet West, Bruce Kaye, and Muriel Porter, all first-class Australian historians, for kindly reading this chapter and making helpful suggestions, most of which I took up.

ployment decreasing: it is almost down to 4 percent of the workforce. In America in 2006, when I looked around, generally I saw much the same as I saw in Australia. Most of the cars were the same; people were dressed the same; the shops had largely the same things in them. In other words, the standard of living is very similar in Australia and America.[2] Yet, like many other affluent Western countries, there is in Australia much inequality in wealth. The majority shares the riches Australia offers, but we have about a million people who live below the poverty line. This means they have at best no disposable income after paying for housing and food. Australia has an inclusive welfare system that means no one is totally destitute, but those who are entirely dependent on welfare are excluded from "the good life" most enjoy.

Most Australians, 82 percent to be exact, live in large cities, mainly in the six state capitals located on the coastline. It is often claimed that Australia is the most urbanized country in the world. Australia is also a profoundly multicultural society. In figures released in June 2004, 23.6 percent of Australians were born overseas and 43 percent had one or both parents born overseas. In 2004–2005, 125,000 new settlers arrived from nearly two hundred countries. Then there are approximately half a million Aborigines and Torres Strait Islanders who have up to 60,000 years of history on this continent. Large numbers of these have poorer health, less education, fewer work opportunities, and lower rates of home ownership than those who have arrived much later. Successive governments have worked hard and budgeted generously in seeking to rectify this affront to our national life, but with limited success.

In Australia, Christianity has not done well. Today the churches find themselves at the margins of Australian society. Sport, if anything, is the national religion. Only 68 percent of Australians identify themselves with any Christian denomination and, among those under 30, only 44 percent. What is more, in this young age group, only 48 percent say they believe in God. The 2001 *National Church Life Survey* revealed that only 8.8 percent of the Australian population attends church once a week. Roman Catholics make up about 50 percent of attendees, Anglicans 12 percent,

---

2. What is most different, I believe, stems mainly from differing politics. Australia's Westminster system allows for no president with executive powers. In addition, in Australia there is far less political polarization, and we have a public health system that provides first-rate medical care for all and a comprehensive welfare system.

Pentecostals about 9 percent, Uniting Church 8 percent, Baptists 7 percent, Lutherans 2.7 percent, Presbyterians 2.3 percent, and The Salvation Army 1.8 percent.[3] When age is added to the equation, the lower the age is, the lower the church attendance. Some of these churches register growth in numbers, but overall church attendance dropped 1 percent between 1996 and 2001. However, it is not just that church attendance is low in Australia. The influence of the churches on the culture is minimal, and antipathy to the churches is high. Some Australian national leaders speak of their Christian faith, but others confess that they are agnostics or atheists, and this meets with no censure. What is more, the inflow of people of other religions into Australia has not helped the churches. Buddhists and Muslims each constitute about 1.5 percent of the population, but their impact is larger than their numbers, especially in the case of Muslims. Their presence and voice reinforces the view that Australia is not even nominally a Christian nation.

Women make up about 60 percent of church attendees, but they are poorly represented in leadership positions, with several of the larger denominations totally opposed to women's ordination. At one level, women do well in Australian society. Girls do better on average at school than boys, and about 54 percent of university graduates are women. The law forbids discrimination against women and makes equal pay for equal work the rule. Violence against women and rape are publicly and legislatively condemned. Marriage is widely seen to be an equal partnership despite the recognition that most men do not pull their weight as they should. Anne Summers writes, "All around [in Australia] we see women doing wonderful things, powerful things, innovative things. We see women acting and achieving in ways that a generation ago seemed almost unimaginable."[4] However, she goes on to show that "the promise of equality has not been met." The number of women in full-time work has not increased in thirty years; women's total average income is just 66 percent of men's; the number of women on welfare has increased to an unprecedented level; childcare is neither adequate nor affordable for many women; the top

3. John Bellamy and Keith Castle, *National Church Life Survey* (Sydney: NCLS Research, 2001). I say "about 9 percent Pentecostals" because, besides the 7 percent given for the Assemblies of God, the largest Pentecostal church, there are several other smaller Pentecostal churches.

4. Anne Summers, *The End of Equality: Work, Babies, and Women's Choices in 21st Century Australia* (Milson's Point, New South Wales: Random House, 2003), 1.

ranks of the powerful public and commercial institutions remain closed to all but a tiny fraction of women, and violence against women remains at epidemic proportions. Sporting opportunities are freely available to women, but sport in Australia is in reality a man's thing.

Australian History

As in every country, our past bears heavily on the present.[5] Our unique Australian history explains many of our national distinctives. We began as a penal colony. When the First Fleet arrived in Sydney Harbor in 1788, the ships unloaded 548 male and 188 female convicts, the soldiers who would guard them, one Anglican chaplain, and one governor. These convicts were the first of the 160,000 who were sent to Australia before transportation ended in 1868. The colony of South Australia, begun in 1836, was the only one to be settled entirely by free settlers. Somewhat more than half the convicts were poor, working class, nominal Anglicans who in England were alienated from the church, and nothing in the harsh Australian environment, where the clergy were allied with their jailers, ameliorated this alienation. The rest were Roman Catholics deported from Ireland who had a strong hatred for all things English, especially the ruling class and the Anglican Church. They were religious and wanted to have their own priests, but for long years they were denied this comfort, an injustice they did not forget.

If religion had a bad start in Australia, so too did women. For the first fifty years, they were in the minority, and the opportunities for them were limited. With few options available to support themselves, most had to choose between becoming a prostitute or the mistress or de facto wife of a soldier or a convict. When the male convicts got "tickets of leave" (parole) or their freedom, most took up the offer of land and began farming in

---

5. In what follows I am indebted to Anne Summers, *Damned Whores and God's Police* (Sydney: Penguin, 1994, updated edition); Muriel Porter, *Land of the Spirit? The Australian Religious Experience* (Geneva: WCC Publications, 1990); and Janet West, *Daughters of Freedom: A History of Women in the Australian Church* (Sutherland, New South Wales: Albatross, 1997). See also M. Hutchinson and E. Campion, eds., *A Long Patient Conflict: Essays on Women and Gender in Australian Christianity* (Sydney: The Center for the Study of Australian Christianity, 1994); and Stuart Piggin, *The Spirit of a Nation: The Story of Australia's Christian Heritage* (Sydney: Strand, 2004), particularly for the contribution of evangelicals. For a strictly sociological perspective, see A. Black, ed., *Religion in Australia: A Sociological Perspective* (Sydney: Allen and Unwin, 1991).

very difficult circumstances. They had to begin from scratch. A home had to be built, the land cleared, the first crops planted, and the Aborigines kept at bay. The women who went with these men shared these hardships, often with the added burdens of pregnancies, child care, water collecting, and cooking. In this bleak period for women, Caroline Chisholm, who came to the colony of New South Wales in 1838 as the wife of an army officer, stands out. She was horrified by the plight of the free settlers who had begun to arrive, especially the single women. A devout Christian, she gave herself tirelessly and sacrificially to helping mainly the women. She met immigrant ships, took girls into her own home, found work for them, and helped couples who were taking up farms "in the bush."

The Transporting of the Churches

The churches that came to Australia were transplants. The Anglican Church arrived with the First Fleet in the person of the chaplain, the Reverend Richard Johnson. He was given little support by those who sent him out and even less from Governor Arthur Phillip. After five years of waiting for a church building to be built by the governor's order, Johnson built a small one at his own expense in 1793. When the governing council chaired by Governor Philip, four years after the church was built, sought to enforce church attendance and "a more sober and orderly manner of spending the Sabbath Day," a hostile response by soldiers, convicts, and freed convicts culminated in the burning down of the church. Muriel Porter observes, "No single incident in Australia's white past reflects so dramatically the fierce resistance to forced religious observance in this society."[6] It was some years before another church was built.

Richard Johnson and the other Church of England chaplains who followed all came with their precious 1662 Prayer Books along with clergy robes, and in due course they built churches exactly like the ones in the villages of England. First an archdeacon was appointed and then a bishop in 1836, followed by other bishops—all of whom came from England. Representative synods in each colony came next. At first, the Church of England assumed the role of the established church with its chaplains appointed as officers of the crown. This, however, was not to last. The other churches, especially the Catholics, and the largely anti-clerical, unreligious population combined to exclude any special privileges for the Church of

---

6. Porter, *Land of the Spirit?*, 11.

England in Australia. In 1836, "the Church Act" basically put all churches on an equal footing.[7] Each church from then on had to raise the money for its clergy and buildings. Despite this legislative setback, the Church of England in Australia continued to think of itself as "the church" and, as such, attracted the colony elites, the politicians in power, and the upwardly mobile. More women than men attended Anglican churches, but their contribution was limited to arranging the flowers, catering, child care, and the annual church fête, as it was in all the churches in England. Possibly their most important contribution was in raising money. Men were wardens, treasurers, and parish vestry/council members; the male clergy did everything else.

The other English churches soon followed. In 1815, the first Methodist minister arrived, then a Presbyterian in 1823, later still a Congregationalist, more Methodists of several varieties, and then, in 1831, the first Baptist minister. All these clergy also transported the churches they knew in England. Muriel Porter sums up the situation eloquently: "Christianity in Australia was largely planted by homesick people."[8] The English rulers would have liked to exclude Roman Catholic worship altogether from the colony. Eventually in 1803, Father John Dixon, an Irish convict, was given permission to say Mass on Sundays, but, after the Irish convicts rebelled the following year, this concession was revoked. It was not until 1820, when two Irish Roman Catholic priests were allowed into the colony to minister to Catholics, that the Mass was regularly said. Unlike the Anglicans, the Catholics wanted to go to church. Services were well attended and the priests held in high regard. By this time, roughly one-quarter of Sydney's population was Catholic, almost entirely of Irish descent. In the Hobart colony, the priest who was sent there found things more difficult because few of the convicts were Catholics. These priests and their successors also transported the church they knew, and, as a result, Australian Catholicism until recently has had a markedly Irish character. From the beginning, the Anglicans in particular, and all the Protestants a little less so, were hostile to the Catholic Church, so that Catholics continued to feel like outsiders and marginalized. The early decision by the Catholic Church to establish a school in each parish as the first priority added to the hostility and division.

7. Dr. Bruce Kaye informs me that the Anglicans still maintained a few privileges in this act.

8. Porter, *Land of the Spirit?*, 33.

We have already noted that South Australia was the only colony entirely settled by free citizens, but it was unique in other ways as well. The vision of the founding fathers was to establish a colony where there would be no established church. It would be a haven for "dissenters"—Methodists, Congregationalists, Baptists, and Quakers who did not share the privileges of the established church in Great Britain. Among the Protestants to come to the colony were two groups of Lutherans fleeing persecution in Prussia, who added a new dimension to the dominant Anglo-Celtic Australian colonies. Very few Catholics came to the colony, but Anglicans were well represented, and within a few years they were in the majority.

Relations between the Aborigines, who had been on the continent for possibly 60,000 years, and the new white settlers were fraught with misunderstanding and conflict.[9] The settlers believed they were entitled to whatever land there was, and, when the Aborigines showed any opposition or killed a settler's animal, the consequences were invariably fatal for the original inhabitants. The British churches at first were not interested in the Aborigines, and the few early attempts to evangelize them failed dismally.[10]

Education

The way education developed in Australia also helps explain the profoundly secular nature of Australian culture. When Governor Darling tried to establish an interdenominational school system for the colony of New South Wales in the late 1820s, he was met with bitter opposition from the Anglicans and the other Protestants. The idea that the Catholics should be part of the education system was anathema to them. The sharp and bitter divide between Protestants and Catholics thwarted every attempt in each colony to establish a comprehensive state-funded education system. In the end, the state governments found the only option was a completely secular system that allowed the Catholics to keep their schools and other churches to build their own schools, all at their own expense.

---

9. The first chaplain, Richard Johnson, tried to befriend the Aborigines. He adopted a young girl, but after eighteen months she ran away.

10. On Aboriginal missions see J. Harris, *One Blood* (Sutherland, New South Wales: Albatross, 1990) and Piggin, *The Spirit of the Nation*, 44–48. Piggin notes that excellent Australian-based missionary work was undertaken in the South Sea Islands, beginning in New Zealand.

State-funded education for boys and girls would be "free, compulsory and secular."[11] Because the Protestants had no army of virtually unpaid priests, brothers, and nuns to run their schools, their fees had to be high. This meant that the Protestant church schools became the domain mainly of the privileged. This was not the case with the Catholic schools.

The nineteenth-century Protestant/Catholic divide, set in a culture that was predominantly irreligious or at best liberal in matters of dogma, led to the establishment of a secular schooling system and also to secular higher education. All the early Australian universities deliberately excluded theology from their curricula. This meant that churches had to establish their own theological colleges and award qualifications themselves.

The Australian Churches

All the churches in Australia in the late nineteenth and early twentieth centuries continued to be a reflection to a large degree of their counterparts in Great Britain, even if they faced different challenges and found themselves in a more religiously hostile or apathetic context. The pattern was, ministers ministered—and they were all men—and congregations congregated—and they were at least 60 percent women. The one exception to this rule was The Salvation Army, founded in England in 1878. Within two years, it had spread to Australia, commencing work in Adelaide, South Australia. From the beginning, Salvation Army officers (their clergy), men and women, stood on an equal footing. All ranks were open to women: they could preach, and they had full voting rights. General William Booth once said, "The best men in my army are the women."[12]

The Catholic Church stands apart in this period as well. In 1838, the first nuns arrived in Australia, and, from then, other Catholic orders sent nuns to form communities. Most arrived from Europe at the request of one of the bishops, but one order, the Order of St. Joseph, started by Mary McKillop, was home-grown. These women worked in parishes, in

11. Dr. Bruce Kaye, on reading this sentence, pointed out to me that, at that time, the word "secular" meant not controlled by the church, rather than non-religious. The act allowed clergy into state schools to give religious education to children belonging to their denomination.

12. R. Collier, *The General Next to God: The Story of William Booth of The Salvation Army* (London: Collins, 1965), 109.

schools, and in hospitals. Often, they found themselves in conflict with their bishop, who was threatened by their independence and initiative. These women, Janet West says, "established a prototype of the independent woman who as teacher, nurse or social worker had a career in her own right. Such a pattern of female independence was to be passed on through convent education to generations of school girls."[13]

For Christian Protestant women who felt God's call to ministry, only one option was open to them: serving God overseas as a missionary. From the 1820s, women were prominent in supporting early Australian missionary work, and, after 1880, women in growing numbers became missionaries themselves. Soon, the majority of Australian missionaries were single women, while most of the men who went as missionaries took with them wives who equally shared their passion for evangelism no matter what the cost.[14] Training colleges for women missionaries were established, and Bible colleges began accepting women. By the 1930s and for at least a decade after the Second World War, the ratio of three single women to every male missionary prevailed in denominational missions such as the Anglican Church Missionary Society and the Australian Baptist Missionary Society and in independent missionary societies such as the Overseas Missionary Fellowship and the Borneo Evangelical Mission.[15] Women in leadership positions and as preachers on the mission field were not seen as a problem by English or Australian evangelicals. Their approach was pragmatic. The Great Commission to preach the gospel to the whole world was primary. Working with other denominations, using laypeople, and mobilizing women were all acceptable and encouraged.

When these heroic missionary women returned home on furlough, they were seldom invited to preach in church. They might be interviewed or invited to read the Bible, but anything beyond that was exceptional. Their main opportunity to tell of their work was found in one or more of the women's groups that met in the church hall.

13. West, *Daughters of Freedom*, 100.

14. See further "'Woman's Peculiar Mission to the Heathen'—Protestant Missionary Wives in Australia, 1788–1900," in *Long Patient Conflict*, 25–44.

15. Hutchinson and Campion, *Long Patient Conflict*, 366.

WOMEN IN CHURCH LEADERSHIP IN AUSTRALIA

The first woman to be ordained in Australia was Winifred Kiek in 1927. She was an exceptional woman in every way. Before coming to Australia with her husband, an Oxford theologian and Congregational minister, she had gained a first class honors' degree from Manchester University and taught school in the slums of that city. On one occasion, she preached to one thousand men. In South Australia, she completed a Bachelor of Divinity degree and began work as a probation officer with juveniles who came before the courts. It was, however, a long wait of ten years before the next woman was ordained in the Australian Congregational Church.

The next church to consider ordaining women was the Methodist Church. This issue was first brought before a synod in Victoria in 1929. Most clergy were opposed to the idea, and, despite several attempts to make progress, nothing was decided for forty years. It was not until 1969 that the church agreed to the ordination of women. The theological argument was that "the ordination of both men and women is a fundamental implication of the Gospel."[16] In 1977, the Uniting Church of Australia was formed by the coming together of the Methodist, Congregational, and Presbyterian churches, with some Presbyterians deciding not to join. The new church inherited thirty-six women ministers from the three constituent churches.

The Presbyterian Church of Australia first ordained women in 1974 in a move partly motivated by the progress being made in moving toward union with the Methodists and the Congregationalists, who had already ordained women. At first, the continuing Presbyterian Church of Australia was an amalgam of mainly liberal, traditional Scottish churchmen and conservative evangelicals. In due course, the conservative evangelicals gained ascendancy. Women in leadership was for most of them objectionable because they believed the Apostle Paul taught that men and men only were to be leaders in the home and the church. Those of liberal conviction were not convinced by this argument nor were some conservative evangelicals. The evangelicals in particular did not accept this interpretation of Paul or the ignoring of the teaching and example of

16. On the theological rationale for this decision, see G. Thompson, "'It has become clear to us . . .' The Justification of the Ordination of Women to the Ministry of the Word in the Uniting Church of Australia," in Cathy Thomson and Vic Pfitzner, eds., *Interface* 8.2 (Oct. 2005), 21–31.

Jesus. Nevertheless, at the National General Assembly in 1992, a motion was passed by 115 votes to 62 not to accept the ordination of women as ministers of the Word and not to accept the ordination of women as elders. All the state assemblies ratified this decision except for New South Wales; it did not agree to exclude women as elders.

The question of the ordination of women came first on the agenda for Baptists in the late 1960s.[17] Initially, there was very little support, and, in the first vote on the matter at the 1976 New South Wales General Council, a motion in favor was overwhelmingly defeated. Nevertheless, at the Victorian General Council one year later, women's ordination in principle was endorsed, and, in 1978, the ordination of the first woman by the Baptist Church of Australia took place. South Australia followed in 1981, Tasmania in 1990, and New South Wales in 1999. In the 2004 Baptist yearbook, fifty-four women are listed as ordained pastors. Many of these women have, however, discovered that finding an appointment as a pastor is not easy. Two things make the Baptist story a bit more complicated than this synopsis of it indicates. First, every Baptist congregation is autonomous, and so an individual congregation can take its own position.[18] Second, Baptists in Australia tend to make ordination secondary to gifting, asking only that those appointed as pastors be "accredited" by their state union.

The Salvation Army continues its policy of equality in ministry, but, in today's world, many Salvation Army women officers are conscious that, in practice, men tend to be elevated or be given preference over women. On the positive side, women officers have for a long time outnumbered men. In 1986, Australia was honored in the appointment of the second woman general of The Salvation Army, Eva Burrows. (The first was Eva Booth, the daughter of William and Catherine Booth, the founders.) General Burrows' spiritual and administrative leadership of the two million members and 27,000 officers of The Salvation Army found worldwide acceptance and was greatly appreciated. No other church in Australia has been able to match the wide community acceptance enjoyed by The

17. I follow the account given by K. R. Manley, *From Wooloomooloo to Eternity: A History of Australian Baptists*, vol. 2, 1914–2005 (Milton Keynes, UK: Paternoster, 2006), 730–36.

18. This is what Stephen Spence emphasizes. See further S. Spence, "Reading Backwards by Looking Forward: Baptists and the Ordination of Women," *Interface*, op. cit., 86–99.

Salvation Army. The overall opinion is that the Army puts into practice what it preaches. It supports service personnel in times of war, provides for the down and out, speaks out on justice issues, and respects women as full human beings with leadership potential.

Pentecostalism began in Australia in 1908 but remained a small religious movement until the 1970s, when charismatic renewal and new church-planting strategies resulted in burgeoning growth.[19] Today, Pentecostal denominations are third in the number of weekly attendees in Australia and have a much higher proportion of young people than any other denomination. Women leaders were prominent in early Australian Pentecostalism—Sarah Jane Lancaster was the first Pentecostal leader, and she, along with other women, spearheaded the spread of Pentecostalism throughout Australia. This "sisterhood" evangelized, preached, planted churches, led churches, published, and fed the poor. By the 1920s, institutionalization, the influence of fundamentalism, and cultural pressures led Pentecostal denominations to place restrictions on the ministry of women. By the 1930s, leadership was almost exclusively in the hands of men. Apart from the occasional exceptional woman, this situation remained until the 1990s when women began again to find acceptance as leaders. Most Australian Pentecostal denominations have experienced a large increase in the number of women pastors in the past fifteen years—for example, in the Christian Revival Crusade in 1990, just 3 percent of pastors were women, whereas, by 2005, 18 percent were women. This change unquestionably reflects cultural change, but other factors are also involved. The growing persuasiveness of the literature arguing that the Bible does not make women's subordination God's ideal, the desire to return to Pentecostal historical practices, and the work of the Spirit in raising up women for leadership have also played important parts in this change. One interesting development in recent years has been the growing prominence of pastors' wives who now comprise a high proportion of women pastors. It seems their intimate connection with the pastor gives them an authority that other women find hard to attain. In some cases, the leadership of the pastor's wife and other women is justified by the "male headship" principle expressed in the idea that they lead on the basis of the "spiritual covering" given by the male pastor. Despite the increasing numbers of women pastors in Pentecostal churches, very few women are

---

19. I express my thanks to Cheryl Catford for this information.

in charge of a congregation as senior pastor, and very few women are represented at the denominational leadership level.

The Lutheran Church of Australia is strongest in South Australia where its one theological seminary, the Australian Lutheran College, is situated. Australian Lutherans are theologically conservatives. It is often said they stand closest to Missouri Synod Lutherans in the USA. In recent years, the debate about the ordination of women has sharply divided the church. At the 2006 annual synod, 50 percent voted in favor, but, as a two-thirds majority is needed to make this change, the motion failed. Behind this debate in the Lutheran Church lies a very high view of the ordained pastor. He is seen as a successor to the twelve apostles, ordained to preach the Word and administer the sacraments. For many Lutheran conservatives—both social and theological—the idea of giving such weighty authority to women is abhorrent. What has fired the debate is that many of the best theological minds in the church have argued strongly that a hermeneutic based on a few texts from the Apostle Paul is inadequate. What must be given priority in appealing to the Bible is the gospel, which sets people free and empowers.

When the question of the ordination of women was placed on the agenda for the Anglican Church of Australia from 1970 onward, the debate was fierce and prolonged.[20] This church has a national synod, which at that time met every three years, but it does not have the power to force any decision on local diocesan synods. To complicate things even more, the church is deeply invested in three theological traditions, if not four: the Anglo Catholics, the liberal Catholics, and the evangelicals, who in Australia are divided between conservative Reformed evangelicals mainly belonging to the Sydney diocese who were trained at Moore Theological College, and more open evangelicals who were mainly from the Melbourne diocese who had trained at Ridley College. The Anglo Catholics and the Sydney Reformed evangelicals were bitterly opposed to the ordination of women for totally different reasons. The Anglo Catholics found the idea of a woman offering the Mass at the altar an abhorrent one. Only a male priesthood could do this. What is more, to ordain women would break with the Catholic tradition as witnessed to by the Roman Catholic

20. What follows is my personal account of the debate. For a complementary and fuller account, see Muriel Porter, "New Wine in New Skins?—The Ordination of Women and the Anglican Church of Australia," *Interface* 8.2 (2005), 62–73.

Church. The Sydney evangelicals, on the other hand, were opposed because they believed passionately that God had given "headship" to men in the home and the church, and this principle excluded women from being ministers in charge and from preaching or teaching in church. On the other side stood the liberal Catholics who believed that women should not be discriminated against, and the Melbourne evangelicals who had been emboldened by the conclusion reached by their world-renowned New Testament scholar, the principal of Ridley Theological College, Dr. Leon Morris. According to Morris, there were no insurmountable theological or biblical arguments against the ordination of women and many in favor.[21] As a two-thirds majority had to be achieved in the national synod before regional synods could act, both sides were frustrated for years. Neither opinion could gain the necessary numbers. Eventually, in 1992, a motion to ordain women to the priesthood was passed by the General Synod. Most dioceses ratified this decision, but a few of the smaller dioceses took some time to agree to this measure, and a very small number, where Anglo Catholic and social conservatism prevail, have still not acted. Sydney diocese has remained implacably hostile to women in leadership in the church. The only debate allowed in that diocese is between those who believe women should not lead or speak in any church context where men are present, even a home Bible study, and those who believe that women can occasionally preach in church with the male minister's consent and possibly lead a home Bible study. Today, the situation in Sydney diocese for women is bleaker than it ever has been, yet the diocese flourishes as great emphasis is given to evangelism and church planting. The diocese sees significant growth each year.

Now the debate has moved to the consecration of women bishops, and the conservative forces have again organized to block this move. Even if this battle is won, possibly on constitutional grounds, the Sydney diocese has said in advance that it will never accept women bishops. Always its opposition is based on the view that the Bible permanently subordinates women to men. Men have been given "headship" by God.

One interesting sidelight to the Sydney Anglican situation is that, in February 2007, the diocesan magazine, *The Southern Cross*, published a special edition asking why Sydney Anglican churches had exactly the same

21. Leon Morris, "The Ministry of Women," L. Morris, J. Gaden, and B. Thiering, *A Woman's Place* (Sydney: Anglican Information Office, 1976), 19–32.

percentage of women (60 percent) in their congregations as Anglicans elsewhere in Australia and most other denominations in the nationwide Australian church. The contributors were puzzled by this fact, because the argument had been for twenty years that, if women were allowed into the pulpit, women soon would be in the majority. On this basis, the leadership of men and men only had been promoted. The only solution with which the contributors to this magazine could come forward was that more manly men were needed as ministers. More testosterone was the answer. The possibility that male-only leadership in the church might attract women and be a deterrent to many men who did not appreciate being bossed around like a child by another man was not even hinted at. The male drive to lead/dominate, especially when women are present, that makes ordination so attractive to young men, was also not commented on.

Closely allied with the Sydney Anglicans is the Australian Fellowship of Evangelical Students (AFES), the largest student ministry in Australia, working in thirty-two universities and in contact with more than four thousand students at any one time. AFES has sixty-eight senior staff workers, twenty-one of whom are women and forty-seven of whom are men, and another fifty-one "apprentices"—staff workers in training.[22] Evangelism is the primary focus, and many students become Christians each year through the AFES. Next in importance for the AFES are biblical teaching and apologetics. When I was actively involved with the AFES thirty years ago as a university chaplain, AFES was a thoroughly egalitarian lay movement. This is now changed. Under the dominant influence of Moore College–trained men, AFES today promulgates a very strong "male headship" theology taught by the clergy who dominate the movement. This is highly significant for the life of the churches, because the many young men nurtured in the AFES who go on to study for ordination assume the premise that God has ordained only men to lead.

The Australian Catholic Church, like every part of the Roman Catholic Church in the world, is bound by Papal rulings. In 1994 in his apostolic letter, "On Reserving Priestly Ordination to Men Alone," Pope John Paul II declared that, because the twelve apostles were all men, the church had no authority to confer priestly ordination on women.[23] A male

22. Information given by Richard Chin, AFES national director.
23. John Paul II, "On Reserving Priestly Ordination to Men Alone" (Homebush, New South Wales: St Paul's, 1994).

priesthood, he pointed out, was "the constant and universal tradition of the Church."[24] For this reason, he ruled that the ordination of women to the priesthood was not a matter open to discussion or revision. Before that time, the ordination of women to the priesthood had been much debated by Australian Catholics, because the declining number of priests was seen as a growing threat to the viability of the church. The Pope's 1994 ruling left Catholic conservative laity, priests, and bishops relieved and the progressives frustrated and angry.

At one level, the contribution of women to the life of the Australian Catholic Church has gone backward because, beginning from the 1960s, the army of nuns that once ran the Catholic schools and hospitals and did pastoral work in the parishes has steadily declined and now has all but disappeared. However, at another level, women have become more prominent. To cope with the decreasing number of priests, many women have been appointed to significant leadership roles as parish pastoral associates in Australian Catholic Church parishes. It is not at all unusual for a Catholic to go to church and find a woman leading a liturgy of the Word, with or without communion, or to have communion brought to one in a nursing home, hospital, or sick bed at home by an authorized lay woman, or to telephone the parish office and be referred to the parish administrator, a woman.

RESPONSE

In the face of the widespread institutional opposition to the ordination of women by the larger churches in Australia, a significant number of Australian Roman Catholic, Lutheran, and Evangelical theologians in the mainline churches have not been convinced by the arguments used to uphold the status quo. They have been particularly critical of the claim that the Bible forbids women to be ordained. They have sought to show that this argument is special pleading. Some of the best work on the Bible has been done by Catholics,[25] but each of the Protestant churches has had evangelical theologians who have argued that the Bible endorses the leadership of women. I have written more on the biblical case for equality than anyone

---

24. "On Reserving Priestly Ordination to Men Alone," 7.

25. For example, see F. J. Maloney, *Woman First Among the Faithful: A New Testament Study* (Melbourne: Dove, 1984); B. Byrne, *Paul and the Christian Woman* (Homebush, New South Wales: St Paul, 1988).

else. In 1977, I published, *Women and their Ministry: A Case for Equal Ministries in the Church Today;*[26] in 1985, *Created Woman: A Fresh Study of the Biblical Teaching,*[27] and in 2002, *The Trinity and Subordinationism: The Contemporary Doctrine of God and the Gender Debate.*[28] As well, I have written numerous articles and debated with evangelicals of opposing views in church papers.[29]

26. Melbourne: Dove Communications, 1977.

27. Canberra: Acorn, 1985.

28. Downers Grove, Ill.: InterVarsity, 2002.

29. Following most evangelical egalitarians, my case is as follows:

- In creation, God made man and woman alike in his image, and to both alike he gave rule over the world. This indicates that, in the created order, man and woman are differentiated yet equals in being and authority.

- Gen 2 does not contradict Gen 1. Created second, or woman as man's helper, does not imply the subordination of women.

- The subordination of women is a consequence of the fall (Gen 3:16). It is an expression of sin.

- Jesus in word and deed affirmed the equal value and leadership potential of men and women. The twelve apostles were all men, but no teaching is given on this mute historical detail. In the patriarchal world of Jesus' day, we would expect community leaders to be men. What is noteworthy are Jesus' affirmations of women.

- Paul's theology of ministry is predicated on the *charismata* (spiritual gifts) given to men and women indiscriminately. His theology is reflected in practice. Paul commends women leading in prayer and prophecy in church (1 Cor 11:3); he speaks of a woman apostle (Rom 16:7); he has women "coworkers" (Rom 16:3, 7; Phil 4:3) and women house church leaders (Col 4:15).

- The three texts that restrict women in some way (1 Cor 11:3–16, 14:33–34; 1 Tim 2:11–12) are all read as apostolic directives seeking to correct behavior by women that was causing offense. The first passage actually speaks positively of women verbally leading in church, simply asking them to cover their heads when they do so.

- The apostolic exhortations to wives and slaves to be subordinate are of the same nature and intent (Col 3:18—4:1; Eph 5:21—6:9; 1 Pet 2:18—3:7). None of them is grounded, nor is 1 Tim 2:11–12, on a creation-given hierarchical social order that is unchanging and unchangeable. First Timothy 2:13 says that woman was created second—these words speak of *chronological* order, not hierarchical social order. In Eph 5:31, Paul does quote Gen 2:24, not to ground woman's permanent subordination in creation, but for just the opposite reason: to stress that, in

As one thinks about the future, it can only be hoped that, when the current church leaders in the Anglican, Lutheran, and Presbyterian churches who have so bitterly opposed the leadership of women retire, fresh thinking informed by a holistic reading of the Bible, as I have outlined it, will prevail. At the moment, there is no movement and absolutely no willingness to discuss afresh what the Bible actually says on the status and ministry of women. One ray of light is the Pentecostal church, the church with the best growth in Australia. It has never had a dogmatic stance against women leading because it has always allowed room for women led by the Spirit to step forward. At present, I am an adjunct professor/teacher at Harvest College in Melbourne, a large Assemblies of God seminary. It is college policy to affirm women in leadership, and, to ensure it, teaching on this matter is given to students.

CONCLUSION

In Australia today, women are fully involved and respected members of society. Most are well educated, articulate, smartly dressed, car-driving human beings. Generally they say they are content with things as they are, even if they wish the "boys" would grow up a bit and in the home do their share of the housework, and, if there are children, do more with them. This widespread contentment by women with things as they are, which annoys committed feminists, allows the prevailing myth that in Australia men and women are "equal" all too often to go unchallenged. The truth is Australia is still very much a man's world. Most top jobs go to men, men on average earn more than women, a much higher percentage of women

---

marriage, man and woman are one.

- When Paul says the man is "the head of the wife" (Eph 5:23), he is speaking of the husband's "leadership," but he then goes on to redefine what this involves in a Christian marriage. It does not involve being served, or having control, or even the casting vote. It is all about *agapē* love. The husband is to lead by serving, even to the point of giving his life for his wife as Christ did for the church.

- In this outline of biblical teaching, the idea that men and women are differentiated simply by "roles" is emphatically rejected. We do not just play out our sexual identity. God has made us men and women. "Role" terminology belongs in the theater and to humanistic sociology texts, not to the domain of biblical theology. I most fully spell out my holistic reading of the Bible on women in *The Trinity and Subordinationism*, part 2.

are on welfare, large numbers of women face violence in the home, and sport remains predominantly a "boys'" thing.

When it comes to church life, there is no room for debate. Women are not equals. They are more in number but less in power and influence. Australian churches are basically bastions of male privilege. Why women acquiesce to this is a mystery to a mere male. Possibly more Christian women are hostile to women in leadership than are men. However, what happens in the church is not of much interest to the majority of Australians. Ninety percent are not involved. One reason for this is that the church in Australia does not stand out as a bright beacon where things are really different on many important matters. Too often, the churches simply reflect the culture, and sometimes the culture at its worst. Nowhere is this truer than with women. When the culture changed and began according equality to women, which most Australians thought was a huge step forward, the churches generally, and evangelicals in particular, decided to take another path. They insisted that women should not be ordained. In the church, they were not equal with men. For those evangelicals who excluded women from ordination because they believed God had given leadership to men and not women (the so called the male "headship" principle), this inequality also extended to the home.

Why Australian church leaders have shown such "intransigent opposition to female ordination" and opposed this move with such "emotional intensity" is an interesting question. The biblical arguments to support it have been tested and shown to be invalid. Stuart Piggin argues that it discloses distinctive elements of the Australian male psyche, a product of Australia's unique history and culture.[30] From the beginning of European settlement, Australia was a man's world. Women had to fit in as best as they could. Over time, what was an historical reality became a cultural presupposition, a presupposition very much under challenge at the beginning of the twenty-first century. The last to see that change is demanded have been Australian church leaders.

30. "From Independence to Domesticity: Masculinity in Australian History and the Female Ordination Debate," in *Long Patient Conflict*, 151–60, quotes p. 158.

12

Biblical Equality in the United States: Signs of Hope and Difficult Challenges

Roberta Hestenes

OVERVIEW

OVER THE LAST CENTURY, accelerating since the 1960s, much of American culture has become visibly and legally open to equal opportunities for women alongside of men in education and employment in both public and private sectors of society. In a country where self-professed Christians make up more than 76.5 percent of the United States population,[1] the changing nature of women's experiences in the home and marketplace interacts with elements of both church and society in complex and dynamic ways. Women work as governors and legislators, astronauts, chief executive officers (CEOs), small business owners and merchants, faculty members and administrators, soldiers, firefighters, and police officers, as well as homemakers, teachers, and service providers in a multitude of different settings. Women are visible as politicians, news reporters, and school bus drivers. Two-income households are common, and sexual discrimination has become illegal in most workplaces. Women now serve as presidents of Harvard, Yale, and the University of Pennsylvania, three of the most prestigious institutions of higher education in America. Female students outnumber male students in most colleges and universities, and they are entering graduate schools of law, business, science, medicine, and other professions in increasing numbers.[2] Disagreements over appropri-

1. "Top Twenty Religions in the United States, 2001," http://www.adherents.com/rel_USA.html#religions (accessed 2008).

2. Mark Mather and Dia Adams, "The Crossover in Female-Male College Enrollment Rates," Population Reference Bureau, http://www.prb.org/Articles/2007/CrossoverinFe

ate male and female roles persist, as do discriminatory practices, negative cultural stereotypes, and sexual abuse and violence. Overall, though, the possibilities for women in American society have expanded enormously during a time of rapid cultural change. Christian women participate in this dynamic culture even as they recognize both positive and negative forces within it. When Christian women serve as "salt" and "light" in so many contexts, this can be seen as a major possibility for Christian witness and for accomplishing good throughout American life.

Over the same time period, openings for women to serve freely and fully in and through the American church and its institutions have grown in somewhat contradictory ways. While the larger culture has tended to focus on demanding equal rights for women, change efforts within the church have often emphasized the need and desirability of recognizing women as created equally in God's image and called equally with men to salvation and all forms of service. Major groups of Christians have acted to remove barriers and provide new opportunities for women through ordination,[3] while other large parts of the American church continue to maintain the necessity of male leadership with formal and informal restrictions on women's activities. Numerous Protestant denominations and thousands of congregations now officially accept and employ women in all types of ministry on the same basis as their male colleagues. But, even as they do so, the meaning and status of ordination itself is shifting within the democratization of American Christianity.[4] Opponents of expanding roles for women not only defend their positions by various biblical arguments, but often cite a need to counterbalance an increasing secular and sexualized culture with high rates of divorce by promoting traditional patterns of marriage and church life. The religious authority of women continues to be an open issue.[5] A woman sensing a call to ministry today may be welcomed and encouraged or challenged and

maleMaleCollegeEnrollmentRates.aspx (accessed 2008).

3. Barbara Brown Zikmund, Adair T. Lummis, and Patricia M. Y. Chang, *Clergy Women: An Uphill Calling* (Louisville, Ky.: Westminster John Knox, 1998), 106–13.

4. Zikmund, Lummis, and Chang, *Clergy Women*, 106–13; Mark Chaves, *Ordaining Women: Culture and Conflict in Religious Organizations* (Cambridge, Mass.: Harvard University Press, 1997).

5. Rebecca Rosen Lum, "Women Fight for Religious Authority," *Contra Costa Times* (Walnut Creek, Calif.) 22 July 2007, A25; Adelle Banks, "Women Clergy Mark Milestones, yet Obstacles Remain," Presbyterian News Service, http://www.pcusa.org/pcnews/2006/06519.htm (accessed 2008).

discouraged, depending on where she finds herself in her particular faith community with its history, policies, and practices. Gaining understanding and perspective on the bigger picture within and beyond one particular congregation or faith community can be important in sorting out how to move forward in following Christ. The interaction between church and culture is inevitably complicated, and the influence and impact of forces supporting and opposing the treatment of women as fully equal, both spiritually and functionally, are still only partially understood.

HISTORICAL ISSUES

There have been women preachers in America since the seventeenth-century arrival of Quaker women in the early colonies, many of whom were severely persecuted, even killed, for testifying to their radical form of Christian faith.[6] By 1740, there were more than 1,400 women preachers in British North America speaking with great fervor in pulpits, streets, and fields during the dramatic religious revivals of the first Great Awakening. Methodist, "new light" Presbyterians, Congregationalists, and even Baptist women in Connecticut and elsewhere were among the women preachers of the first and, later, the second Great Awakening. As the fires of revival died down, so did the large numbers of women preachers who had given enthusiastic witness to their faith, but who had not sought equality in the formal structures of the church.[7] Some of these women and their spiritual descendants became leaders in the abolition movement against slavery, launched and sustained the first feminist movement, then later went on to found numerous societies for social betterment that had a major and permanent impact on American life.

Among the results of revival was the founding of Oberlin College in Ohio by abolitionist Presbyterians and Congregationalists in 1833. With leading revivalist Charles Finney as its second president, Oberlin became the first college in America to admit African Americans regularly as students and to become coeducational. Even though Oberlin initially

6. Rebecca Larson, *Daughters of Light: Quaker Women Preaching and Prophesying in the Colonies and Abroad, 1700–1775* (New York: University of North Carolina Press, 1999), 14.

7. Louis Billington, "'Female Laborers in the Church': Women Preachers in the Northeastern United States. 1790–1840," *Journal of American Studies* 19 (1985); Aaron Spencer Fogleman, *Jesus Is Female: Moravians and Radical Religion in Early America (Early American Studies)* (Philadelphia: University of Pennsylvania Press, 2007), 81–87.

withheld her degree, graduate Antoinette Brown preached regularly and was called by a congregational church, where she became America's first ordained clergywoman in 1853. When abolitionist women were repeatedly scorned and denied their right to speak out publicly against slavery, the first women's rights movement was born and grew, even in the face of strong opposition.[8] During the tumultuous decades of abolitionist debate, civil war and its aftermath, and crusades for temperance and other social reforms, feminist women and men began to reexamine the Scriptures commonly cited in defense of traditional male predominance. They challenged traditional interpretations of crucial texts concerning God's will for women and published and distributed their conclusions.

Many of those who came to understand the Bible as supportive of women's rights in church and society continued to affirm a high view of biblical authority as normative for faith and life. They actively declared their faith in Christ as they organized and challenged restrictive practices that treated women as inferior or second-class citizens. Efforts to change congregational and denominational policies that favored men and excluded women were met with strong resistance, but some change began. Enterprising Christian women began their own organizations and mission societies within and outside of existing Christian structures when they found doors to service and outreach closed to them because of their gender. This first feminist movement was strongly Christian in its origins and proponents, and the impact of the movement was broad and deep in American life, probably reaching a cultural climax in 1920 when women finally gained the right to vote in national elections.

Most historic Protestant denominations and communions, with the major exception of groups like the Southern Baptists, Missouri Synod Lutherans, and theologically dispensational independents, have removed the formal rules prohibiting the ordination and calling of women to all positions in the church.[9] They have become increasingly open and officially nondiscriminatory toward women even though informal patterns favoring male leadership persist. The numbers of women clergy are

---

8. For a brief historical overview of the history of evangelical feminism, see Rebecca Merrill Groothuis, *Women Caught in the Conflict: The Culture War between Traditionalism and Feminism* (Grand Rapids: Baker, 1994), 31–64.

9. For a partial list, including forty-four denominations and the dates they granted full clergy rights to women, see Chaves, *Ordaining Women,* 16–17.

growing dramatically.[10] After thirty-seven years of struggle, The Christian Reformed Church has become one of the most recent of more than eighty denominations to remove the last constitutional barriers to women as elders and clergy with voting power in the governing bodies of the church.[11] Positive and enthusiastic responses and support for women serving as Christian leaders are notable across the United States. Yet, among holiness churches and Pentecostals who officially recognize women, including more than one thousand women clergy in the Assemblies of God, there are lower numbers of women clergy today than there were fifty years ago in spite of a small recent upward trend. Significant opposition to women being treated as fully and functionally equal to men in marriage and in the church continues to exist within the large conservative, or evangelical, movement in America.[12] In its congregations, women are denied pulpits, podiums, and worship leadership as battles over women's "place" sharpen and intensify. Many congregations refuse to acknowledge or address the existence or possibility that any sort of equal rights or serious efforts to welcome women's leadership gifts could be biblically based, theologically sound, or practically beneficial.

During the last few decades, tens of thousands of women have become elders, deacons, pastors, and officially recognized leaders in Christian congregations, institutions, and denominations while some conservative or evangelical church bodies have tightened their standards against informal as well as formal leadership roles for women. A few women have risen to the highest positions in their communions. Bishop Vashti McKenzie became the first woman bishop of the African Methodist Episcopal Church in 2003. Katherine Jefferts Schori was consecrated in 2006 as the presiding bishop of the Episcopal Church in America. Sharon E. Watkins serves as the president of the Christian Church (Disciples of Christ). Examples of women's progress include the twelve bishops and almost 12,000 women (27 percent of the whole) who have been ordained as clergy within the United Methodist Church alone. Women make up about 25 percent of active clergy in the Evangelical Lutheran Church of America and have grown to more than three thousand in the Presbyterian Church,

10. Banks, "Women Clergy Mark Milestones, yet Obstacles Remain."

11. "Christian Reformed Ok Female Ministers," *Christian Century* (10 July 2007): 14.

12. Throughout this paper, these terms are used in their common popular meanings rather than as precise categories of differentiation.

USA. Across the country, about six hundred women have been ordained in Baptist churches, with a surprising, though minority, number of them in Southern Baptist churches. It is no longer unusual for women to serve as solo pastors in small or struggling churches while larger churches with multiple clergy on staff often include at least one ordained woman in the mix.

TIMES OF ENCOURAGEMENT

During the later years of the first wave of feminism, large numbers of conservative Bible institutes and schools were founded with high percentages of women students who were equipped and sent out to become evangelists, church planters, social reformers, and a major force in the great expansion of worldwide missionary activity. American women missionaries, both single and married, went courageously and faithfully all over the world as powerful witnesses to the gospel of Jesus Christ.[13] Holiness and Pentecostal women emerged as gifted and authorized leaders in the early decades of the founding and growth of their movements. Whether officially sanctioned or not, inside their homes and beyond them, Christian women have always been integral to the life, growth, and impact of Christianity in America. Women form a majority of the membership of Christian congregations in America and have always been important contributors to the progress of the gospel in their families, churches, and communities as well as in worldwide missions. Every Christian community has its history of women of courage who moved forward in faith in spite of the problems they faced.[14] One encouraging sign of hope today is the way in which this exciting history of women's contributions to the cause of Christ is being recaptured and made available in scholarly studies and publications by new generations of biographers, scholars, and researchers. More research, publication, and widespread distribution of this great legacy is still needed. Knowing and building on the work that other committed Christians have done rather than starting all over again

13. Janette Hassey, *No Time for Silence: Evangelical Women in Public Ministry around the Turn of the Century* (Grand Rapids.: Academic Books, Zondervan, 1986). This book is especially helpful on the little-known history of the Moody Bible Institute and similar conservative Bible schools of the period.

14. A recent resource on the history of women in a large African American denomination is Anthea D. Butler, *Women in the Church of God in Christ: Making a Sanctified World* (New York: University of North Carolina Press, 2007).

in each new generation is an important ingredient in making positive changes that endure.

The beginning of the Evangelical Women's Caucus in 1974 by members of theologically conservative but socially progressive Evangelicals for Social Action brought women with evangelical backgrounds together, along with a few supportive men, to encourage sustained efforts to promote egalitarian relationships among women and men and to discourage female passivity. This effort has seen rich results, even though the original membership divided over the issue of homosexuality in the mid 1980s.[15] In 1987, the conservative Council on Biblical Manhood and Womanhood was organized to uphold male headship over women in home and church as a biblical requirement. In the same year, Christians for Biblical Equality (CBE) was formed to support mutuality and partnership among Christian women and men. Today, CBE includes members from more than eighty denominations "who believe that the Bible, properly interpreted, teaches the fundamental equality of women and men of all ethnicities and economic classes based on the teachings of Scripture. . . ."

There are other reasons for encouragement. Over the last forty years, women have entered theological seminaries in record numbers, often making up one-third to one-half of the student population in their desire to prepare for Christian service. Many biblical and theological scholars, including increasing numbers in traditionally conservative and evangelical seminaries and colleges, have become convinced of the scriptural foundations for mutuality within Christian marriage and biblical equality in all aspects of church life. Some have been willing to risk or lose their positions because of these convictions. There is also a slow growth in the numbers of women serving in positions of influence in Christian higher education as faculty members, deans, provosts, and presidents. Women exercise influence as authors and speakers and lead several large ministry organizations that equip women and men as Bible teachers and small group leaders. These ministries help to educate part of an American population that has been characterized by respected researchers, such as George Gallup, Jr., and George Barna, as biblically illiterate and spiritually immature.

---

15. For a thorough and detailed analysis of the issue of homosexuality and the Evangelical Women's Caucus, see Pamela D. H. Cochran, *Evangelical Feminism: A History* (New York: New York University Press, 2005), 77–109.

CONTEMPORARY ISSUES

Although women enter clergy and pastoral positions in greater numbers, their experiences differ widely. The most positive experiences seem to occur in congregations or organizations that choose "a woman we know" to take up an enhanced or new role traditionally assumed by men. Such a woman has often grown up or been converted within the church family and exhibits acceptance of important core values as she demonstrates her competence and willingness to work hard to meet the needs of people. External credentials like theological study and degrees, preaching and teaching invitations, and volunteer service can enhance her acceptance within her home faith community. Making a successful transition outside of or beyond the initial community of acceptance can be hard to navigate. Many women benefit from creating or joining strong networks that include well-respected and influential people where their passion and gifts can become more widely known and commended. Seeking or responding to invitations to serve as conference speakers, volunteer board members, or occasional seminar leaders or faculty members give women increased visibility and credibility.

Women clergy, even when chosen and welcomed, still face difficulties beyond the ordinary problems that accompany any ministry assignment.[16] Pockets of resistance to female leadership can take any of the issues that routinely challenge congregations and institutions and turn them into informal or formal referendums on the suitability of female leadership. Anonymous letters, threats of withdrawal of financial support, gossip, and personal attacks make ministry more difficult in any circumstances. Single women serving in small towns or rural locations can be lonely. Low compensation and minimal benefits are the reality for many women who serve in tiny or small, yoked or struggling congregations or in parachurch youth ministries with few possibilities of upward mobility comparable to male colleagues with similar backgrounds, training, and experience.

Probably the most difficult reality for parish women clergy is the lack of openness to women as senior pastors in large multiple-staff churches, even when women have the necessary vision, gifts, experience, and skills to serve well. Getting the first and second job, or interim positions, in a

---

16. Julie Ingersoll, *Evangelical Christian Women: War Stories in the Gender Battles* (New York: New York University Press, 2003), 61–96.

church can be relatively easy. But trying to break through the glass ceiling, which keeps women out of the highest or most influential positions, can be difficult, if not impossible.[17] Congregations appear to have less trouble when women become leaders as "sisters" serving under a male "father" who is senior pastor or bishop than when women seek to fill such roles themselves. Traditional patriarchal family patterns and system dynamics exert a powerful influence, whether forthrightly defended or unrecognized and unacknowledged, over very long periods of time. When the typical challenges of any church ministry also include reduced mobility or unfair accusations of selfish ambition, lack of affirmation, the demand for experience and success without providing a way to obtain that experience or resources to succeed, or clear marginality within "old boy" networks, talented women can be discouraged from beginning or continuing to serve in church ministry. Those who pioneer and persevere deserve respect, resources, and help.

In summary, the long journey toward full equality and acceptance for women has met with some encouraging success along with strong continued opposition and some setbacks. The fulfillment of Christ's great commission in Matthew 28 is not possible without the full engagement and deployment of the spiritual gifts and abilities belonging to all members of the worldwide body of Christ, female and male. The challenges of mission and ministry are too great, and the need to reach billions of suffering and lost people is too demanding, for women to be excluded or restricted from exercising their callings and using all of the gifts that God has given them. There is a continuing risk that traditional teaching and severe limitations placed on women who offer their gifts for service will damage evangelistic outreach among new generations of women outside of the church who need to know that the gospel is good news for them. Much is at stake. With all the progress that has been made, the need remains to recognize and work to overcome major obstacles that still discourage many women in their desire to follow Christ with the full blessing and support of the church. It will take continued faith and confidence in God, courage and the willingness to take risks, increased research and education, persistence, and advocacy if the American church

---

17. For a study of two southern women pastors who broke through the stained glass ceiling, see: Sally B. Purvis, *The Stained Glass Ceiling: Churches and Their Women Pastors* (Louisville, KY: Westminster John Knox, 1995).

is to be transformed into a more complete reflection of Jesus Christ and a sign of God's kingdom "on earth as it is in heaven."

IT IS NOT FINISHED

The increasing acceptance of women in ministry can be interpreted as meaning that efforts are no longer needed to work for change. Young women seminarians can be tempted to believe that the struggle for equality has been fought and won.

It is sobering to note, however, that most of the growth in the acceptance of women exists in denominations that, while still maintaining millions of members, are significantly declining in membership and societal influence. Further, many of these same denominations are now sharply divided or threatening to be torn apart over the issue of ordaining gays, lesbians, the bisexual, and transgendered (GLBTs) to the pastoral offices of the church. For biblically conservative women affected by these debates, it is particularly painful to see issues of women's ordination and the ordination of gays and lesbians joined together as if they were identical. There are many passages and examples in Scripture that can be understood clearly and directly as affirming women in ministry, alongside are a few notable texts that seem, on the surface, to limit women and thus demand careful study and respectful dialogue. Biblical feminists disagree with the intertwining of these issues because of the difference in the texts and the way they are used to support these very different struggles for change. There are no texts in Scripture, in either the Old or New Testaments, that affirm gay or lesbian sexual behavior, and there is a consistent collection of texts from both the Old and New Testaments that treat such behavior as sin along with other forms of sexual immorality and other kinds of sin, such as greed and idolatry. Christian women who have experienced hostility and discrimination in the church often are offended by speeches and actions expressing ungodly hatred and disgust toward homosexuals. Even so, they seek to uphold biblical standards for godly living while desiring to love God and their neighbors.

THE CUTTING EDGE

Across the whole spectrum of diverse theological traditions that make up American Protestant Christianity, it is clear that women have made some important, although uneven, inroads, which are likely to continue and grow. The vast majority of visible Christian leadership, however, continues to be male; glass walls and ceilings are still firmly in place.[18] These limit women's access and mobility in using all of their gifts for service at all levels of the church. These walls and ceilings need to be acknowledged and broken down by patient, deliberate action and advocacy by both men and women at local, regional, and national levels.[19] Women should not have to bear this burden alone. Men need to move beyond mere toleration and tokenism, where it exists, and take deliberate affirmative steps to seek fairness and justice for women in their circle of influence. Women need wise mentors of both genders who can be prayerful and thoughtful guides as they seek their way forward. Spiritual friendship and deliberate advocacy can make an enormous difference. It is also true that women have been able to organize and support efforts for change within pluralistic denominations in ways that are quite difficult to do in the multiplicity of more conservative or independent environments. This is one reason why women need support groups to help them persevere in challenging contexts where they face misunderstanding, loneliness, or hardship. Organizations like Christians for Biblical Equality take on a special importance for biblically conservative women in unsupportive situations. Working for positive change is much easier with the companionship of sisters and brothers who provide a place for Christian community, prayer, encouragement, and practical help for women in ministry.

While large parts of the American church remain divided and polarized around their understandings of what is biblical and appropriate behavior for women in the church, family, and society, the focus and shape of the debate continues to shift somewhat from decade to decade. In general, more change has occurred within theologically pluralistic Protestant denominations than in the large majority of avowedly conservative or evangelical denominations and independent congregations. Even within the evangelical movement, it is noteworthy that there are significant pacesetting churches that support women in ministry, like Willow Creek Community Church and its association, which link thou-

18. For contemporary data, see the statistical and research Web sites of denominations, e.g., http://www.pcusa.org/research (accessed 2008); http://archives.umc.org/ (accessed 2008); and the Evangelical Lutheran Church, Department of Research and Evaluation.

19. Carol E. Becker, *Leading Women: How Church Women Can Avoid Leadership Traps and Negotiate the Gender Maze* (Nashville: Abingdon, 1996), 175–85.

sands of churches together to develop "fully devoted followers of Christ." May their tribe increase.

Different responses to women's rights and roles today often reflect the particular history of American Christianity in the twentieth century as it became deeply divided in its response to the rise of Darwinism, biblical higher criticism, and numerous economic and social forces. The fundamentalist versus modernist controversies of the early and mid twentieth century split the American church, and the role of women, unfortunately, became one of the battlefronts that remains to this day. Fundamentalists concerned to uphold the authority of Scripture tended to focus on biblical texts that appear on the surface to restrict and limit the authority of women, while they downplayed or ignored texts that could be understood as supportive of women's gifts and full equality with men. Opposing parties exported their different convictions and perspectives on the gospel and the role of women into global mission structures. Some groups still tend to emphasize one aspect of the gospel message in contrast to another by taking the message of the gospel and separating it into two opposed emphases on *either* conversion *or* compassion, the centrality of the Cross and Resurrection *or* the imperatives of the social gospel focused on loving one's neighbor. Too complicated to review in depth here, this deep polarization within and between congregations and denominations over doctrine, scriptural authority, and the relationship of the church to science and culture left evangelical feminist women and their supporters caught uneasily in the middle, facing misunderstanding or stereotyping from multiple directions.[20] When male authority and dominance are insisted upon as requirements of Christian orthodoxy, biblical feminists, who adhere to essential Christian beliefs as expressed in Scripture and the historic confessions of the church, find themselves having to defend their very identity as Christian believers.

Biblical feminists are those supportive *both* of biblical orthodoxy and authority *and* the call for women to be free to use all of their gifts, including gifts of preaching and teaching, in the ministries of the church. Accused by those at either extreme as being either "too liberal and radical" or "hopelessly conservative and obsessed with Paul," biblical feminists have to define, defend, and advocate for their views in two directions simultaneously because they do not fit into the simplistic categories often

---

20. Groothuis, *Women Caught in the Conflict,* 175–85, 199–216.

assigned to them. This means that we must know clearly what we believe and why we believe it if we are not to lose our way. Narrow slogans, personal attacks, or cultural captivity are unworthy of the gospel, whether the pressures come from the left or the right. Only the rediscovery of the wholeness of the gospel as given in Scripture and incarnated in Jesus Christ's life, death, and resurrection takes us forward in our efforts to be faithful disciples. The power of the Holy Spirit makes it possible for us to grow in love and humility as we engage in a genuinely respectful dialogue that works to maintain the unity of the faith while acknowledging serious differences. Differences among Christians over biblical interpretations of the role of women should not be allowed to become destroyers of unity and fellowship in the faith. Knowing that we belong to God our Savior gives us hope and a foundation that can hold us firmly even in the midst of the most painful disagreements with fellow Christians.

There is no substitute for risk taking and courage in situations that are oppressive or forbidding in their openness to the use of women's gifts. Because of the large numbers of diverse denominations and communions within American Christianity, women who are blocked in one part of the Christian community sometimes move outside of their home faith community into one that is more welcoming. This can be spiritually and emotionally liberating as well as painful, and many women discover they are called to remain in the congregations and denominations to which they presently belong as faithful servants and courageous witnesses.

While the interpretation of biblical texts and their authority has long been central to controversies over roles for women, other lines of argument have been important as well. It was not uncommon during the 1940s and 1950s for conservative Christian books and periodicals to argue that women should not be allowed to study Greek, or preach, or teach in the church because of their physical, intellectual, and psychological vulnerability and inferiority to men. Scientific research and the increasing number of women performing successfully in a wide variety of occupations provide evidence that contradicts these traditional assumptions and have rendered that line of argument less and less persuasive. Women now serving in the Senate and House of Representatives, state governors, scientists, CEOs, academics, doctors, biblical scholars, and theologians, as well as Olympic athletes, provide some of the contemporary female role models that influence many young women today. Differences between males and females exist, but such differences are less and less accepted in the larger culture, or within the church, as reasons for male dominance, privilege, or discrimination against women.

The founding of the conservative Council on Biblical Manhood and Womanhood provided a focal point for anti-equalitarian arguments that insist on the necessity of male "headship" or rule in the family and church. They assert that, while women are spiritually equal to men through their baptism in Christ, women were meant by God to be functionally subordinate to men in actual practice. Women are thus "complementary" to men and they need to be under male authority in marriage and ministry. Biblical feminists see this argument as inherently illogical and inconsistent with biblical examples of outstanding women and biblical teaching on mutuality and participation of women in the body of Christ. In addressing these issues, there are no easy substitutes or shortcuts for careful, thorough, and patient exegesis and understanding of all the pertinent texts, even though it is hard and sometimes complicated work. Providentially, there is significant literature available through the Web site at www.equalitydepot.com that can be helpful.

CLARIFYING AND DRAWING CLEAR LINES

The broad secular feminist movement in America became more radicalized and splintered during the last years of the twentieth century. A radicalized post-Christian feminism has emerged on the extreme left. These voices are often heard as broadly representative when they actually are a distinct minority. They attack historically orthodox understandings of the Trinity and Christology, refusing to address God as "Father" and rejecting Jesus as Savior because he is male. Some promote agendas of goddess worship, lesbian relationships, and the supposed superiority of peaceful feminine spirituality over supposedly aggressive "patriarchal" male Christianity. The visibility of these radical views in the media and on university campuses has caused a negative reaction among orthodox Christians to the very word "feminist." The word "feminist," defined as "a person believing in social, political, and economic equality of the sexes," is used frequently in conservative circles as a derogatory term embracing the most extreme examples of pro-female, anti-male bias, which attacks traditional institutions like marriage and the family. Clarifying and drawing clear lines between those with such radical and revisionist views and those seeking greater biblical fidelity in the treatment of women is important and necessary.

ACTION FOR TODAY

With all of the efforts and mixed progress made thus far, where do we go from here? Scholarship, publications, and visibility for the Christian commitment to women's dignity, worth, and equality must continue and expand. Respectful efforts must continue to engage traditionalist or "complementarian" arguments in persuasive ways whenever and wherever possible. Women must respond in faithful obedience to the call of God on their lives wherever that call takes them. Listening to God speak by the Holy Spirit though Scripture and seeking the wisdom of mature Christians can embolden us to respond to the needs around us with courage and determination. Demonstrating our beliefs through lives of love, sacrificial service, and moral integrity is one of our most powerful ways to bear witness and influence others. What else can be done?

Here are seven concrete suggestions for attention and action:

1. Maintain biblical faithfulness along with humility and servanthood while expanding opportunities and dismantling barriers to women's growth and service wherever possible. Stay rooted in prayer and Christian community while working for change.

2. Examine and reshape youth ministries in the local church to take young women as seriously as God does. Give them multiple opportunities to speak publicly about their faith. Provide healthy mentors and models of women followers of Christ. Address biblical and social issues on the relationships between women and men in singleness and marriage so that students, male and female, are equipped to meet the challenges of single and married life with a biblical worldview, relational understanding, and skill. Don't avoid dealing with these issues because they are awkward, complex, or controversial. There may never be another time of such availability and openness to lay down important foundations in these students' lives.

3. Expand outreach ministries on college and university campuses to reach young women and men with the news that the gospel is good news for everyone, including women. Develop and provide apologetic resources that address feminist issues and alternative spiritualities with

thoughtful Christian perspectives and illustrations. Do not lose the battle for women's minds and souls through default, neglect, or indifference.

4. Consider the music, media, and Bible versions used in worship and other gatherings. Are they inclusive of women in positive ways? Much of contemporary praise music uses male language exclusively. Biblical translations like the NRSV, the TNIV, and the New Living Translation are faithful to the original Greek and Hebrew while using inclusive language where appropriate.

5. Become intentional and proactive in recommending and encouraging gifted women in positions that have traditionally excluded them, whether as clergy, board members, or senior leaders and heads of ministries. Help women to get their second or third calls on the same basis as men. Do not settle for tokenism or satisfaction with the presence of a few women while remaining indifferent or exclusionary to many others. Encourage women to explore expanding their spheres of service as God gives them the opportunity.

6. Expand research and publication efforts on biblical, theological, historical, and pastoral issues related to women; fund scholarships. Encourage evangelical women to write. Broaden seminary curriculums to integrate women's history and contemporary issues into the mainstream of required study. Develop systematic programs of spiritual direction, Christian community, and field education that nourish and develop women preparing for ministry. Redesign doctor of ministry programs to reach out to women in substantive ways.

7. Practice advocacy for girls and women whenever and wherever possible, especially reaching out to women of poverty and victims of abuse. Provide scholarships for education, conference participation, and support involvement in organizations supportive of opportunities for women's growth and service.

In conclusion, there are many modes of supportive activism and many reasons for hope. Therefore, take more risks. Trust Christ boldly. Live with passion and purpose. People who live like this can change the world!

Conclusion

Aída Besançon Spencer

W HEN I WAS WRITING my defense of the ministry of women, I entitled my book *Beyond the Curse*,[1] because Genesis 3:16 has been and continues to be important as a defining influence on global societies. Even though "your desire shall be for your husband and he shall rule over you" may not technically be a "curse," it does indicate God's ramifications for sin as they affect women. Husbands and men can oppressively rule over women, and women can even desire to be oppressed, while other men and women have become engaged in a power struggle, not in a cooperative, mutually enhancing relationship. Death instead of life has permeated throughout all societies. Adam and Eve's sin has had rebounding ramifications for relationships. First, Cain murdered his brother Abel (Gen 4:1–16), later the greedy murderer Lamech added bigamy, taking two wives (Gen 4:19), then the sons of God continued choosing wives in a way that grieved the Spirit of God (Gen 6:2–3): "The wickedness of humankind was great in the earth" (Gen 6:5 NRSV). Abram asked Sarai to feign that she was his sister in Egypt and in Gerar for his own self-preservation (Gen 12:11–13, 20:1–2), while Sarai used Hagar to give her an heir and afterwards thrust her out (Gen 16:2–3, 6, 21:10). Lot was ready to offer his own virgin daughters to the attacking men of Sodom (Gen 19:5–8). But then Lot's daughters used their father to obtain heirs (Gen 19:32–36). The oppression of women by men, men by women, men by men, and women by women is ongoing. But, God's desire for the world is not for humans to oppress one another, but rather to move "beyond the curse" and have God's law written on their hearts: "No longer shall they teach one another, or say to each other, 'Know the Lord,' for they shall all know me, from the least of them to the greatest, says the Lord; for I

---

1. Aída Besançon Spencer, *Beyond the Curse: Women Called to Ministry* (Peabody, Mass.: Hendrickson, 1985).

will forgive their iniquity, and remember their sin no more" (Jer 31:34 NRSV). And, indeed, enlightened by the gospel, the Christians in Rome were renowned for being able to instruct one another (Rom 15:14; see also Col 3:16). Those in Christ are now no longer "male and female" but "one in Christ Jesus," because all are heirs (Gal 3:28–29).

What have I learned from reading these chapters about the challenges and successes of gender and ministry in countries around the globe? First, I will highlight important concerns from each nation and make comparisons among them, and, second, I will collate positive steps for action from the chapters.

COMPARISONS AMONG NATIONS

There are some countries where the Christians originally brought in great reform for women (India, China, United States). In other countries, the Christians followed changes in the secular world (Africa). Christian reformation needs to continue both in the church and in the society. A number of authors stressed that Christian education is always a key, as Paul commands in 1 Timothy 2:11 ("Let a woman learn") (India, China, Korean America, Africa, African America, Europe, Australia, United States). The biblical foundation for women in leadership needs to be explained to men as well as women, and both need to be encouraged. In India and China, Christians were the ones who brought education to girls. In these cultures, female infanticide, abortion, and prostitution are problems. The husband is treated as a god. Additional problems in India are dowries and greed, the lack of freedom for women to marry the man of their choice, and women not being treated as independent.

Sometimes, societal changes bring negative ramifications, for example, an increase in divorce (China, Africa). Challenges to which we should be alert are maintaining women in leadership during the process of institutionalization (China, Hispanic America, Australia, United States) and recruiting women into leadership roles in already established institutions (Korean America, Africa, African America, Australia, United States). Female missionaries can be a great model for equality (China, Africa, Brazilians in the United States). So, it is important for women not to be self-centered, but to open doors for other women (China, Africa). In regard to displaced populations, some nationalities are more conservative in the United States than in their original countries (e.g., Chinese America, Korean America).

Christianity teaches the value of a human being created in God's image and recreated when redeemed by Christ. A number of authors (India, Korean America, Africa, African America) cited the importance of viewing men and women as created in God's image and having equal value and worth. But, as one author cautioned, since Christ valued women,[2] should not Christians also advance the particular value of the female and the need for justice for the female (India)? "He shall rule over you"—as a consequence of the fall—certainly explains the injustices against women and the entitlement of men, but it should never be used as an excuse to treat women unjustly and in a devalued way.

Every society has its ideal for a woman and a man. What is the Christian ideal? Certainly, Proverbs 31 shows that God's revelation supports the independent capabilities of women.[3] A dilemma for Christians exists when Scripture appeals to Christians to accommodate society in order to evangelize it (e.g., 1 Pet 2:13-15, 3:1).[4] But, where does accommodation for evangelistic purposes clash with the Christian's need to be prophetic and countercultural (India, Africa)?

Several authors asked: How does one handle the clash of tradition and Christian values (Korean America, Africa, African America)? The word of God and education are important not just for women, but also for the church (Korean America, African America). Community, too, is important among Christian change agents (China, Korean America, Africa, Europe, United States). An attractive vision is made of the full church—all its members—unleashed, its energy used for good.

In contrast to India, China, and Korean America, the situation of Brazilian and Native American women was not clearly in all ways worse before this culture embraced the Christian faith. Still, authors from Brazil, Korean America, Africa, and the United States felt that the subordination of the wife in the home limits her freedom to minister. In Korean America,

2. A. Spencer, *Beyond the Curse,* ch. 2; "Jesus' Treatment of Women in the Gospels," *Discovering Biblical Equality: Complementarity without Hierarchy,* eds. Ronald W. Pierce and Rebecca Merrill Groothuis (Downers Grove: InterVarsity, 2004), ch. 7.

3. William David Spencer, "Diamond or Diamond Mine?" *Priscilla Papers* 16:2 (Spring 2002): 16–17.

4. See A. Spencer, "Peter's Pedagogical Method in 1 Peter 3:6," *Bulletin for Biblical Research* 10:1 (2000): 107–19.

African America, and Native America, being part of a minority that is in some ways oppressed by a majority puts limitations on gender roles. The societal and familial structures of African America and Native America were greatly destroyed by the process of enslavement and political oppression. The destruction of the Native American cultures is an important reminder to Christians to discern gender roles and native familial and societal relationships before blindly suggesting change of roles. It seems Christianity does help with more biblical ideals of sexual faithfulness (also India, China). Native Americans remind us of the importance of women having not only influence but also political and religious power. What a great difference in impact authentic Christianity has over nominal Christianity!

Paul commands the church in Corinth to "give recognition" to the coworkers and workers (1 Cor 16:16, 18). Even though some translations render verse 18 as male exclusive (for example, "men" [NIV, TNIV, TEV, ESV]), the Greek is plural, gender-inclusive ("such people" [NRSV, KJV, NLT, CEV, REB]). Moreover, Stephana could be a female or male.[5] The difficulty in some Hispanic churches has been that women indeed have been working hard in ministry, but their leadership has not been appreciated properly. Women lead, but are not recognized publicly by being nominated to positions of authority. When institutions are finally created by women, men, not women, are placed in leadership. Coworkers who devote themselves to ministry should "be subject to" and respected by those to whom they minister (1 Cor 16:16; 1 Thess 5:12–13), even as Paul asked for recognition of and expressed respect for Phoebe, the minister of Cenchreae (Rom 16:1–2).

Both Australia and the United States have organized forces opposing the treatment of women as equals, but, in Australia in 2008, there appears to be little willingness between opposing groups to discuss what the Bible says about the ministry of women. In both countries, the majority of believers are women, but the majority of visible leaders are male. In both countries, there are few women senior pastors of multiple-staff churches or in the most influential denominational positions. Women preachers are more numerous in times of revivals and mission (United States,

---

5. Aída Besançon Spencer, "'El Hogar' as Ministry Team: Stephana(s)'s Household," *Hispanic Christian Thought at the Dawn of the 21st Century: Apuntes in Honor of Justo L. González*, eds. Alvin Padilla, Roberto Goizueta, and Eldin Villafañe (Nashville: Abingdon, 2005), ch. 6.

Hispanic America, Europe, Australia), but they are not recognized when the church becomes institutionalized. Women excel more where they have been known in the church, for example, as a pastor's wife who becomes the pastor. Sadly, in cultures where men predominate, the church reflects the culture (as in Australia, India, Korean America, Hispanic America, Europe). The importance of perseverance was cited for the United States, India, African America, and Latin America. Even when women are working as recognized leaders in the church, their leadership as a female can be challenged when any problem occurs; they can be left out of the "old boy" networks, and they can be required to have more credentials in leadership without being provided any opportunities to get the experience necessary (United States, African America).

To what extent has the gospel been diluted and reshaped by cultural or ethnic traditions? On the one hand, the Native American situation raised the question of whether European cultures harmed positive gender values already existing. On the other hand, was the European culture really Christlike in its ecclesiastical structures? The European traditions may have diluted and reshaped Christ's good news. It turned a Christian fellowship of equals into a hierarchy of male dominance.[6] Even while women were allowed to enter foreign missions, but not preach at home, seeing the leadership of these female missionaries in Africa and Brazil affected the Africans' and Brazilians' own views of female leadership. Full equality of women in the church entails the church allowing qualified women (as well as men) to teach, preach, pastor, and lead, to give the sacraments, to serve all people, not just other women, children, the sick, and the poor. The priesthood of all believers[7] should be a real-life model for the ministry of the church, not merely a theoretical principle. Together as men and women, in Africa, indigenous America, India, China, Australia, Europe, and the United States, the church needs to become a prophetic voice in society, facing issues of justice and compassion: relief work, broken families, evangelism, showing Christ's love, yet confronting sin. Christianity needs to affect individual salvation *and* the welfare of society.

---

6. See also William David Spencer, "The Chaining of the Church," *Christian History* 7, no. 1 (17): 25; Ronald A. N. Kydd, *Charismatic Gifts in the Early Church* (Peabody, Mass.: Hendrickson, 1988).

7. 1 Pet 2:5; Rev 1:6, 5:10; Exod 19:6; Isa 61:6.

Many cultures have a variety of attitudes to Christianity—post-Christian or never Christian—but none is authentically Christian.[8]

Despite the doubt of some, equality is a biblical concept. Literally, "equality"[9] has to do with being the same in length (Rev 21:16), being consistent in testimony (Mark 14:56, 59), receiving the same wage (Matt 20:12), and being identical in personhood and rank (John 5:18; Phil 2:6). Equality flows from the nature of God as "impartial."[10] Watching to recognize our analogous situations with others can help us to treat those who may appear subservient as an equal in rank (Col 4:1) and as an equal in benefits (Acts 11:17; 2 Pet 1:1). Where the Bible may assess equality differently than do others is that it recognizes that equality is not based on sameness. All do not have the same economic benefits, yet we are to give or receive until we end up at the same place (2 Cor 8:13–14). All may receive the same pay, even though they do not "deserve" it, having worked the same number of hours (Matt 20:12). So, it is *not* equal pay for equal work, but equal pay for any work. We also are not to give simply to receive (Luke 6:34), and someone may choose not to have all the benefits they

---

8. Ronald Sider, citing different studies, notes that those with a "biblical worldview," who demonstrate a genuinely different thought and behavior, are a small group (9 percent of the 40 percent in the United States who are "born-again"). *The Scandal of the Evangelical Conscience: Why Are Christians Living Just Like the Rest of the World?* (Grand Rapids: Baker, 2005), 128. According to the World Christian Database, "Great Commission Christians" are "believers in Jesus Christ who are aware of the implications of Christ's Great Commission, who have accepted its personal challenge in their lives and ministries, are attempting to obey his commands and mandates, and who are seeking to influence the body of Christ to implement it." It claims the percentages of Great Commission Christians in the total population (2005) are: USA (33.89 percent), Australia (33.71 percent), South Korea (28.56 percent), Zimbabwe (25.03 percent), Europe (23.71 percent), Brazil (14.4 percent), Spanish-speaking Latin America (8.28 percent), China (7.43 percent), and India (4.64 percent). Within the USA, WCD has statistics for "Christian" or "Affiliated Christian." An "Affiliated Christian" is someone whose name is entered on the church's books. The percentages of Affiliated Christians are: USA (65.7 percent), Latino/a American (84.3 percent), Native American (74.44 percent), African American (71 percent), Anglo U.S. (62.57 percent), Korean American (62 percent), Chinese American (21.66 percent), and Indian American (10 percent). Accessed 7 March 2008 by Bert Hickman, Research Associate, Center for the Study of Global Christianity, Gordon-Conwell Theological Seminary, South Hamilton, Massachusetts, USA.

9. *Isos, isotēs, isotimos, isopsuchos.*

10. The negative of *prosōpolēmpteō, prosōpolēmptēs, prosōpolēmpsia,* "not to receive a face": Matt 22:16; Acts 10:34; Rom 2:11; Gal 2:6; Eph 6:9; James 2:1; 1 Pet 1:17; Deut 10:17–18. See also 1 Sam 16:7; Gal 3:26–29.

deserve because of a greater goal (Phil 2:6). Biblically, men and women, although different, are equal in being and rank and benefits.

POSITIVE STEPS FOR ACTION

Progress has occurred in education and employment of women in every country. But spiritual equality has not always been reflected in functional equality. All our writers agree that biblical feminism or biblical egalitarianism supports biblical orthodoxy and authority as well as the freedom for women and men to use all their gifts in the church and society.

In summary, the contributors have offered many helpful steps to bring transformation to individuals, congregations, institutions, and societies. Indeed, change is accomplished individual by individual, congregation by congregation, denomination by denomination, and society by society. Godly change involves analysis, setting goals, amassing resources, and using techniques to reach its goals in a Christlike manner. Thus, (1) Christians need to be proactive, bold, willing to change, and persevering. (2) A crucial foundation is comprised of the living out or modeling of *authentic Christianity*, the modeling of the dignity and equality of women and men in church and home, the modeling of the love of Christ, and the just confrontation of sin. (3) *Prayer* is key for dependence on God for transformation. (4) Those who differ with us are not necessarily our enemies. They may simply be uninformed. Therefore, a recurring theme is the necessity for *education*—clarifying the biblical basis for gender equality. Education can be done by preaching and teaching in the church; at conferences, seminars, and workshops; in educational institutions; in keeping dialogue with those who differ with us in the church; and as an apologetic to the larger society. Moreover, music, media, and resources need to be evaluated in regard to being inclusive of the voice of women and men.

(5) Women need to encourage, help, and *advocate* for other women, including mentoring young women. (6) Men need to respect, encourage, and advocate for women. (7) Thus, women's *confidence* can be built up. (8) Thereby, we can create mutual *support networks* of prayer, sharing of concerns and resources, and strategizing locally, nationally, and internationally. (9) As biblical equality is worked out in *marriages*, marriages are helped to become companionships, husband and wife each operating in areas of giftedness, husband and wife becoming able to serve Christ

together as a couple in their areas of gifts and strengths. Christian heterosexual marriage recognizes the uniqueness of unity in the diversity of male and female.

(10) Encouragement needs to become proactive, in *recommending* and appointing women to lead in the church and in other institutions. (11) But believers should not allow themselves to be limited to transformation of the church; they should also look outward to the transformation of society. Christians need to be a *prophetic voice in society* today, as they were in the past—especially being aware of and engaging in social issues that affect women. (12) New models for *leadership* will be needed, (13) as well as *financial resources.*

The task may appear to be overwhelming, but the resources will be drawn from and distributed over a larger group of people. In addition, each of us has a unique gift and unique calling. No one but God is responsible for everything! What, then, will be the appeal of instituting full gender equality? The appeal will be increased freedom, wisdom, love, justice, truth, creativity, and self-understanding; and decreased fear. Marriages and churches will be healthier and happier. People will spend their time better in encouraging rather than discouraging one another. Churches will strive to create a radical paradigm living beyond the curse, reaching back to the roots of God's intention when the command to rule the earth was given jointly to men and women. Most of all, more believers will be equipped and mobilized for service. Evangelism will be more appealing to the young and to society. A more appealing model of Christianity will be broadcast, because, as we stated in the preface, men and women will more reflect the perfect love and equality and harmony within the Triune Godhead.

Bibliography

1. REFORM MOVEMENTS: HOW THEY REVIVE THE CHURCH

Bebbington, David. *Evangelicalism in Modern Britain: A History from 1730s to the 1980s*. Grand Rapids: Baker, 1989.

Cunningham, Loren, David Joel Hamilton, and Janice Rogers. *Why Not Women? A Fresh Look at Women in Missions, Ministry and Leadership*. Seattle: YWAM Publishing, 2000.

Douglass, Fredrick. http://gbgm-umc.org/UMW/bible/douglass.stm Accessed 18 April 2008.

———. *Life and Times of Frederick Douglass: His Early Life as a Slave, His Escape from Bondage, and His Complete History*. New York: Collier, 1892.

Fee, Gordon. *Listening to the Spirit in the Text*. Grand Rapids: Eerdmans, 2000.

Giles, Kevin. *The Trinity and Subordinationism: The Doctrine of God and the Contemporary Gender Debate*. Downers Grove, IL: InterVarsity, 2002.

———. *Jesus and the Father: Modern Evangelicals Reinvent the Doctrine of the Trinity*. Grand Rapids: Zondervan, 2006.

Grudem, Wayne. "Should We Move Beyond the New Testament to a Better Ethic? An Analysis of William J. Webb, *Slaves, Women and Homosexuals: Exploring the Hermeneutics of Cultural Analysis*." *JETS* 47, no. 2 (June 2004): 299–346.

———. *Evangelical Feminism and Biblical Truth: An Analysis of More than One Hundred Disputed Questions*. Sisters, OR: Multnomah, 2004.

Lausanne Issue Group 24. Occasional Paper No. 53, *Empowering Women and Men to Use Their Gifts Together in Advancing the Gospel*, edited by Alvera Mickelsen. St. Paul: Christians for Biblical Equality, 2005.

Noll, Mark. *The Rise of Evangelicalism: The Age of Edwards, Whitefield, and the Wesleys*. Downers Grove, Ill.: InterVarsity, 2003.

Reasoner, Mark. "Chapter 16 in Paul's Letter to the Romans: Dispensable Tagalong or Valuable Envelope?" *Priscilla Papers* 20, no. 4 (Autumn 2006): 11–17.

Robert, Dana L. *American Women in Mission: A Social History of Their Thought and Practice*. Macon, Ga.: Mercer University Press, 2005.

Sanders, Catherine Edwards. *Wicca's Charm*. Colorado Springs: Waterbrook, 2005.

Schemm, Peter R. "Kevin Giles's *The Trinity and Subordinationism*: A Review Article." *Journal for Biblical Manhood and Womanhood* 7, no. 2 (Fall 2002): 67–78.

Spencer, Aída Besançon, Donna F. G. Hailson, Catherine Clark Kroeger, and William David Spencer. *The Goddess Revival*. Grand Rapids: Baker, 1995.

Sumner, Sarah. "Forging a Middle Way Between Complementarians and Egalitarians." In *Women, Ministry, and the Gospel: Exploring New Paradigms,* edited by Mark Husbands and Timothy Larsen, 266–88. Downers Grove, Ill.: IVP, 2007.

Swartley, Willard. *Slavery, Sabbath, War, and Women: Case Issues in Biblical Interpretation.* Scottdale, Pa.: Herald, 1983.

Tracy, Steven, "Headship with a Heart: How Biblical Patriarchy Actually Prevents Abuse." *Christianity Today* (February 2003). http://www.ctlibrary.com/ct/2003/february/5.50. html. Accessed 18 April 2008.

Webb, William J. *Slaves, Women, and Homosexuals: Exploring the Hermeneutics of Cultural Analysis.* Downers Grove, Ill.: InterVarsity, 2001.

Wilberforce, William. 1788 House of Commons address. http://satucket.com/lectionary/ William_Wilberforce.htm. Accessed 1 May 2008.

Willard, Frances. *Glimpses of Fifty Years: The Autobiography of an American Woman.* Chicago: H.J. Smith, 1889.

2. STEPS FORWARD ON A JOURNEY IN INDIA

Jeyaraj, Nirmala, ed. *Women and Society.* Madurai: Lady Doak College, 2001.

Mangalwadi, Ruth. *William Carey: A Tribute by an Indian Woman.* New Delhi: Nivedit Good Books, 1993.

Memon, Rithu, ed. *Women Who Dared.* India: National Book Trust, 2002.

O'Neill, Mary Aquin. *Women, Justice and the Bible.* 2003. http://www.msawomen.org/ works/works_lecture_2003_womenjusticebible.htm.

Roy, Benoy Bhusan, and Pranati Ray. *Zenana Mission: The Role of Christian Missionaries for the Education of Women in 19th Century Bengal.* Delhi: ISPCK, 1998.

Tucker, Ruth, and Walter Liefeld. *Daughters of the Church.* Grand Rapids: Zondervan, 1987.

3. THE PATH OF BIBLICAL EQUALITY FOR THE CHINESE WOMEN

Chao, Jonathan, and Rosanna Chong. *A History of Christianity in Socialist China, 1949–1997.* Taiwan: CMI Publishing Co., 1997.*

Drycker, Alison R. "The Role of the Y.W.C.A. in the Development of the Chinese Women's Movement, 1890–1927." *Social Service Review* 53 (1979): 425.

Hsia, Hsiao Hung. *Women of Late Qing and Contemporary China.* Beijing: Beijing University Publishers, 2004.*

Kristof, Nicholas D., and Sherryl WuDunn. *China Wakes: The Struggle for the Soul of a Rising Power.* New York: Vintage Books, 1995.

Kwok, Pui-lan. *Chinese Women and Christianity, 1860–1927.* Atlanta: Scholars Press, 1992.

Leung, Ka-lun. *Evangelists and Revivalists of Modern China.* Hong Kong: Alliance Bible Seminary, 1999.*

———. *The Rural Churches of Mainland China since 1978.* Hong Kong: Alliance Bible Seminary, March 1999.*

Liu, Wing Chung. *Women and History.* Hong Kong: Hong Kong Educational Publishing Co., 1993.*

Marquand, Robert. "Women in China Finally Making a Great Leap Forward." *Christian Science Monitor,* 17 December 2004.

Tucker, Ruth. *From Jerusalem to Irian Jaya.* Grand Rapids: Zondervan, 1983.

Wu, Silas. *Dora Yu: Harbinger of Christian Church Revival in 20th Century China.* Boston: Pishon River Publications, 2000.*

Yang, Fenggang. "Gender and Generation in a Chinese Christian Church." In *Asian American Religions: The Making and Remaking of Borders and Boundaries,* edited by Fenggang Yang and Tony Carnes, 205–22. New York: New York University Press, 2004.

Yau, Cecilia, Dora Wang, and Lily Lee. *Gender Reconciliation: Men and Women Become One in Christ.* Petaluma, Calif.: Fullness in Christ Fellowship, 2004.*

———. *A Passion for Fullness: Examining the Woman's Identity and Roles from Biblical, Historical and Sociological Perspectives.* 2nd ed. Hong Kong: China Graduate School of Theology, 2004.*

Zhang, Ning. "A Conflict of Interests: Current Problems in Educational Reform." In *Economic Reform and Social Change in China,* edited by Andrew Watson, 144–70. London: Routledge, 1992.

* The preceding books are written in Chinese.

4. CHALLENGING THE PATRIARCHAL ETHOS: GENDER EQUALITY IN THE KOREAN AMERICAN CHURCH

Aristotle. *The Works of Aristotle–Politics.* Vol.10. Translated by Benjamin Jowett. Oxford: Clarendon, 1921.

Balswick, Judith K., and Jack O. Balswick. "Marriage as a Partnership of Equals." In *Discovering Biblical Equality: Complementarity without Hierarchy,* edited by Ronald W. Pierce and Rebecca Merrill Groothuis, 144–70. Downers Grove, Ill.: InterVarsity, 2005.

Belleville, Linda L. "Women Leaders in the Bible." In *Discovering Biblical Equality: Complementarity without Hierarchy,* edited by Ronald W. Pierce and Rebecca Merrill Groothuis, 110–25. Downers Grove, Ill.: InterVarsity, 2005.

———. *Women Leaders and the Church: Three Crucial Questions.* Grand Rapids: Baker, 2000.

Cha, Peter, and Grace May. "Gender Relations in Healthy Households." In *Growing Healthy Asian American Churches,* edited by Peter Cha, S. Steve Kang, and Helen Lee, 164–82. Downers Grove, Ill.: InterVarsity, 2006.

Chan, Sucheng. *Asian Americans: An Interpretive History.* New York: Twayne, 1991.

Chong, Kelly H. "What It Means to Be Christian: The Role of Religion in the Construction of Ethnic Identity and Boundary among Second-generation Korean Americans." *Sociology of Religion* 59 (1998): 259–86.

Choung, James. "Can Women Teach?: An Exegesis of 1 Timothy 2:11–15 and 1 Corinthians 14:33–40. Unpublished Paper. La Jolla, Calif., 2006.

Chung, Ruth. "Reflections on a Korean American Journey." In *Struggle for Ethnic Identity: Narratives by Asian American Professionals,* edited by Pyong Gap Min and Rose Kim, 59–68. Walnut Creek, Calif.: Altamira, 1999.

Davison, Lisa Wilson. *Preaching the Women of the Bible.* St. Louis: Chalice, 2006.

de Leon, Christie Heller. "Sticks, Stones and Stereotypes." In *More than Serving Tea: Asian American Women on Expectations, Relationships, Leadership and Faith,* edited by Nikki A. Toyama and Tracy Gee, 19–35. Downers Grove, Ill.: InterVarsity, 2006.

Fong, Ken Uyeda. *Pursuing the Pearl: A Comprehensive Resource for Multi-Asian Ministry.* Valley Forge, Pa.: Judson, 1999.

Giles, Kevin. "Post-1970s Evangelical Responses to the Emancipation of Women." *Priscilla Papers* 20, no. 4 (2006): 46–52.

Groothuis, Rebecca Merrill. "'Equal in Being, Unequal in Role.'" In *Discovering Biblical Equality: Complementarity without Hierarchy,* edited by Ronald W. Pierce and Rebecca Merrill Groothuis, 301–33. Downers Grove, Ill.: InterVarsity, 2005.

Gudykunst, William B. *Asian American Ethnicity and Communication.* London: Sage, 2001.

Haddad, Mimi. "Egalitarian Pioneers: Betty Friedan or Catherine Booth?" *Priscilla Papers* 20, no. 4 (2006): 53–59.

Khang, Kathy. "Pulled by Expectations." In *More than Serving Tea: Asian American Women on Expectations, Relationships, Leadership and Faith,* edited by Nikki A. Toyama and Tracy Gee, 36–49. Downers Grove, Ill.: InterVarsity, 2006.

Kim, Illsoo. *New Urban Immigrants: The Korean Community in New York.* Princeton: Princeton University Press, 1981.

Kim, Jason Hyungkyun. "The Effects of Assimilation within the Korean Immigrant Church: Intergenerational Conflicts between the First and Second Generation Korean Christians in Two Chicago Suburban Churches." Ph.D. diss., Trinity International University, 1999.

Kim, Jung Ha. "Cartography of Korean American Protestant Faith Communities in the United States." In *Religions in Asian America: Building Faith Communities,* edited by Pyong Gap Min and Jung Ha Kim, 185–213. Walnut Creek, Calif.: Altamira, 2002.

———. "The Labor of Compassion: Voices of Churched Korean American Women." In *New Spiritual Homes: Religion and Asian Americans,* edited by David K. Yoo, 202–17. Honolulu: University of Hawaii Press, 1999.

Kim, Kwang Chung, R. Stephen Warner, and Ho-Youn Kwon. "Korean American Religion in International Perspective." In *Korean Americans and Their Religions: Pilgrims and Missionaries from a Different Shore,* edited by Ho-Youn Kwon, Kwang Chung Kim, and R. Stephen Warner, 3–24. University Park: Pennsylvania State University Press, 2001.

Kim, Matthew D. *Preaching to Second Generation Korean Americans: Towards a Possible Selves Contextual Homiletic.* New York: Peter Lang, 2007.

———. "Preaching to Second Generation Korean Americans: Towards a Possible Selves Contextual Homiletic." Ph.D. diss., University of Edinburgh, 2006.

———. "From Corporate Silence to Real Talk: A New Contextual Homiletic for Second Generation Korean Americans." M.Th. diss., University of Edinburgh. Ann Arbor: UMI, 2004.

Kim, Nak-In. "A Model Ministry to Transitional and Second Generation Korean-Americans." D.Min. diss., School of Theology at Claremont, 1991.

Kim, Rose. "My Trek." In *Struggle for Ethnic Identity: Narratives by Asian American Professionals,* edited by Pyong Gap Min and Rose Kim, 49–58. Walnut Creek, Calif.: Altamira, 1999.

Bibliography

Kim, Stephen S. "Seeking Home in North America: Colonialism in Asia; Confrontation in North America." In *People on the Way: Asian North Americans Discovering Christ, Culture, and Community,* edited by David Ng, 1–23. Valley Forge, Pa.: Judson, 1996.

Kitano, Harry H. L., and Roger Daniels. *Asian Americans: Emerging Minorities.* Upper Saddle River, N.J.: Prentice-Hall, 1988.

Lee, Inn Sook. "Korean American Women and Ethnic Identity." In *Korean American Ministry,* edited by Sang Hyun Lee and John V. Moore, 192–214. Louisville, Ky.: General Assembly Council PCUSA, 1987.

Li, Chenyang, ed. *The Sage and the Second Sex: Confucianism, Ethics, and Gender.* Chicago: Carus, 2000.

Lundell, In-Gyeong Kim. *Bridging the Gaps: Contextualization among Korean Nazarene Churches in America.* New York: Peter Lang, 1995.

Mathews, Alice P. "Preaching to the Whole Church." In *Preaching to a Shifting Culture: 12 Perspectives on Communicating that Connects,* edited by Scott M. Gibson, 147–60. Grand Rapids: Baker, 2004.

———. *Preaching that Speaks to Women.* Grand Rapids: Baker, 2003.

Min, Pyong Gap. "A Literature Review with a Focus on Major Themes." In *Religions in Asian America: Building Faith Communities,* edited by Pyong Gap Min and Jung Ha Kim, 15–36. Walnut Creek, Calif.: Altamira, 2002.

———. "The Structure and Social Functions of Korean Immigrant Churches in the United States." *International Migration Review* 26 (1992): 1370–94.

Min, Pyong Gap, and Jung Ha Kim, eds. *Religions in Asian America: Building Faith Communities.* Walnut Creek, Calif.: Altamira, 2002.

Noll, Mark A. *The Scandal of the Evangelical Mind.* Grand Rapids: Eerdmans, 1994.

Oh, Myungseon. "Study on Appropriate Leadership Pattern for the Korean Church in Post-modern Era." *Journal of Asian Mission* 5, no. 1 (2003): 131–45.

Patterson, Wayne. *The Korean Frontier in America: Immigration to Hawaii, 1896–1910.* Honolulu: University of Hawaii Press, 1988.

Pierce, Ronald W. "Contemporary Evangelicals for Gender Equality." In *Discovering Biblical Equality: Complementarity without Hierarchy,* edited by Ronald W. Pierce and Rebecca Merrill Groothuis, 58–75. Downers Grove, Ill.: InterVarsity, 2005.

Robinson, Haddon W. *Biblical Preaching.* 2nd ed. Grand Rapids: Baker, 2001.

Shin, Eui Hang, and Hyung Park. "An Analysis of Causes of Schisms in Ethnic Churches: The Case of Korean-American Churches." *Sociological Analysis* 49 (1988): 234–48.

Stuart, Douglas. *Old Testament Exegesis: A Handbook for Students and Pastors.* 3d ed. Louisville, Ky.: Westminster/John Knox, 2001.

Toyama, Nikki A. "Perfectionist Tendencies." In *More than Serving Tea: Asian American Women on Expectations, Relationships, Leadership and Faith,* edited by Nikki A. Toyama and Tracy Gee, 50–68. Downers Grove, Ill.: InterVarsity, 2006.

Tseng, Timothy, et al. *Asian American Religious Leadership Today: A Preliminary Inquiry.* Pulpit and Pew: Research on Pastoral Leadership. Durham: Duke Divinity School, 2005.

U.S. Government Census. http://www.census.gov/prod/cen2000/doc/sf4.pdf.

Wright, N. T. "The Biblical Basis for Women's Service in the Church." *Priscilla Papers* 20, no. 4 (2006): 5–10.

Yao, Xinzhong. *An Introduction to Confucianism.* Cambridge: Cambridge University Press, 2000.

Yoon, In-Jin. *On My Own: Korean Businesses and Race Relations in America*. Chicago: University of Chicago Press, 1997.

5. BIBLICAL EQUALITY IN ZIMBABWE, AFRICA

Acts of Parliament of Zimbabwe. Harare, Zimbabwe: Government Printers, 1996.

Apostolic Faith Mission in Zimbabwe, Constitution and Regulations. Harare, Zimbabwe: Mardon Printers, 2003.

Ellsberg, Mary, and Lori Heise. *Researching Violence against Women*. World Health Organization. Geneva, Switzerland: PATH, 2005.

Murefu, Agnes. Interview at her home. 998 Chitunya Road, Chitungwiza, Zimbabwe. 17 June 2007.

Murefu, Constantine Matiyenga. *Biblical Foundation for Believers*. Harare: Faith Printers Production, 2001.

Siamanzime, Brendah. "The Reporter." Zambian National Television Channel. 9 a.m. 11 February 2007.

6. GIFTED FOR LEADERSHIP: GENDER EQUALITY FROM AN AFRICAN AMERICAN PERSPECTIVE

Barna, George. *Single Focus: Understanding Single Adults*. Ventura, Calif.: Regal, 2003.

Christoff, Nicholas B. *Saturday Night Sunday Morning: Singles and the Church*. San Francisco: Harper & Row, 1978.

Chrysostom, John. Works of St. Chrysostom, Homily IX, 1 Timothy 2:11–15, *Nicene and Post-Nicene Fathers First Series*. 1889. Reprint, Peabody, Mass.: Hendrickson, 2004.

———. Works of St. Chrysostom, Homily XI, 1 Timothy 3:8–10, *Nicene and Post-Nicene Fathers First Series*. 1889. Reprint, Peabody, MA: Hendrickson, 2004.

Cohen, Abraham. *Everyman's Talmud: The Major Teachings of the Rabbinic Sages*. New York: Schocken, 1949.

Collier, Jarvis. *The Biblical Challenge for Christian Singles*. Nashville: Townsend, 1998.

Evans, James H., Jr., *We Have Been Believers: An African-American Systematic Theology*. Minneapolis: Fortress, 1992.

Farrington, Debra K. "Singled Out." *U.S. Catholic* 67, no. 9 (2002): 50.

Feinberg, Margaret. "Singular Mission Field." *Christianity Today* 45, no. 8 (2001): 33.

Higginbotham, Evelyn Brooks. *Righteous Discontent: The Women's Movement in the Black Baptist Church, 1880–1920*. Cambridge, Mass.: Harvard University Press, 1993.

Kroeger, Richard Clark, and Catherine Clark Kroeger. *I Suffer Not a Woman: Rethinking 1 Timothy 2:11–15 in Light of Ancient Evidence*. Grand Rapids: Baker, 1992.

LaRue, Cleophus J., ed. *This Is My Story: Testimonies and Sermons of Black Women in Ministry*. Louisville, Ky.: Westminster John Knox, 2005.

Lincoln, C. Eric, and Lawrence H. Mamiya. *The Black Church in the African American Experience*. Durham, N.C.: Duke University Press, 1990.

McMickle, Marvin A. *An Encyclopedia of African American Christian Heritage*. Valley Forge, Pa.: Judson, 2002.

Mitchell, Ella Pearson. *Those Preaching Women*. Valley Forge, Pa.: Judson, 1985.

Mitchell, Henry H. *Black Church Beginnings: The Long Hidden Realities of the First Years*. Grand Rapids: Eerdmans, 2004.

Sanders, Cheryl J. *Empowerment Ethics for a Liberated People: A Path to African American Social Transformation.* Minneapolis: Fortress, 1995.

———. "The Woman as Preacher." In *African American Religious Studies: An Interdisciplinary Anthology,* edited by Gayraud S. Wilmore, 373–91. 1989. Reprint, Durham, N.C.: Duke University Press, 1992.

Taylor, Clarence. *The Black Churches of Brooklyn.* New York: Columbia University Press, 1994.

Thayer, Joseph H. *Thayer's Greek-English Lexicon of the New Testament.* 1896. Reprint, Peabody, Mass.: Hendrickson, 1997.

Walker, Theodore, Jr. *Empower the People: Social Ethics for the African-American Church.* Maryknoll, N.Y.: Orbis, 1991.

Wiggins, Daphne C. *Righteous Content: Black Women's Perspectives of Church and Faith.* New York: New York University Press, 2005.

Wilmore, Gayraud S., ed. *African American Religious Studies: An Interdisciplinary Anthology.* 2nd ed. Durham, N.C.: Duke University Press, 1992.

7. EQUALITY AND NATIVE AMERICANS IN NORTH AMERICA

Adams, Nehemiah. *The Life of John Eliot: With an Account of the Early Missionary Efforts among the Indians of New England.* Vol. 3 of The Lives of the Church Fathers of New England. Boston: Massachusetts Sabbath School Society, 1847.

Bjornlund, Lydia. *Women of Colonial America.* Women in History. New York: Thomson/ Gale, 2004.

Bubar, Rowe W., and Irene S. Vernon. *Social Life and Issues.* Contemporary Native American Issues. Broomall, Pa..: Chelsea House, 2006.

Cogley, Richard W. *John Eliot's Mission to the Indians before King Philip's War.* Cambridge, Mass.: Harvard University, 1999.

Demos, John. *The Tried and the True: Native American Women Confronting Colonization.* Vol. 1 of *The Young Oxford History of Women in the United States of America,* edited by Nancy F. Cott. New York: Oxford, 1995.

Eliot, John. *The Christian Commonwealth: or, The Civil Policy of The Rising Kingdom of Jesus Christ.* London: Livewell Chapman, 1659. Reprint in facsimile, Research Library of Colonial America. New York: Arno, 1972.

Hirschfelder, Arlene, and Paulette Molin. *Encyclopedia of Native American Religions,* 2d ed. New York: Facts on File, 2000.

Jemison, Mary. "Mary Jemison Becomes an Iroquois." In *Native American Testimony: A Chronicle of Indian-White Relations from Prophecy to the Present, 1492–1992,* edited by Peter Nabokov, 73–78. 2d ed. New York: Viking, 1991.

Johnston, Charles. *A Narrative of the Incidents Attending the Capture, Detention, and Ransom of Charles Johnston, etc.* New York: J.&J. Harper, 1827. Reprint, Cleveland: Burrows Brothers, 1905.

Josephy, Alvin M., Jr., "American Indians." In *Collier's Encyclopedia,* Vol. 12, edited by William D. Halsey and Bernard Johnston, 642–89. New York: Macmillan, 1987.

Las Casas, Bartolomé de. *History of the Indies.* Translated and edited by Andrée Collard. New York: Harper, 1971.

Mitchell, Rudy. "New England's Native Americans." *Emmanuel Research Review* 32 (November, 2007). http:/www.egc.org/research/issue_32.html. Accessed 12 January 2008.

Mullin, Molly H. "Women." In *American Indians.*, Vol. 3. Edited by the Editors of Salem Press, 865–68. Englewood Cliffs, N.J.: Salem Press, 1995.

Nabokov, Peter, ed. *Native American Testimony: A Chronicle of Indian-White Relations from Prophecy to the Present, 1492-1992.* 2nd ed. New York: Viking, 1991.

Popick, Jacqui, "Native American Women, Past, Present, and Future." *Lethbridge Undergraduate Research Journal* 1, no. 1 (2006). http://www.lurj.org/article.php/vol1n1/running.xml. Accessed 21 January 2008.

Prezzano, Susan C. "Warfare, Women, and Households: The Development of Iroquois Culture." In *Women in Prehistory: North American and Mesoamerica,* edited by Cheryl Claassen and Rosemary A. Joyce, 88–99. Regendering the Past. Philadelphia: University of Pennsylvania, 1997.

Rowlandson, Mary. "The Captivity of Mary Rowlandson." In *The Portable North American Indian Reader,* edited by Frederick W. Turner, III, 312–60. New York: Viking, 1974.

Seaver, James Everett. *A Narrative of the Life of Mrs. Mary Jemison.* New York: J.D. Bemis, 1824.

Snow, Dean R. *The Iroquois.* The Peoples of America. Cambridge, Mass.: Blackwell, 1994.

Spencer, Aída Besançon Spencer. "How God's Spirit Worked a Revolution in Hawaii in 1819–1825." *Priscilla Papers* 19, no. 3 (Summer 2005): 5–11.

Spencer, Aída Besançon, and William David Spencer, eds. *The Global God: Multicultural Evangelical Views of God.* Grand Rapids: Baker, 1998.

Treat, James. *Native and Christian: Indigenous Voices on Religious Identity in the United States and Canada.* New York: Routledge, 1996.

Winslow, Ola Elizabeth. *John Eliot: "Apostle to the Indians."* Boston: Houghton Mifflin, 1968.

8. BIBLICAL EQUALITY AND UNITED STATES LATINO CHURCHES

Agosto, Efrain. "Paul's Use of Greco-Roman Conventions of Commendation." Ph.D. diss., Boston University, 1996.

Adams, Anna. "Perception Matters: Pentecostal Latinas in Allentown, Pennsylvania." In *A Reader in Latina Feminist Theology: Religion and Justice,* edited by María Pilar Aquino, Daisy L. Machado, and Jeanette Rodríguez, 98–113. Austin: University of Texas Press, 2002.

Aquino, María Pilar. "Directions and Foundations of Hispanic/Latino Theology: Toward a *Mestiza* Theology of Liberation." *Journal of Hispanic/Latino Theology* (Nov. 1993): 5–21.

———. "Latina Feminist Theology." In *A Reader in Latina Feminist Theology: Religion and Justice,* edited by María Pilar Aquino, Daisy L. Machado and Jeanette Rodríquez, 133–60. Austin: University of Texas Press, 2002.

Aquino, María Pilar, Daisy L. Machado, and Jeanette Rodríguez, eds. *Religion, Feminism and Justice: An Introduction to Latina Feminist Theology.* Austin: University of Texas Press, 2002.

Bibliography

Barton, Paul, and David Maldonado, eds. *Hispanic Christianity within Mainline Protestant Traditions: A Bibliography.* Decatur, Ga.: AETH Books, 1998.

Bauer, Walter. *A Greek-English Lexicon of the New Testament and Other Early Christian Literature.* Translated, adapted, revised, and augmented by W. F. Arndt, F. W. Gingrich, and F. W. Danker. 2d ed.; Chicago: University Press, 1979.

Benavides, Luis E. *Latino Christianity: History, Ministry, and Theology (The New England Methodist Situation),* Commission on Archives and History, Conference Commission on Archives and History, Conference Committee on Hispanic/Latino Ministry, 2005.

Brooten, Bernadette J. "Junia." In *Women in Scripture,* edited by Carol L. Meyers, Toni Craven, and Ross S. Kraemer, 107. Grand Rapids: Eerdmans, 2000.

————. "Junia . . . Outstanding Among the Apostles' (Romans 16:7)." In *Women Priests: A Catholic Commentary on the Vatican Declaration,* edited by Arlene Swidler and Leonard Swidler, 141–44. New York: Paulist 1977.

Carcaño, Minerva Garza. "Una perspectiva bíblico-teológica sobre la mujer en el ministerio ordenado." *Apuntes* (Summer 1990): 27–35.

Cicero. *Epistulae ad familiares.* 3 Volumes. Translated by W. Glynn Williams. Loeb Classical Library. Cambridge, Mass.: Harvard University Press, 1972.

Cotter, Wendy. "Women's Authority Roles in Paul's Churches." *Novum Testamentum* 36, no. 4 (1994): 350–72.

Dahl, Nils A. "Euodia and Syntyche and Paul's Letter to the Philippians." In *The Social World of the First Christians,* edited by L. Michael White and O. Larry Yarbrough, 3–15. Minneapolis: Fortress, 1995.

De La Torre, Miguel A. "Confesiones de un Macho Cubano." *Perspectivas* (Summer 2001): 65–87.

Dondried, Karl P., ed. *The Romans Debate.* Peabody, Mass.: Hendrickson, 1995.

Dunnam, Maxie D. *Galatians, Ephesians, Philippians, Colossians, Philemon.* Communicator's Commentary. Waco, Tex.: Word, 1982.

Ellis, Earle E. "Co-workers." In *Dictionary of Paul and his Letters,* edited by Gerald F. Hawthorne, Ralph P. Martin, and Daniel G. Reid. Downers Grove, Ill.: InterVarsity, 1993.

Espin, Orlando O. "The State of U. S. Latino/a Theology: An Understanding." *Perspectivas* (Fall, 2000): 19–55.

Fee, Gordon. *Paul's Letter to the Philippians.* Grand Rapids: Eerdmans, 1995.

Fitzgerald, John T. "Philippians in the Light of Some Ancient Discussions of Friendship." In *Friendship, Flattery, and Frankness of Speech,* edited by John T. Fitzgerald, 141–62. Leiden: E. J. Brill, 1996.

Francis, Fred O. and J. Paul Sampley. *Pauline Parallels.* Minneapolis: Fortress, 1992.

Furnish, Victor Paul. *The Moral Teaching of Paul.* Nashville: Abingdon, 1985.

Gaventa, Beverly R. "Romans." *Women's Bible Commentary.* Louisville, Ky.: Westminster John Knox, 1998.

González-Tejera, Awilda. *Intercession in Paul's Letters in Light of Graeco-Roman Practices of Intercession.* Ann Arbor: Pro-Quest, 2002.

Hays, Richard B. *First Corinthians.* Interpretation. Louisville, Ky.: John Knox, 1997.

Hooker, Morna D. "The Letter to the Philippians." *The New Interpreter's Bible.* Vol. XI. Nashville: Abingdon, 2000.

Hull, Gretchen G. "Biblical Feminist: A Christian Response to Sexism." *ESA Advocate* (Oct. 1990): 14–25.

Bibliography

Inscriptiones Graecae. Berlin: Preussiche Akademie der Wissenschaften, 1873–.

Isasi-Díaz, Ada María. "'Apuntes' for a Hispanic Woman Theology of Liberation." *Apuntes* (Fall 1986): 61–71.

Jaquette, James L. *Discerning What Counts*. SBLDS 146. Atlanta: Scholars, 1995.

Keener, Craig. S. "Man and Woman." In *Dictionary of Paul and his Letters*, edited by Gerald F. Hawthorne, Ralph P. Martin, and Daniel G. Reid. Downers Grove, Ill.: InterVarsity, 1993.

Lampe, Peter. "The Roman Christians of Romans 16." In *The Romans Debate*, edited by Karl P. Donfried, 216–30. Peabody, Mass.: Hendrickson, 1995.

Liddell, H. G., and R. Scott. *An Intermediate Greek-English Lexicon*. Oxford: Clarendon, 1997.

Lightfoot, J. B. *St. Paul's Epistle to the Philippians*. London: Macmillan, 1894.

Loya, Gloria Inés. "The Hispanic Women: *Pasionaria* and *Pastor* of the Hispanic Community." In *Frontiers of Hispanic Theology in the United States*, edited by Allan Figueroa, 124–33. New York: Orbis, 1992.

Maldonado, Zaida. "U.S. Hispanic/Latino Identity and Protestant Experience: A Brief Introduction for the Seminarian." *Perspectivas* (Fall 2003): 93–110.

Malinowski, Francis X. "The Brave Women of Philippi." *Biblical Theology Bulletin* 15 (1985): 60–63.

Marshall, A. J. "Roman Women and the Provinces." *Ancient Society* 6 (1975): 108–27.

Martell, Loida. "Women Doing Theology: Una Perspectiva Evangélica." *Apuntes* (Fall 1994): 68–85.

Martínez, Aquiles Ernesto. "Imágenes Feministas en Santiago: Optica de género y destellos de liberación." *Apuntes* (Fall 1998): 67.

Meeks, Wayne A. *The First Urban Christians*. New Haven: Yale University Press, 1983.

Moody, Linda A. *Women Encounter God: Theology across the Boundaries of Difference*. New York: Orbis, 1996.

Osiek, Carolyn. *Philippians, Philemon*. Abingdon New Testament Commentaries. Nashville: Abingdon, 2000.

Perkins, Pheme. "Christology, Friendship, and Status: The Rhetoric of Philippians." *Society of Biblical Literature Seminar Papers* 26 (1987): 509–20.

Peterlin, Davorin. *Paul's Letter to the Philippians in the Light of Disunity in the Church*. Leiden: E. J. Brill, 1995.

Rodríguez, Jeanette. "Experience as a Resource for Feminist Thought." *Journal of Hispanic/Latino Theology* (Nov. 1993): 68–76.

———. "Latina Activist: Toward an Inclusive Spirituality of Being in the World." In *A Reader in Latina Feminist Theology: Religion and Justice*, edited by María Pilar Aquino, Daisy L. Machado, and Jeanette Rodríguez, 114–30. Austin: University of Texas Press, 2002.

Sampley, J. Paul. *Walking Between the Times*. Minneapolis: Fortress, 1991.

Silva, Moisés. *Philippians*. Baker Exegetical Commentary of the New Testament. Grand Rapids: Baker, 1992.

Spencer, Aída Besançon. *Beyond the Curse: Women Called to Ministry*. Nashville: Thomas Nelson, 1985. Reprint, Peabody, Mass.: Hendrickson, 1989.

———. "'El Hogar' as Ministry Team: Stephana(s)'s Household." In *Hispanic Christian Thought at the Dawn of the 21st Century: Apuntes in Honor of Justo L. González*, edited by Alvin Padilla, Roberto Goizueta, and Eldin Villafañe, 69–77. Nashville: Abingdon, 2005.

Tacitus. *Agricola. Germania. Dialogus.* Translated by M. Hutton and W. Peterson. Loeb Classical Library. Cambridge, Mass.: Harvard University Press, 1914.

Thiselton, Anthony C. *The First Epistle to the Corinthians.* The New International Greek Testament Commentary. Grand Rapids: Eerdmans, 2000.

Wire, Antoinette C. *The Corinthian Women Prophets.* Minneapolis: Fortress, 1990.

Witherington, Ben III. *Friendship and Finances in Philippi.* The New Testament in Context. Valley Forge, Pa.: Trinity, 1994.

9. BIBLICAL EQUALITY AMONG PASTORING COUPLES IN THE NEW ENGLAND PORTUGUESE DISTRICT OF THE INTERNATIONAL CHURCH OF THE FOURSQUARE GOSPEL

DeBiaggi, Sylvia Duarte Dantes. *Changing Gender Roles: Brazilian Immigrant Families in the United States.* New York: LFB Scholarly Publishing, LLC, 2002.

Burgess, Stanley M., and Gary B. McGee, eds. *Dictionary of Pentecostal and Charismatic Movements.* Grand Rapids: Regency Reference Library, 1989.

Corporate Bylaws of the International Church of the Foursquare Gospel. 2007 edition. Los Angeles.

Handbook for the Operation of Foursquare Churches. Los Angeles.

Marques, Cairo. "Coisas Nossas." *A Publication of the New England Portuguese District of Foursquare Churches for District Ministers.* Malden, Mass., 2007.

Schell, Steve, ed. *Women in Leadership Ministry.* Los Angeles: Foursquare Media, 2007.

Synan, Vinson. *The Twentieth Century Pentecostal Explosion.* Altamonte Springs, Fla.: Creation House, 1987.

Van Cleave, Nathaniel M. "The First Branches of the Vine." *The Vine and the Branches: A History of the International Church of the Foursquare Gospel.* Los Angeles: International Church of the Foursquare Gospel, 1992.

10. THE CAUSE OF THE GOSPEL FOR MEN AND WOMEN IN EUROPE

Boccia, Maria L. "Hidden History of Women Leaders of the Church." *Journal of Biblical Equality* (September 1990): 66.

Calvin, John. *Commentary on the Epistles of Paul the Apostle to the Corinthians.* Edinburgh: Calvin Translation Society, 1848.

Fell, Margaret. "Women's Speaking Justified, Proved, and Allowed of by the Scriptures, All such as speak by the Spirit and Power of the Lord Jesus. And how Women were the first that Preached the Tidings of the Resurrection of Jesus, and were sent by Christ's own Command, before he Ascended to the Father, John 20:17," *A Brief Collection of Remarkable Passages and Occurrences Relating to the Birth, Education, Life, Conversion, Travels, Services, and Deep Suffering of the Ancient, Eminent, and Faithful Servant of the Lord, Margaret Fell, But by her Second Marriage, Margaret Fox Together with Sundry of her Epistles, Books, and Christian Testimonies to Friends and Others' and also to those in Supreme Authority, in the several late Revolutions of Government.* London: J. Sowle, 1710.

Grenz, Stanley J. *Women in the Church: A Biblical Theology of Women in Ministry.* Downer's Grove, Ill.: Intervarsity Press, 1995.

Groothuis, Rebecca Merrill. *Good News for Women: A Biblical Picture of Gender Equality.* Grand Rapids: Baker Books, 1997.

Hyatt, Susan C. *In the Spirit We're Equal: The Spirit, the Bible, and Women: A Revival Perspective.* Dallas: Hyatt Press, 1998.

Ignatius. "To the Trallians." In *The Apostolic Fathers,* edited by Michael W. Holmes. Grand Rapids: Baker, 1992.

Langton, Edward. *History of the Moravian Church.* London: George Allen & Unwin, 1956.

Nixson, Rosie. *Liberating Women for the Gospel: Women in Evangelism.* London: Hodder & Stoughton, 1973.

Scholz, Emanuel. *Die Frau im Verkündigungs-und Zeugendienst der Gemeinde.* Marburg an der Lahn: Verlag der Francke Buchhandlung, 1964.

Storkey, Elaine. *Created or Constructed? The Great Gender Debate.* Guildford: Paternoster Press, 2000.

Werner, Elke. *Frauen verändern ihre Welt: Wege zu verantwortlicher Mitarbeit und Leiterschaft.* Holzgerlingen: Hänssler, 1999.

Wualben, Lars. *A History of the Christian Church.* New York: Thomas Nelson, 1933.

11. A LONG HARD STRUGGLE: THE AUSTRALIAN STORY AND THE AUSTRALIAN CHURCHES AND WOMEN

Bellamy, J., and K. Castle. *National Church Life Survey.* Sydney: NCLS Research, 2001.

Black, A., ed. *Religion in Australia: A Sociological Perspective.* Sydney: Allen and Unwin, 1991.

Giles, Kevin. *Created Woman: A Fresh Study of the Biblical Teaching.* Canberra: Acorn, 1985.

———. *The Trinity and Subordinationism: The Doctrine of God and the Contemporary Gender Debate.* Downers Grove, Ill.: InterVarsity, 2002.

———. *Women and Their Ministry: A Case for Equal Ministries in the Church Today.* Melbourne: Dove Communications, 1977.

Hutchinson M., and E. Campion, eds. *A Long Patient Conflict: Essays on Women and Gender in Australian Christianity.* Sydney: The Center for the Study of Australian Christianity, 1994.

Mackay, H. *Advance Australia Where? How We've Changed, Why We've Changed, and What Will Happen Next.* Sydney: Hachette, 2007.

Piggin, S. *The Spirit of a Nation: The Story of Australia's Christian Heritage.* Sydney: Strand, 2004.

Porter, M. *Land of the Spirit? The Australian Religious Experience.* Geneva: WCC Publications, 1990.

Summers, A. *Damned Whores and God's Police.* Sydney: Penguin, 1994, updated edition.

———. *The End of Equality: Work, Babies, and Women's Choices in 21st Century Australia.* Milson's Point, NSW: Random House, 2003.

West, J. *Daughters of Freedom: A History of Women in the Australian Church.* Sutherland, NSW: Albatross, 1997.

12. BIBLICAL EQUALITY IN THE UNITED STATES

Banks, Adelle, M. "Women Clergy Mark Milestones, yet Obstacles Remain." Presbyterian News Service, http://www.pcusa.org/pcnews/2006/06519.htm. Accessed 2008.

Becker, Carol E. *Leading Women: How Church Women Can Avoid Leadership Traps and Negotiate the Gender Maze.* Nashville: Abingdon, 1996.

Billington, Louis. "'Female Laborers in the Church': Women Preachers in the Northeastern United States, 1790–1840." *Journal of American Studies* 19 (1985): 369–94.

Butler, Anthea D. *Women in the Church of God in Christ: Making a Sanctified World.* New York: University of North Carolina Press, 2007.

Chaves, Mark. *Ordaining Women: Culture and Conflict in Religious Organizations.* Cambridge, Mass.: Harvard University Press, 1997.

"Christian Reformed Ok Female Ministers." *Christian Century,* 10 July 2007, 14.

Cochran, Pamela D. H. *Evangelical Feminism: A History.* New York: New York University Press, 2005.

Fogleman, Aaron Spencer. *Jesus Is Female: Moravians and Radical Religion in Early America.* Early American Studies. Philadelphia: University of Pennsylvania Press, 2007.

Groothuis, Rebecca Merrill. *Women Caught in the Conflict: The Culture War between Traditionalism and Feminism.* Grand Rapids: Baker, 1994.

Hassey, Janette. *No Time for Silence: Evangelical Women in Public Ministry around the Turn of the Century.* Grand Rapids: Zondervan, 1986.

Ingersoll, Julie. *Evangelical Christian Women: War Stories in the Gender Battles.* New York: New York University Press, 2003.

Larson, Rebecca. *Daughters of Light: Quaker Women Preaching and Prophesying in the Colonies and Abroad, 1700–1775.* New York: University of North Carolina Press, 1999.

Lum, Rebecca Rosen. "Women Fight for Religious Authority." *Contra Costa Times* (Walnut Creek, Calif.), 22 July 2007, A25, 28.

Mather, Mark, and Dia Adams. "The Crossover in Female-Male College Enrollment Rates." Population Reference Bureau, http://www.prb.org/Articles/2007/Crossover inFemaleMaleCollegeEnrollmentRates.aspx. Accessed 2008.

Purvis, Sally B. *The Stained Glass Ceiling: Churches and Their Women Pastors.* Louisville, Ky.: Westminster John Knox, 1995.

"Top Twenty Religions in the United States, 2001." http://www.adherents.com/rel_USA .html#religions. Accessed 2008.

Zikmund, Barbara Brown, Adair T. Lummis, and Patricia M. Y. Chang. *Clergy Women: An Uphill Calling.* Louisville, Ky.: Westminster John Knox, 1998.

CONCLUSION

Kydd, Ronald A. N. *Charismatic Gifts in the Early Church.* Peabody, Mass.: Hendrickson, 1984.

Sider, Ronald. *The Scandal of the Evangelical Conscience: Why Are Christians Living Just Like the Rest of the World?* Grand Rapids: Baker, 2005.

Spencer, Aída Besançon. *Beyond the Curse: Women Called to Ministry.* Peabody, Mass.: Hendrickson, 1985.

Bibliography

————. "'El Hogar' as Ministry Team: Stephana(s)'s Household." In *Hispanic Christian Thought at the Dawn of the 21st Century: Apuntes in Honor of Justo L. González,* edited by Alvin Padilla, Roberto Goizueta, and Eldin Villafañe, 69–77. Nashville: Abingdon, 2005.

————."Jesus' Treatment of Women in the Gospels." In *Discovering Biblical Equality: Complementarity without Hierarchy,* edited by Ronald W. Pierce and Rebecca Merrill Groothuis, 126–41. Downers Grove, Ill.: InterVarsity, 2004.

————. "Peter's Pedagogical Method in 1 Peter 3:6." *Bulletin for Biblical Research* 10, no.1 (2000): 107–19.

Spencer, William David. "The Chaining of the Church." *Christian History* 7, no. 1 (17): 25.

————. "Diamond or Diamond Mine?" *Priscilla Papers* 16, no. 2 (Spring 2002): 16–17.

Scripture Index

Subject Index

Evangelical Women's Caucus, 201

Evangelicals for Social Action, 201

evangelism: evangelists. *See* missions

Eve. *See* Adam

families, African, 71–74; Native American, 107–8, 214; European, 170. *See also* marriage; gender, roles

Fee, Gordon, 2

Fell, Margaret, 165–66

feminism: feminists, 8, 17, 20, 27, 50, 56, 75, 78, 106, 145, 147, 169, 193, 197–98, 200, 204, 206–9, 217

Finney, Charles, 197

Fitzgerald, John T., 136

foot binding, 37–40, 51

Foote, Julia A., 83

Fort Washington Baptist Church, xii, 88–91, 96, 98–99, 101

Gandhi, Indira, 22

Gaventa, Beverly Roberts, 140

gender, equality, xix–xx, 12, 33, 46, 49, 52–53, 56, 58–60, 62–63, 67–72, 75–79, 81–85, 87–89, 91–92, 94–95, 98–102, 106, 110, 118–19, 126, 136, 140, 144–46, 148–49, 173, 178–79, 186, 191–92, 194, 197, 201, 203–4, 206, 208–209, 212, 215, 217–18; God's intention, xviii–xix; identity, 27, 61–61, 172–73, 207–8; reformation, xix, 2–3, 5, 8–15, 17–20, 35, 38, 51, 68–69, 79, 82–83, 99–100, 146–47, 170, 174–75, 193, 202–3, 205, 209–10, 212–15, 217–18; roles, 27–28, 33–34, 56, 59–60, 63–65, 68, 70–74, 78, 101, 106–7, 109–10, 119, 145, 152–53, 163, 174, 193, 214. *See also* God, image of; equality

Giles, Kevin, ix, 59, 65, 192

god: husband as, 28, 37, 212

God, image of, 27, 79, 93–94, 98, 100, 172–73, 192, 196, 213. *See also* gender

goddess, xvii, 14, 22–23, 79–80, 208

Gookin, Daniel, 122

Gordon, A. J., 2, 20

Gordon, Philip (Ti-Bish-Ko-Gi-Jik), 123

Greco-Roman, 52, 59, 66, 132, 134, 136–37

Grenz, Stanley, 167

Groothuis, Rebecca Merrill, 63

Gudykunst, William, 54

headship, 5, 18–19, 52, 187, 189–90, 193–94, 201, 208

hermeneutics, 3, 9–16, 20, 50, 62, 145, 198, 201, 207, 209. *See also* Scripture

hierarchy: and nonhierarchy, 55–56, 62, 84, 106, 109, 118, 144, 163, 168, 215

Higginbotham, Evelyn, 82

homosexuality: homosexuals, 61, 172–73, 201, 204

Hope for Europe, 171, 173

Hopkins, John Henry, 9

Hoscott, Cynthia Teecomwas, 123

house churches, 48–49, 192

Hughes, Jennie V., 44

Hull, Gretchen Gaebelein, 20

Hung Hsiu-ch'uan, 40

Hyatt, Susan, 165

Ignatius, 164

immigration: immigrants, 49, 53–59, 153, 156, 169, 171, 173, 180, 212–13

institutionalization, 44, 187, 212

International Church of the Foursquare Gospel (ICFG), xiii–xiv, 150–61